Mrs. AMBASSADOR

AMBASSADOR

THE LIFE AND POLITICS OF
Eugenie Anderson

MARY DUPONT

MINNESOTA
HISTORICAL
SOCIETY PRESS

The publication of this book was supported though a generous grant from the Eugenie M. Anderson Women in Public Affairs Fund.

mnhspress.org

The Minnesota Historical Society Press is a member of the Association of University Presses.

Manufactured in the United States of America

10 9 8 7 6 5 4 3 2 1

∞ The paper used in this publication meets the minimum requirements of the American National Standard for Information Sciences—Permanence for Printed Library Materials, ANSI Z39.48-1984.

International Standard Book Number
ISBN: 978-1-68134-127-9 (paper)
ISBN: 978-1-68134-128-6 (e-book)

Library of Congress Cataloging-in-Publication Data available upon request.

This and other Minnesota Historical Society Press books are available from popular e-book vendors.

CONTENTS

Mrs, AMBASSADOR

AUTHOR'S NOTE

*A*LL BIOGRAPHIES START WITH THE SAME COMmitment: that the subject is worthy of our attention. From there, the writer has countless choices to consider and a thousand narrative paths to follow or abandon. No single biography can, or should, capture and relay every detail from the subject's life; therefore, each biography becomes a story based on choices. I approached this biography of my grandmother knowing that I would be discarding almost all of my own memories and associations and relying, almost exclusively, on the words of others—most importantly, on Eugenie Anderson's own firsthand words. I deliberately chose to incorporate hefty amounts of citations in Eugenie's own voice, invoking her logic and her cadence, allowing the reader not only to experience her verbal and written words but also to note the omissions. I also made a conscious choice to favor many firsthand voices of Eugenie's contemporaries as her story progressed: from early family letters; Minnesota historians (versus national authors); journalists in their lingo of the day; later reminiscences and personal letters by family members and political colleagues; and reflections by women about women in politics and society. In narrowing this biography to a discussion of Anderson's place in mid-twentieth-century opportunities for women, specifically in diplomacy, as well as her personal life, I deliberately abandoned other narrative paths—paths I am confident are already

3

or are yet to be covered in excellent fashion by other historians and political writers.

Eugenie Anderson was my grandmother. I offer this portrait of one interpretation of her life based on an interweaving of private and public aspects that felt particularly compelling to me in our ever-changing political and social climate.

PREFACE

UGENIE MOORE ANDERSON WAS A CONSTANT PRES-
ence and an active influence on the American political
scene in the mid-twentieth century. She achieved a
historic diplomatic status when President Truman appointed her
the first woman to the rank of Ambassador for the United States in
1949. Over the course of her career, international news and images
of her engaged readers of thousands of papers across the country
and the world, through her high-level appointments to postwar
Denmark, Communist Bulgaria, and the United Nations. Until
now, however, the story of her life, combined with her experience
as a woman in politics, her involvement in the Minnesota DFL
Party and the national Democratic Party, and the effect she had
on the history of Minnesota and the country, has not been told.
Walter Mondale says: "Eugenie was one of the giants of the DFL
Party . . . a gifted, scholarly, kindly, totally aware person. Probably
[Hubert] Humphrey's best friend."[1]

Eugenie was not in a position to ask if a woman could have it
all; rather, she concerned herself with protecting the democratic
system that would enable *other* women, and men, to pursue such
questions.

This biography of Minnesota's Eugenie Anderson will explore
not only how her life was influenced as a woman by the politics
and expectations of her century but how *she* directly influenced
twentieth-century politics and history. Jo Freeman, feminist
author and civil rights activist whose work spans over fifty years,

wrote, "It took the concentrated efforts of both insiders and out-siders to hoist women's political participation beyond the level of tokenism." Eugenie began, naturally, as an outsider. Friend, adviser, and campaigner for future vice president Hubert Humphrey, she launched her own career after meeting the women who were insid-ers: Eleanor Roosevelt and Democratic National Committee vice chairman India Edwards. It was through the combined sponsorship of Minnesota men like Humphrey and Governor Orville Freeman, and women with direct ties to the White House like Roosevelt and Edwards, that Eugenie burst into national view, seemingly from nowhere. Her own strategies for staying in the game proved just as valuable as sponsorship by others. Eugenie said: "The important thing for any woman in public life is to forget first that she *is* a woman and concentrate on her objectives."[2]

Eugenie Anderson was not a proclaimed feminist. But her parameters and expectations of feminism were very different than they are for women today. When Eugenie said of feminism, "That aggressive attitude won't get a woman any place," she was speaking, out loud, to the press, in 1949. Jo Freeman stated in her book *A Room at a Time*: "Context is crucial to political history. It is impos-sible to understand what people say or do in the political arena without knowing the influences upon them and those whom they are trying to influence. Otherwise one runs the risk of seeing the past through the eyes of the present, and distorting both."[3]

In post-World War II America, there was no active women's movement. There had never been a woman president, woman prime minister, or female—anywhere in the world—*elected* to lead a democratic nation. One single woman, Margaret Chase Smith, had ever been elected to the US Senate. Suffrage had been adopted thirty years before, and the current social climate in America dic-tated that women should be grateful for peace after victory in the world war, grateful that their men were home and dominating the workplace, grateful that they could raise children in a free country, and grateful that they had the right to vote and choose candidates.

Wilfrid Sheed described the era in his biography of Ambassador Clare Boothe Luce: "The summer was 1949. . . . The whole forefront of American life had a strange gleam to it, like a starlet's smile, as wartime propaganda turned its incandescence on peace and tried to make it glow like World War II: patriotism, religion, optimism, for its own sweet sake—anything to ward off depression."[4]

Not until 1963, when Betty Friedan published her groundbreaking social study, *The Feminine Mystique*, would the "strange gleam" of postwar gender stereotypes and conditions come into sharper scrutiny; eventually, by the end of the 1960s, the conversation led into the second wave of feminism in the United States. So while it may seem anachronistic to apply ideas in *The Feminine Mystique* to the path of Eugenie Anderson's career (which began almost twenty years before its publication), the fact that the subject matter of the book examines and discusses those very years makes it a perfect reflection on the women's issues and challenges that Eugenie faced.[5]

When Eugenie joined politics, her objective was not feminism, women's rights, or anything that would draw attention to her gender. She wanted to fight tyrants and bullies, and the bigger and tougher and higher up they were, the stronger she wanted to protest. She wanted to meet them on diplomatic ground and argue, intellectually and morally, why they were wrong. She wanted to lend her voice to the support of democracy and human rights, and if she had to do it in a skirt, well, then, she'd wear a skirt and wear it like silk shantung armor. An avid student of political history, and traumatized by (not through experiencing, but through understanding) the horrific crimes of Nazi Germany and other totalitarian regimes in the first half of the century, Eugenie focused her beams on Soviet Communism and the effects of Stalinism. Her work and championing of the North Atlantic Treaty Organization (NATO) and President Truman's Marshall Plan exemplified everything she believed about international cooperation and resistance to the spread of Communism. In a letter to Hubert Humphrey, she wrote: "Sometimes I feel that a far greater danger to our survival than H-bombs or nuclear warfare, is Western *fear* of these things. The Soviet Union is masterful about exploiting our fears."[6]

It is hard not to draw parallels to our own position in time, as we live through each day now listening to debates over interrelationships between the highest levels of power in America and Russia. In 1963, based in Communist Bulgaria, Eugenie wrote home to her family: "I was absolutely shocked to see that recent picture of [Ambassador] Harriman and Khrushchev embracing each other on reaching the test-ban agreement. It is one thing to reach such an agreement—but it is quite unnecessary (and unwise in my opinion) for an American official to be carried away by it." Most of the nation reacted the same way in 2018 when President Trump publicly congratulated Russian President Putin on his "electoral" victory. One of the strongest female voices in American politics today, former senator and secretary of state Hillary Clinton, still sees a global threat from the Kremlin. Clinton wrote: "Now that the Russians have infected us and seen how weak our defenses are, they'll keep at it. Maybe other foreign powers will join them. They'll also continue targeting our friends and allies. Their ultimate goal is to undermine—perhaps even destroy—Western democracy itself."[7]

Above all, Eugenie Anderson wanted to be known for advocating democratic ideals. If being the "first woman" in any given role helped her spread the message of that goal, then it was useful. If representing women helped provide an example that all people, regardless of gender, color, race, or creed, could join the democratic process, then it was useful. But when those same situations—any emphasis on her femininity—jeopardized her very presence at the tables where policy was made and democracy was at stake, then calling attention to her gender was *not* useful, and she blazed forward, relying on hard work, loyalty to her political sponsors, and the adept camouflaging of blatant sexist challenges. Her bottom line was to keep communication lines open to promote peaceful diplomatic solutions to conflicts anywhere on the globe. Civil rights. Human rights. Persistent, and inevitable, conversations about women's rights were always in the background of those larger ideals. While Eugenie dealt with sexism every day of her life, she employed every bit of personal stamina to keep its power over her to a minimum. And she succeeded far more often than she failed. Hillary Clinton wrote: "It can also be deeply rewarding to be a woman in politics. You know that just by being in the room, you're making government more representative of the people. You're bringing a vital perspective that would otherwise go unheard."[8]

Eugenie kept her place in the room. This is her story.

Studio portrait of the Moore family in 1912, during Rev. Moore's posting to the Methodist Church in Dexter, Iowa. Clockwise from top: Ruth Moore (Stanley), age nine; Ezekiel A. Moore, age thirty-nine; Helen Eugenie Moore (Anderson), age three; Flora Belle McMillen Moore, age thirty-eight; Mary Katharine Moore (Biederman), age one; Julie Moore (Ross Stanley), age seven. The youngest sibling, William J. Moore, was born a year later. *Anderson family collection.*

One
LEAVING the TOWER

From private to public life, the phases may seem disconnected,
but they are not. Each phase prepared me in some way for the next
and influenced what I became. In talking to young women, I have often
said that women's lives come in segments, dictated in part by biology.
I have also said that this is actually an advantage because it allows
women to explore different paths. It is important, however, to have
some guiding star. For me that star has always been faith in
the democratic promise that each person should be able
to go as far as her or his own talents will allow.

MADELEINE K. ALBRIGHT, *FASCISM*

EUGENIE ANDERSON'S PUBLIC STATEMENTS REGARD-
ing her initial spark of interest in politics always highlighted her first trip to Europe in 1937. In her 1971 reminiscences, she said, "The news of the world that was beginning to
reach us more with the radio and the rise of Hitler, events in Europe
that seemed to be leading toward a World War began to penetrate
even into our ivory tower." Declarations to colleagues, to the press,
and to anyone who asked over the course of her career received the
same overview of motivation for her need to get involved:

> The day that we crossed the border from France to Germany I
> remember that the first thing I saw were little boys marching in
> the street, little four- and five-year-old boys in uniform and goose-
> stepping. And I remember my horror at this sight and being sud-
> denly really afraid of what was happening there and of the menace
> that this represented for our country, too.

I realized that I didn't know anything about what was really happening in Europe, although I was aware that there was a very dangerous growth there with fascism and Hitler and I did feel that there was certainly going to be a war. . . . I read a great deal and I also soon after that realized that I knew nothing about our own government and I joined the League of Women Voters.[1]

It is true that Eugenie was spurred into action, in part, because of her broadened view of the world and the dangerous possibilities of fascist regimes and growing isolationism. But that trip to Europe, and its consequences on her choice to get involved in politics, was only one factor coming at the tail end of Eugenie's youth and early experiences. She hinted at the wider story when she told the interviewer in 1971, "I began to realize that there was this aspect of my personality that somehow didn't find expression with a family." At this point in the interview, the conversation centered on 1936 in the timeline: before Eugenie's pivotal trip to Europe. This chapter illustrates the deeper picture behind Genie's inspirations and life ambitions.[2]

Eugenie was born in May 1909, in a tiny town in southwest Iowa called Adair. Her father, Ezekiel Arrowsmith Moore, was a Methodist minister; her mother, Flora Belle McMillen Moore, a homemaker. Genie was acknowledged to be the family's "prettiest baby." At birth, she was the third of three girls; in 1911 and 1912, another sister and a long-awaited brother followed, fixing Genie firmly at the center of five quite brilliant, energetic children. She always stood out.

As Genie approached adolescence, several events occurred that changed America, and the world, through the course of the twentieth century. First, from April 1917 to November 1918, the United States participated in the Great War, later called World War I. When asked by the interviewer if she remembered anything about that war, Eugenie replied yes, most definitely. She stated: "[My father and a friend] were the first ones in Corning [Iowa] to be informed of the Armistice having been signed on November 11 in 1918. . . .

And we did organize very quickly that morning a little parade and marched through the town spreading the word."[3]

Second, also in 1917, the Russian Revolution took place. Third, the 1918-19 influenza pandemic wiped out millions of people—more than those killed in the Great War—across the globe. Fourth, in October 1919, the United States found itself under a full-scale prohibition of alcohol under the Volstead Act. And lastly, of special interest in light of Genie's future as a woman in politics, the Nineteenth Amendment was ratified on August 18, 1920, finally giving women the right to vote. Genie was eleven years old; her mother was forty-six.

It is easy to see the stresses of the 1920s and '30s that ran headlong into World War II. Some conservative American citizens

November 1918, Corning, Iowa. Celebrating the victory of the Allies in the Great War, Genie Moore, age nine (far left), portrays Great Britain. Three friends depict the United States, France, and Germany (lurking in the bushes, far right). *Anderson family collection.*

retreated to a stronger isolationist stance, voting for politicians who promised to keep the United States separate and safe from conflict overseas and dangerous interdependencies. They feared and ridiculed the sissy socialists and liberals. The uppity women. Was it any wonder, they said, that America fell into the Great Depression? But for every traditional isolationist view, there were competing ideologies for expanding America's role and responsibility to the world. It is particularly interesting that the pattern of Genie's life would reflect a certain similar stereotype of American image for each decade she lived through. Innocent, untested, and naïve from 1909 to 1917. Adolescent, living carefree and discovering freedom in the Roaring Twenties.

Besides national and global events between 1917 and 1920, a death in Genie's family would have brought her a more acute awareness of adult grief and reality. Grandma Lottie, her mother's mother, died in November 1919. By accounts, Lottie was senile and quite a handful. And yet she was the mother of Genie's mother, and the first close relative that Genie would have seen buried. The passing of a very old person can generate all kinds of forgotten stories, memories of others long gone, and shifts in attitudes among generations who suddenly view themselves and their place in history as forever altered. So within the following year after Lottie's death, Genie's mother, Flora Belle, found herself in the strange position of being an adult orphan, and also of being a mature woman allowed to vote for the first time. The fundamental fracture of it must have been very hard for Flora, who was highly sensitive to changes in family dynamics, and exhibited to young Genie the significance of mortality and evolving family.

The Moore children "worshipped" their father. The Rev. Ezekiel Moore loved to talk—and he talked all the time. Eugenie reminisced: "My father was a man with a very strong sense of social indignation and a passion for social justice . . . he was always getting into difficulties with his parish because of it. He just couldn't, you know, stay out of controversial issues. He had to take a stand on what he thought was right or against what he thought was wrong." Genie was probably not unique among middle-class young women in the 1920s, who, while they were born and raised to respect and obey their father's authority, protection, and alpha position in the family, were also faced with a new challenge to their attitudes concerning their mothers. Suddenly, the assumptions of women's meekness and subservience were fundamentally altered by the Nineteenth Amendment. Women who wanted a voice no longer had to put on a banner and expose themselves in the street demanding suffrage—they could go to the polls on election day and privately vote for whomever or whatever they wished, and no one, not even their husbands, would know which boxes they checked.[4]

Because of Rev. Moore's job, along with his tendency to make trouble in his own parishes (for example, sermonizing on temperance and the evils of alcohol while members of the church board made a fair amount of money bootlegging during Prohibition), the Moore family moved quite often around the state of Iowa. Eugenie lived in five or six different towns growing up. The social energy it must have required to switch communities, schools, and friends probably gave her a solid psychological background for diplomacy. She was also forced to attend three different colleges, when she would have preferred to stay at the first one. Graduating young from high school, at age sixteen, Eugenie first enrolled at Stephens College in Missouri, where she became part of a tight circle of close girlfriends and gloried in her studies. But there was not enough money to keep her at Stephens, so Eugenie transferred to Simpson College in Iowa, closer to home. She was quite unhappy with the provincial quality of Simpson. Near the end of that sophomore year, Flora Belle suffered from illness, and Eugenie moved home for a year to take care of her parents, her younger siblings, and the house. Flora Belle taught her to cook—not just a dish here or a dessert there, but real family cooking.

By the fall of 1929, Eugenie's family had recovered enough that she felt able to continue on with university studies. With a

Eugenie Moore, age nineteen, in 1928. *Anderson family collection.*

scholarship in music, Eugenie enrolled in her junior year at Carleton College in Northfield, Minnesota. Flora Belle had taught all of her children to play the piano, and Genie's overwhelming love of music had blossomed into a passion for the compositions and theory of the old masters as well as an interdisciplinary approach to music with philosophy and art. She wrote poetry. She immersed herself in Beethoven. It was at this point in time—when Eugenie's youthful idealism and sense of potential romance and adventure were most open to fate—that she met John Pierce Anderson.

Twenty-two years old, tall and thin, with the brooding facial contours of an intellectual artist, John materialized like a dream, the older brother of Eugenie's classmate Elizabeth Anderson, with whom Eugenie shared music classes, long academic discussions, and nighttime bus rides to and from classical music concerts in Minneapolis and St. Paul. Excitement buzzed in the girls' dormitory anytime one of them caught a glimpse of the handsome and mysterious John Anderson on campus. But he was just as quickly gone, driving Liz back to their home in Red Wing for weekends—the home called Tower View.

John and Elizabeth were two of the four children of Alexander and Lydia Anderson. Alexander Pierce, or A. P., as he was often called, had made a substantial living from the invention, development, and patenting of air-puffing grain into cereal, among other endeavors in botanical and mechanical sciences. At the time John was shuttling his sister Liz to and from Carleton College, their father, A. P., was sixty-eight years old and only semiretired. Minnesota historian Larry Millett wrote, "Although botany was Anderson's chief field of study, he was something of a mad scientist at heart, a restless tinkerer who loved experimenting with new ideas." A. P. and his wife, Lydia, fifty-four, lived a rather active lifestyle on a rather isolated piece of land. Some called it a farm, others referred to it as an estate: Tower View was both—a sheltered, self-sufficient haven outside Red Wing, Minnesota, a tall brick water tower with a fairy-tale aerie and conical roof at its center—physically and metaphorically. Neither A. P. nor Lydia had been born wealthy. On the contrary, A. P. was born during the Civil War to poor, recent Swedish immigrants in a rough cabin next to their first dugout in Featherstone Township, Goodhue County, Minnesota. Lydia was born in the working-class streets of Glasgow, Scotland, near the shipyards on the River Clyde, where her father sailed in and out for months at a time as a quartermaster with the Royal Merchant Marine. Lydia's mother had died of tuberculosis when Lydia was only six years old.[5]

A. P., uninterested in public opinion or ostentation, did not build his tower strictly for appearances; he built it to provide water for a nine-hundred-acre farm, two working scientific laboratories, and his own large family and staff. Lydia, too, was not a stereotypical rich housewife. She did not join Twin Cities social circles or seek out alliances with society women or travel extensively for exposure. Instead, she hosted quiet meetings for the Women's Christian Temperance Union at Tower View; spent winters in the territory of Hawaii with A. P. and the children (quite off the grid and not at all popular in the 1920s); and encouraged her offspring to run free like sturdy farm folk rather than hold back like the delicate elite. Her three daughters rode horses, raised chickens, and shot guns wearing britches with their hair cut short like boys. They took long expeditions along the Cannon River bottoms, collecting and cataloging thousands of insects and specimens. John terrified his mother by climbing up the ladder on the outside of the tower aerie to the red-tiled roof above, crouching on the steeply pitched edge of the witch's hat 115 feet above the ground. Only Lydia went to church regularly. The Andersons became a well-known presence in Red Wing, yet they kept close to themselves and preferred their own company in the shadow of the tower rather than mixing more constantly in society.

After high school, John wanted to study art. He was not an outstanding student, but he managed to gain entrance to Yale University, rooming with Ralph Sargent, the fiancé of his older sister

Louise. John's son, Hans Anderson, remembered his father's bitter memories of Yale, which ended in failure and a return to Minnesota.

> Ralph was very jovial and sarcastic and outgoing. . . . And he would tease John about painting. And John didn't go to class—after a very short time there, he wouldn't go to class—and he told me once that he often fell off his chair because he was so drunk. And the president of Yale University invited him for dinner more than once because he was the son of this very rich guy back in Minnesota. And John remembers going to these dinners and being completely unable to even speak, because he was with all these special people. And he had a terrible time. And he ended up dropping out and going home.[6]

John Anderson, though brilliant, sensitive, and talented in many forms of art and mechanical science, battled a lifelong illness of addiction and chemical dependency, which probably began with the substantial abuse of alcohol when he left home and found himself surrounded by unsympathetic, elitist strangers in the halls of Yale. He did not fit the environment and could not adapt to its expectations. After writing to Tower View to inform his parents that he was dropping out, John received a reply from his father:

> April 19, 1929
> Dear John,
> . . . I have just now read your letter—a good one and it shows you are earnestly and honestly trying to do the best thing & right thing for yourself, now and always. We ask no more and you can be sure that you will find what you seek. . . . It is the law of the universe to be humble. . . . It is only after many years that one can really see how fortunate, and after all, how dependent and insignificant we all are in this *small world*, in *this large universe* of ours. . . .
> Your father. A. P. Anderson[7]

A key to John's character, throughout his life, was the unusual relationship he had with his parents. On the one hand, both A. P. and Lydia were ahead of their time in the way they raised all of the children to be freethinkers, intellectually ambitious, physically brave (regardless of gender), and consciously humble and benevolent, generous neighbors and citizens. And yet, with their only son, John, the indulgent love and devotion that they showed him resulted in a tie between John and Tower View that was never sufficiently relaxed.

Reminiscing about the early months of 1930, Eugenie described how she and her Carleton roommate took a bus to St. Paul for a piano concert and spotted Elizabeth and John Anderson high above them in the lofty balcony:

John Anderson in his art studio, converted from a small farm building at Tower View, Red Wing, Minnesota, 1932. *Anderson family collection.*

After the concert, the Andersons stopped and asked us if they could take us to the station. And that was how I met my husband . . . they took us to Walgreen's Drug Store and the four of us had coffee there and I remember that I was instantly enthralled by my future husband's appearance because he was very unusual looking. He had quite long hair, which in those days was uncommon. He looked like a poet or an artist. He had very large eyes. He was very thin and serious looking. He was, I thought, very romantic looking and he was a quiet man.

Apparently, Eugenie had made a strong impression on John, too. Instead of returning to Red Wing that night, he and Liz drove all the way down to Carleton College and convinced the dormitory housemother to allow Eugenie (who had just returned by bus), to come *back* out with them in the middle of the night. "We got to Tower View about 3 a.m.," Eugenie recalled.

We didn't go to bed that night, we stayed up listening to music, the phonograph. I can remember that in the morning about sunrise we thought we'd better get some fresh air and we walked out toward Red Wing along the road when the sun was coming up. . . . We had lots of long discussions about music and the arts and philosophy. I don't think we ever talked anything about politics. In fact I'm sure we didn't. We never talked about anything personal. This was a very rarified atmosphere in which we were living at that time. I must say we were all of us in an ivory tower.[8]

John and Eugenie saw each other occasionally through Eugenie's spring semester. In the summer of 1930, she went home to Iowa. And pined for John. Ezekiel and Flora Belle Moore took Eugenie and her younger sister, Mary, on an extended road trip to Oregon in July, returning home to Des Moines at the end of the month. Within a day or two, John Anderson was knocking on the Moores' front door, and any pretense of a platonic relationship was abandoned. He invited Eugenie to spend the second week of August at Tower View, and by the end of that week, they had become engaged, to the shock and disapproval of both sets of parents. A. P. and Lydia feared for John's dangerously spontaneous proposal, and Ezekiel and Flora Belle wanted Eugenie to finish college first and get her degree.

None of them had a prayer against the romantic whirlwind of the affair. Eugenie's love letters to John after their engagement were filled with giddy astonishment and breathless anticipation. Eugenie professed herself "unbelievably certain and bewildered and full—all at the same time." She sent him quotations about the lovers Odysseus and Penelope (written by Homer about 800 BCE), and Jerome and Sophie from the new novel about a white man and a black girl in jazz-age Seattle, *The Game of Love and Death*. Eugenie wrote, "All the time that I have been reading or lying here in the dark alone I have been thinking about what our lives—I am not sure if I can yet say our life—can be, must be." She gushes on, writing out the complete text of an Emily Dickinson love poem, even speculating on what sort of a man Jesus really *was*. The girl was pixie-mazed in love, spouting Homer, Beethoven, German philosophy, Christian theory, best-selling novels, and intricate poetry.[9]

Without John's letters to compare, his responses are unknown. But he was equally committed to the engagement—that is certain, since he ignored his much-honored parents' misgivings. The initial plan was to find an apartment in Paris and set up studios where John would continue with his painting and art studies, and Eugenie would devote herself to the piano, Beethoven, and Bach. It is clear from Eugenie's letters that she had her heart set on Paris. One could easily believe, in this mad flush of love and good fortune, she felt Paris was her destiny. Compromise, however, was necessary, and A. P. and Lydia evidently told John that while they couldn't stop him from getting married, they could refuse to pay for a life in Paris. Eugenie wrote:

> Can it be that we are really making definite plans to be together? And you are very sure that your Father's and Mother's opposition is not too much? . . . perhaps it is wise to choose Paris, for one cannot be sure when it will come again. But I also understand your feeling

about New York and I too think that there is a vast amount to absorb there—more than I shall be capable of for a long time.—

And so it seems to be still finally your decision. And I shall not make application for a passport until you write again more definitely.[10]

Eugenie scribbled a postscript in the margin of a letter, gratitude for the wedding gift she had received from Lydia, John's mother: the order of a Steinway grand piano. "And can you think of a piano," she wrote, "such a piano—and me, and you, and together?"[11]

So the wedding took place, in the living room of the Moores' modest parsonage in Des Moines, Iowa, officiated by Rev. Ezekiel A. Moore. Only the immediate family attended, no photographer was hired, and the bride did not wear a white gown. Someone took candid photos on the front lawn after the ceremony. Thirty seconds of black-and-white movie film exist showing the ebullient bride peeking out under a cloche hat and a dark-suited groom, in a fedora like a Hollywood movie star, boarding a train for Chicago. They smile and wave, and they are gone.

The first three days of the couple's honeymoon were spent in the city of Chicago, in the company of Charles Biederman, a young artist to whom Eugenie had been introduced the year prior by her older sister Julie Moore. Julie and Charles were both students at the Art Institute of Chicago, and it was Julie and Eugenie Moore who introduced Charles to John Anderson, and the bond that the men formed, for better or for worse, shaped the rest of both families' lives. Certainly, spending one's honeymoon in 1930 with a third party is indicative of their youthful and modern ideas. About four days after the wedding, the Andersons boarded their second train, bound for New York City.

Eugenie had been accepted to what is now the Juilliard School (then called the Institute of Musical Art) to study the piano. The newlyweds had arrangements to stay at the New Yorker Hotel while they hunted for the right apartment with enough space for the Steinway grand piano and good northern light for a painter's studio.

September 1, 1930. John P. Anderson, twenty-three, and Eugenie Moore, twenty-one, were married in a simple ceremony in the living room of the Moores' Des Moines, Iowa, parsonage, offici-ated by the bride's father, Rev. Ezekiel A. Moore. *Anderson family collection.*

As soon as they arrived, a letter met them from John's mother, Lydia. A. P. had suffered a serious anemia attack, was briefly hospitalized, and then was brought home to Tower View to recuperate. Within the next two weeks, Lydia herself would be sent away for a rest cure. The exhaustion incurred by A. P.'s illness and John's precipitous wedding and departure put her close to collapse, and she was bundled off to the Battle Creek Sanitarium in Michigan. No one knew at the time (including Lydia) that she was in the early stages of breast cancer. Little sister Jean, fourteen years old, wrote to John in New York, wondering about his new apartment and "the way you have it fixed." She extols the home farm pumpkins and bushels of squashes and sunflowers, all stacked up. "I wish you could be here to see them," she closes. The trouble was, John wished he could be there, too.[12]

The bedevilment of alcoholism cannot be underestimated. Like cancer, it does not choose people based on health or bad intentions. It is a disease: you can treat it for a lifetime, but it will never be cured. John Anderson suffered from this illness, and while you could say that he "won the war" by living to the age of ninety-one with relatively few other physical ailments, you could also say that he fought innumerable battles day by day, year by year. Some he won; many he lost. John and Eugenie had been married for just over three months when John confronted his wife in their New York apartment kitchen and told her that their marriage had been a grave mistake and that he wanted a divorce. In response, Eugenie fled the apartment, still wearing her kitchen apron, and leaped onto a train out of Manhattan. She took it to the end of the line on Long Island and walked out onto a beach overlooking the Atlantic Ocean. There she stood, sobbing, when a kindly stranger asked her if she was all right, if she needed help. The intervention resulted in Eugenie's turning her back on the sea and going home to the apartment.[13]

As with most of John's previous troubles and dilemmas, the handling of this one was taken over by his parents. Eugenie wrote to them of John's pronouncement, and they immediately responded with authority. There would be no divorce. The newlyweds must honor their vows, accept responsibility, and learn how to "pull together like a good team of horses." John, trapped by his addiction to alcohol (and dependency on his parents) more than his regrets over a whirlwind marriage, had what was then called a "nervous breakdown." A. P. and Lydia arranged for him to be sent to Chicago and committed to the psychiatric ward at the Henrotin Hospital on North La Salle Street. Everyone was told that John had a serious digestive complaint and had exhausted himself working in New York. Even his sisters thought that he was on a special diet and recuperating from bad health that had nothing to do with the truth of his substance abuse. For several months, Eugenie was not allowed to visit him. The entire experience, thinly documented by family letters and certainly never spoken of in years to come, smacks of frighteningly antiquated treatments for alcoholism and depression. John was sequestered in a locked ward without an advocate. A letter from Lydia refers to the mixed nature of his fellow inpatients:

> By the way I was wondering if you should not change your room to another floor. I sort of feel a bit nervous over your room being so near the policemen and the gangsters. Ask Dr. W. right away. It would be no trick for your room to be used as a hiding place if gangsters decided to make trouble, so I think you better get out of there. Tell Dr. W. I am the one who wants the change. As soon as that police man makes a move to get out of the hospital there is going to be trouble.[14]

Eugenie remained in New York, alone in the apartment, trying to keep up with her music studies. She wrote letters to John describing the sound of her piano, the wind and the sun and how they felt as she walked along the East River, the possibility of apartments with larger windows and better light. She asked: "If we are at Tower View next year in the farm house, what kind of a studio is there? Maybe you could have a skylight fixed! Think how straightly one can walk there! But I like to walk erectly here by the river too." Near the letter's conclusion, she confessed: "The house is very quiet. Every slightest sound is amplified now, especially when it is dark." Lastly, she mentions her attachment to a Cézanne mounted print of *The Boy in the Red Vest*. Among the family's collection of photographs is a picture from Eugenie's bedroom in about 1993: there on the wall over her bed is the Cézanne print of *The Boy in the Red Vest*, and its presence on the wall illustrated much about Eugenie and John's enduring strength over a lifetime of painful compromises and choices.[15]

Eugenie in early married years, about 1932, with John's parents, Alexander P. Anderson and Lydia M. Anderson, at Tower View in Red Wing, Minnesota. *Anderson family collection.*

Their marriage could have ended here, but in the spring of 1931, John and Eugenie, influenced by the probability that A. P. and Lydia would cut them off financially if they divorced, and also young and strong enough to bounce back from bad times, chose to start over. John spent some time in New York at the apartment, spent more time at "home" in Minnesota, and visited Charles Biederman in Chicago. Eugenie persevered at Juilliard. On her summer holidays, in July 1931, the young married couple traveled to Highlands, North Carolina, where A. P. and Lydia Anderson still owned and maintained a large house on some property in the Blue Ridge Mountains, a veritable paradise retreat. Part of the time, they shared the house and their vacation time with John's sisters. Eugenie felt very left out when the rambunctious, hearty Andersons took off for all-day picnics on horseback, leaving Eugenie behind because she didn't ride. While at Highlands, John wrote home to his parents that he and Eugenie had decided to pack up in New York and move back to Minnesota and Tower View. The elder Andersons agreed: they offered the large white frame farmhouse (built in 1925 for a farm manager's family) on ten acres along the east side of the property to John and Eugenie as a permanent residence. The house boasted two stories and a full basement, spacious, airy rooms, four bedrooms on the second level, three modern bathrooms, a four-car garage, and plenty of grounds for both privacy and future buildings if required.

So while John and Eugenie anticipated their move back to Minnesota, A. P. and Lydia began preparing for their annual winter in Hawaii. Before they left, however, A. P. voiced his concerns over John's apparent plans to invite Charles Biederman to cohabit the farmhouse with himself and Genie. A. P. wrote: "Now as to Charles B[i]ederman. *Bederman* is a good name & I am sure that he is a very fine going man. As Mother wrote, we all have our own way of doing things. Mother & myself have so many people & obligations on our mind—among which our children, that we cannot add more to our efforts. This is just a note in ans. to your letter. Hope you are keeping up your *standard weight*. I understand you are."[16]

In other words, Charles was not welcome as a rent-free resident at Tower View. John went back and forth between Highlands, North Carolina, and New York City throughout the summer and fall. Eugenie went back to New York to facilitate the transfer of her music studies and the contents of their apartment. But then they seemed to waffle on whether or not to go to Minnesota; Charles Biederman might have had something to do with their failure to commit. The notion of Paris came up again. Should they all go? Letters imply that while John was working on his art (both he and Charles were painting), he was also not feeling well. Both of his parents inquire about his diet and offer advice after an "appendicitis scare." In actuality, John was experimenting with drugs in addition to alcohol, putting strain on both his physical and mental health.[17]

At the end of May 1932, the Andersons arrived in Red Wing, closely followed by Charles, who had just returned from an unsatisfactory voyage of artistic discovery (subsidized by John) to Biederman's father's roots in Prague, Czechoslovakia. Eugenie reminisced:

> [Charles] came back and he spent I believe almost six months at Red Wing living with us at that time. He had one of the upstairs rooms for his studio; John had his studio in a converted chicken house . . . and I had my piano in the downstairs living room, which I learned later that my practicing, especially of Bach . . . drove Charles almost crazy because he was trying to paint in the room upstairs and there was no sound proofing or anything. . . . I think that we had all thought in the beginning that we might be able to just continue this indefinitely but that wasn't practical.[18]

It isn't likely that Eugenie, John, or Charles were paying any attention to the political scene, certainly not in Minnesota, nor even nationally. A. P. and Lydia Anderson were Republicans. John didn't vote. November 1932 ushered in the beginning of the Franklin D. Roosevelt years. Most of the country was grappling with the Great Depression, but because of A. P.'s safe investments and freedom from vulnerable dependencies (he owned a lot of land outright without debt and ran it with the combined talents of a farmer and a savvy businessman), the Andersons were not affected by the stock market crash. Eugenie wrote: "John was painting and, once again, even though we were living in New York when the Depression was beginning, I don't remember of being very touched by it . . . we were aware there were growing numbers of unemployed people and occasional breadlines." While the likes of Floyd B. Olson and Elmer Benson made their mark on Minnesota (during the high tide of the Farmer-Labor Party from 1930 to 1938), Eugenie lived mostly oblivious, delving even more deeply into a concentration on the life's work of Johann Sebastian Bach. Knowing that she could not aspire to be a concert pianist (being too far away from urban centers of activity and lacking the touch of genius necessary), she told herself that she would become the world's greatest expert on Bach. She studied at Carleton College, driving back and forth several times a week from Red Wing. Both she and John read constantly about art and philosophy and music theory, and they kept up a steady correspondence with Biederman, who had set up a studio in Chicago under John's patronage.[19]

While John had always previously declared that he did not want children, Eugenie became pregnant early in 1934. She is very clear in her reminiscences that at this point "I didn't plan to have a career. I wanted to have a family. And as a matter of fact, after we had Johanna, and I thought she was so wonderful, I thought we should have five children, which my husband didn't think was a very good idea."[20]

As Eugenie's first pregnancy advanced, she felt healthy and strong; she was but twenty-five years old. But through the spring and summer of 1934, as Eugenie glowed with the excitement of impending motherhood, Lydia Anderson was succumbing to the final stages of incurable breast cancer. While the family story differs according to who tells it, several people, including Eugenie herself, have repeated Lydia's great advice to her daughter-in-law, as they walked around the sunlit meadows of the Tower View estate the summer before Lydia died. Eugenie's version is recorded in her

Portrait of Eugenie Anderson by Charles Biederman, about 1930-31. The painting's style is highly reminiscent of Paul Cézanne's *The Boy in the Red Vest. Author's collection.*

reminiscences: "[Lydia] urged me to do something besides have a family. . . . 'Oh, you must do this because you will always feel that you should have if you don't.' She said, 'I have always felt that I should have done something creative that was just my own work.' And I expressed surprise and said, 'But you had a wonderful family. This was your creation.' She said, 'It is not the same.' . . . Now, this was quite unusual for a mother-in-law, I think."[21]

Other versions of "the talk" clarify that not only did Lydia encourage Eugenie to find a creative outlet, or by extension a career outside of her family, but she advised it in part believing that her son, John, was not capable of great change—was perhaps not even capable of permanently leaving Tower View. If Eugenie wanted to see the world, or experience life in a way that differed from making a home on this Minnesota farm, she would have to carve it out for herself. Moreover, Lydia absolutely thought that Eugenie should do just that.[22]

John and Eugenie's first child was born in the late autumn of 1934, a girl named Elizabeth Johanna. She arrived a month too late to meet her grandmother Lydia, who had died on September 27 at age fifty-eight. All of the Andersons went into deep mourning for their beloved mother and equated Lydia's loss with a seismic shift away from the utopian quality of Tower View's first twenty years. Throughout 1935 and 1936, both John and Eugenie made several trips to New York City, where they still kept an apartment, and where Charles Biederman was also living and working in his own place. Galleries were beginning to take notice, and Biederman worked feverishly and constantly, continually developing his techniques and theories. His relationship with John only strengthened, and they kept plots afoot to bring their New Art to the public eye.

Once again, Charles was invited to stay for an extended visit at Tower View, in the summer of 1936. These would be the final months in which Charles Biederman merely painted on a flat canvas: his ideas were moving toward three-dimensional collage, sculpture, and eventually what he would call "constructionism," or later, "structurism." And all of it was theorized, formulated, and planned between both Charles and John Anderson. They also agreed that it was necessary for Charles to go to Paris, to study, create new work, and be involved in the art movements there. As had been their standard arrangement, John funded the endeavor in return for a number of finished works when Charles came back. Biederman sailed off to Europe and was quickly immersed in the Paris art world, mingling and learning from the exhibits of Pablo Picasso, Piet Mondrian, Juan Gris, Georges Braque, Fernand Léger, and Joan Miró. Modern art enthusiasts would no doubt put such an epoch in Paris at the top of their time machine wish lists. Charles was there. John was not.

Biederman spent enough time in the cafés of Paris to sense the widespread and growing fear of Hitler's Germany. Writing to John Anderson in the spring of 1937, Biederman said, "Imagine Al Capone running the United States and you have a not exaggerated picture of today's Germany."[23]

It was Eugenie who felt the urge to witness history, to make a temporary break from Minnesota and travel to Europe, where she had never gone before. Eugenie later said: "The news of the world that was beginning to reach us more with the radio and the rise of Hitler, events in Europe that seemed to be leading toward a World War began to penetrate even into our ivory tower.... I wanted John to go but he didn't want to go ... my friends encouraged me and I finally decided I would go." For whatever reason, John declined the opportunity. Perhaps their marriage was especially difficult at this point, or perhaps he was depressed and unable to find the energy for overseas travel. Their daughter was about two and a half years old. Eugenie arranged for her sister Mary Moore Pine to come and stay with Johanna while she was away. John was a loving father, but not an active participant in childcare when his children were very young, which wasn't unusual for the times.[24]

And so Eugenie traveled. This was the milestone that she cited to anyone who asked, ten, twenty, thirty years later, and for the rest of her life. She explained it to the reporters who wanted to know what inspired the first woman ambassador of the United States. She used it in her speeches when she visited the counties of Minnesota to gain support for her Senate campaign. And she harkened back to it even in the 1980s, when she was serving dinner at the table at Tower View, wearing a clean kitchen apron. In the streets of Berlin in 1937, she saw the young boys marching in rows, even

Salzburg, Austria. One of the only existing photographs of Eugenie Anderson in the spring of 1937 when she visited Europe for the first time. *Anderson family collection.*

goose-stepping, holding out their hands to say "Heil, Hitler," and it made her sick to her stomach. The threatening atmosphere of Germany and other places where extreme anti-Semitism was erupting must have seemed surreal when viewed against the other objectives of Eugenie's tour. She went to Arles, France, to worship at the altar of Van Gogh. Salzburg, Vienna, Amsterdam, Bonn. Every great region and city revealed to her the manifestation of everything she had been reading about and dreaming about for ten years: music, art, language, architecture, philosophy. She fell in love with the world—the good, the bad, and the ugly altogether.

Later, Eugenie would publicly say that the first immediate action she took at home upon returning from this voyage was to join the League of Women Voters. This is true, but not the whole truth. To family members, Eugenie admitted that her other reaction to the experience was to want another child. Hans Anderson recalls a talk he had with John in 1982: "And [John] said 'well for the first three years of your life,' he said, 'I had absolutely nothing to do with you.' My mother had told me many times before that that he didn't want to have children at *all*, and that after Johanna was born, he certainly didn't want to have any more, and she said 'I tricked him and got pregnant again.'"[25]

Eugenie's first impulse, as a woman, coming home to her beautiful daughter and privileged American life, was to build on that utopia and share it with another human being—another creation of her own. This she accomplished within a few weeks of returning. Her other reaction, which was a much more academic decision based on being a person and a citizen, regardless of her gender, was to begin investigating her outlets for political involvement. It began with study: "I read a great deal and I also soon after that realized that I knew nothing about our own government." Peggy Lamson, author of *Few Are Chosen: American Women in Political Life Today*, wrote: "[Anderson's] action was not merely symbolic; she immersed herself in League activities, learning all that she could about her own country, its government, and its relation to the shrinking world. By the time World War II began she was a committed internationalist."[26]

It was never an option for Eugenie to simply put on lipstick and drive to her meetings, maybe stuff a few envelopes, or make phone calls. It would never have occurred to her that attendance could be superficial, perfunctory, or just a lark. She was not trying out the League of Women Voters to see what they could do for her or whether they could fill a social void in her daily life. She was there to see what *she* could do for the democracy of the United States, which, in her mind, was the primary beacon of hope for a world perched on the brink of another world war. Lamson wrote in 1968: "All too often, I suspect, women who say they would like to enter public life hover on the brink and then turn back because they tell themselves it would not be fair to their husbands to go forward. They then regret their retreat as a sacrifice when it is, in fact, an excuse. The likelihood is that they were not really drawn to public life as activists but only as interested observers."[27]

Lamson's words of fifty years ago are fairly harsh on women. But their sentiment is indicative of what Eugenie may have believed even as she embarked on her personal fact-finding mission in 1937. As it will become increasingly clear through this biographical exploration of Eugenie's career, she did not see herself as represented by most feminist beliefs. Over many years, she more or less denied the tenets of the "feminine mystique": that she began as a housewife with dissatisfied stirrings who silently pondered the hopeless, existential "Is this all?" She also made it clear that it was not her *primary* goal to be a role model, a spokesperson, or any kind of champion for women's rights. She saw women's rights as human rights, bottom line. It was the promotion and expansion of human rights, protected by civil rights, that she later spent her time and energy advocating.[28]

The summer of 1937, while Eugenie was gestating and cogitating the state of the world, John Anderson was hitting a strong creative period himself. Charles Biederman left Paris and moved back to

New York at the end of June, then came to stay at Tower View for the month of August. Biederman's biographers note, "He and John worked on sculpture, including a project made in concrete now in the collection at the Minneapolis Institute of Art. . . . These collaborative efforts were productive, and the men were sincerely appreciative of one another's abilities." Charles also enjoyed the frequent visits of Eugenie's sister Mary Moore Pine to Tower View. She was married, but not happily so, and both Charles and Mary harbored a secret crush on the other.[29]

In the early spring of 1938, Eugenie gave birth to her second child and named him Hans Pierce. The year following Hans's birth was a difficult one for Eugenie. While intense, productive work and good relations between artists supplied John with energy and enthusiasm, it also created a loud, busy atmosphere around the farmhouse much of the time. Many letters from Eugenie's mother and sisters inquired after Eugenie's state of mind and physical well-being, in recognition of her late nights talking, cleaning up, and listening to John and Charles and their endless debates and plans for their art advancement and publication of their theories—as well as her early mornings feeding Hans before dawn. By day, John and Charles spent all of their time in the many different spaces of the Tower View estate that facilitated studios for drawing and design; workshops for sculpture, model making, spray-painting, and gluing; and laboratories for wood- and metalworking, soldering, and multimedia construction. The year 1938 was exceptionally important for both of them. For Eugenie, however, as much as she loved and reveled in her two children, life stagnated, and the Andersons' marriage suffered. Seriously debilitated by sleep deprivation by the end of the year, Eugenie made plans to leave Tower View temporarily and seek respite near her own family. In February 1939, Eugenie took the two children on the train down to New Orleans, where her brother and his wife lived. Mary Moore Pine, recently separated from her husband and filing for a divorce, was also living there and working as a secretary to a medical doctor. Their mother,

Flora Belle Moore, joined the family circus for long visits as well. A nanny was hired to look after the children so that Eugenie could spend time alone or with family and friends.

Elizabeth Anderson, now married to Ray Hedin and living in Chicago, wrote to Eugenie in February 1939. She reported that John appeared at the Hedins' door in Chicago one night, an unexpected surprise visit, and that "he looked better than I've seen him for a long time and must have gained weight." One can only speculate what John's family thought about John and Eugenie's unconventional marriage, in which each party seemed to operate independently of the other in work, child rearing, travel, and almost all aspects of daily life. Five years had passed since the death of Lydia Anderson, and while A. P. persisted in working and living at Tower View and wintering in Hawaii or Florida, he was lonely and isolated without his daughters, who had all moved away. One curt line in the same letter from Elizabeth (above) hints at a relationship that later came to have great significance to all of the Andersons. Liz wrote: "Saw Vinnie. She is fine and working hard as ever." Vinnie Eleanor Munson, fifty and never married, was a housekeeper at the big house at Tower View. She had worked there as a maid for many years, long before Lydia died, and probably took care of increasing numbers of details and tasks for A. P. as he grew older. Vinnie always loved Eugenie, and the admiration was mutual. Vinnie was a frequent babysitter to Hans and Johanna when Eugenie was in residence in Minnesota. In 1939, whether or not A. P. and Vinnie were romantically or sexually involved, they no doubt had a caring relationship beyond that of employer and employee. Vinnie's trust in Eugenie's friendship would help her immensely in years to come.[30]

Eugenie spent two months in New Orleans and returned to Tower View with the children in the spring. Mary Moore Pine's divorce was finalized on May 15, 1939 (a process that included her ex-husband's parents' threats to sue her for attorney and court costs, which Mary ultimately had to pay in full). Mary also toyed with joining the Communist Party, having been introduced to it

Sisters, Eugenie and Mary, 1938. *Anderson family collection.*

by a man she was casually dating. "I have been seriously thinking about it," she wrote, "and I might decide to do it yet. I wouldn't tell anyone but you, however, if I did it."[31]

The two younger Moore sisters, while they had always been close, grew doubly attached in these years of the late 1930s. They relied heavily on each other for moral support and a sympathetic ear when each needed to legitimize, or just recognize, ongoing struggles with their spouses. Both of them had grown away from any strong ties with the Christian religion; both of them were highly drawn to intellectual pursuits within their own minds and outward in discussion with others, the favorite topics being art, music, and philosophy. And they were both seeking meaning and purpose for themselves as individuals, outside the roles of wife or mother. Mary was very keen to hear from all walks of life at lectures and meetings for labor unions, civil rights, modern psychology and medicine, sexual freedom, and, among political possibilities, the Communist Party. She was only twenty-eight years old, divorced, without children, and extremely attractive. Trouble was, she just couldn't get Charles Biederman out of her system. In one letter, she joked: "I had several dates with one of the Communists and he did his best to make me one too. . . . He is very attractive physically, but his mind is so adamantly communist that I naturally and instinctively shy away from him. He promptly asked me to be his sweetheart and I as promptly refused, so I don't imagine I'll see much of him now." A month later, Mary inquired after Charles, who had been staying with John and Genie for some weeks. "I was much interested to hear about the change in Charles B.," she wrote. "If he is considering getting married—well that is most amazing of all. Ask him if I would do?"[32]

Charles probably overstayed his welcome at Tower View (it certainly wasn't the first time). Letters between Eugenie and her mother and sisters again dwelt on the unrelenting and tiring nature of motherhood, in addition to hosting. Eugenie admitted that "I have been living a very irregular life since Charles came, and I feel as if I have been primarily in search of sleep." In September, the German invasion of Poland and escalating crash into World War II took over the news and everyone's attention. Sometime during the fall of 1939, both Charles and Mary took up, separately, residences in Chicago and began to see each other frequently. Biederman's biographer interpreted that "the Andersons watched Mary and Charles' developing relationship with some trepidation but also with sincere good will toward both of them."[33]

Early in 1940, Eugenie and her sister-in-law Elizabeth Anderson Hedin decided to develop a nursery school in Red Wing, combining their organizational talents with their desire to foster early education and help families of all income levels. They had both read extensively on the benefit of social and educational interaction for little ones under school age, particularly the work coming out of the Institute of Child Development at the University of Minnesota. It was a deliberate step in Eugenie's quest for finding civic (proto-political) involvement, even though she was still nonpartisan and unaware of the intricacies of the two major parties. "At that time I didn't have any idea of becoming involved," she reminisced. "I guess because my parents had been Republicans, John's parents were Republican. Everybody probably thought we would be Republicans too." The nursery school project lasted for about two years, closing soon after the United States entered into the war; gas rationing kept anyone living at Tower View with limited means to drive into town.[34]

The month before America was drawn into World War II, Eugenie's last living grandparent, Eliza Jane Arrowsmith Moore, died in Long Beach, California. She was ninety-one years old, a human bridge of memory and blood connection to the previous century and even the Civil War. While the death might seem tangential here, the lives and heritage of our grandparents, and past generations, have a huge, often unexamined impact on our own histories—indeed, our futures. In 1941, Eugenie had no conscious thought of entering public life as a diplomat or a voice for anyone or any group. She was

Anderson family, 1940: Hans, age two; Eugenie, age thirty-one; John, age thirty-three; Johanna, age five. *Anderson family collection.*

focused on her family and her young children, pouring her energy into a nursery school and maintaining an unconventional marriage. And yet, I can't help remembering the bedtime stories Genie told to me at Tower View when I was young. She told me about *her* grandparents, the Moores and the McMillens. One of my favorite stories was about her grandfather Willie Moore, who ran away to join the Union Army when he was only fourteen years old. His twin brother, Jimmy, ran away, too. Genie told me: You are only here listening to my story because my grandfather's discharge from Abraham Lincoln arrived in time, and he marched back home where he could recover, grow older, and marry Eliza Jane Arrowsmith. Will's twin brother, Jim, was not so lucky. He died, on Sherman's march to Atlanta, with a sniper's bullet in his spine. He was seventeen.

Eugenie understood the connections between generations. She honored them, and she studied them. While most of her time was consumed by childcare and domestic necessities, she continually joined in John and Charles's (and other family members') discussions about the interconnections among science and art, philosophy and music, semantics and historical progression. Eugenie always had a great interest and capacity, probably unexpressed at the time, for seeing the silvery threads between family and history, not in an intellectual or theoretical way but in a very real, sensory, urgent manner. Mothers spend a lot of time inhaling the heady fragrance of their children's hair and sweet shoulders. It reminds them of what their own mothers must have experienced. When Eliza Jane died in November 1941, the Moore family gathered to mourn her passing and reflect on all that had changed since that old woman had been a tiny baby on a pioneer farm in 1850. They couldn't know, of course, that Pearl Harbor would be bombed by the Japanese in less than a month's time. But they did know that Fate's decision in the Civil War had been to choose one twin and not the other. Did Eugenie ask herself: What is my fate? And did her unconscious reply: *Do something about it?*

The week before Pearl Harbor, Charles Biederman and Mary Moore informed John and Eugenie that they wanted to get married. Their intention was to take the train from Chicago to Red Wing, planning to have a civil ceremony with only John and Eugenie for witnesses; then the Japanese arrived in Hawaii, and America was drawn into World War II. Charles wrote: "Mary and I have decided to go through with our plans as previously arranged, regardless of the implication of my age-vulnerability to soldiering. . . . Please give no information about Mary and me until it's over with. I was so busy today, Mary had to buy the ring." The Biedermans were married on Christmas Day 1941.[35]

Eugenie did what most women of her age did after war was declared: she volunteered with the local Red Cross, as well as the war bond drive. She reminisced: "I do remember that I gave a good many speeches for the War Bond Drive and for the Red Cross. . . . I became aware of the fact that I enjoyed making speeches and I enjoyed talking to people and trying to persuade people to do something." The activity also drove her to think more deeply about history and consequences. "The League [of Women Voters] was beginning to study the United Nations. And I felt that this was a wonderful hope for the prevention of future wars . . . [partly] because of my son's age. . . . And I think that this awareness of mine that isolationism was not the way to prevent wars was propelling me more and more toward political activity." It was also at this point that Eugenie began to rely more heavily on household and nanny help. Vinnie came over often from the big house at Tower View. Several other women were employed to clean, organize, and look after the children, who at eight and almost four years old were decidedly out of babyhood.[36]

A very important element of World War II that affected John and Charles was the draft. As the months went by, the draft was increased to include men of older ages and also those with children. As artists and self-employed individuals, John and Charles were easy candidates to be drafted, and they conspired together to find ways to avoid it. Although Biederman had been writing a great manifesto (over eight hundred pages at this point), with Mary proofreading and editing, different occupations needed to be found that would secure both Charles's and John's value to society outside of the armed services. In the meantime, Mary became pregnant. While Mary prepared for her first child and spent a great deal of time with Eugenie, Johanna, and Hans, John hit upon the means by which he and Charles could exonerate themselves from the draft.

Saying goodbye to Hans at home, about 1940. Eugenie drove round-trip from Red Wing to the Twin Cities during her many years of collaboration with the DFL, Hubert Humphrey, and the ADA. Before that, she spent several years volunteering and working for the League of Women Voters and other activities. *Anderson family collection.*

Using the laboratories and mechanical facilities at the Tower View estate, and setting up a partnership called the Anderson Institute, they contracted with the government to run a series of medical experiments. The first involved using volunteer (or what were *called* volunteer) patients at the Hastings mental hospital and inmates of the Stillwater state prison, monitoring their wounds and testing procedures to keep them from getting infected. Subsequent experimental work moved away from this area of medicine, and the men were asked to design equipment that would provide information on the effects of oxygen deprivation on the brain. (Apparently, the army wanted to know why dive-bombing pilots often blacked out.) "Biederman and Anderson invented a pressurized neck-cuff that would gradually starve the brain of oxygen. They watched for signs of unconsciousness and noted the onset and duration of blackouts in their subjects. They tested it on prisoners at Stillwater and mental patients at Hastings. They also tested it on themselves, suffering their own discomfort before trying it on others."[37]

As the war intensified, Charles and Mary welcomed their baby daughter, Anna, into the world in early 1943. Anderson and Biederman succeeded in avoiding the draft, but they were also prohibited from working on the new art that they had designed since war rationing kept metal and plastic virtually unobtainable. Meanwhile, the big house next door at Tower View was empty—A. P. Anderson was spending the winter in Florida, accompanied by Vinnie, who had become his nurse as well as his companion. Hans Anderson warmly reminisced about his eccentric old grandfather, who made a fortune on puffed grain, loved farming, wrote sentimental poetry, and ran around the estate fields flapping his arms as he contemplated the physics of helicopter blades.

> Alexander took [my cousin] Hugh and I down to the edge of the field in back of the whole Tower View, this big field, and the sun would go down on the other side, the other end of it, to the west. We would all lie down on the ground and he had this enormous . . . World War I lever-action rifle . . . and he would wait until a gopher would stick

its head up and it would be silhouetted by the light, and he'd pull the trigger. And he often would hit them! And they would just vaporize. [laughs] He *hated* gophers! . . . from his growing up in the fields of Minnesota, plowing and stuff, and the crops . . . even as an old man . . . if he only would kill one, it would be a good evening.[38]

A. P. died in Miami, Florida, at age seventy-nine, with Vinnie—his wife—by his side.

They had been married in Florida, in secret. None of the children were told, and none of them knew, even as they were untangling the red tape to have A. P.'s body transported back to Minnesota. It took some time and some doing (wartime only complicated issues). Vinnie would have come back with the body to the empty big house at Tower View, where everyone expected her to carry on as a house-keeper and manager. She was terrified and distraught. And it was to Eugenie that she turned for advice and support. At the recep-tion after the funeral (at which Vinnie probably had to help serve), she approached Eugenie, drew her aside, and told her that she and Alexander had been married. *How do I tell them? What will happen?* It transpired that Eugenie was the one to break the news to John, Louise, Elizabeth, and Jean. A lot of time had passed since Euge-nie was the newcomer to the Anderson family, but in many ways she was still the odd one out; she must have found it very difficult to be the liaison in this sensitive situation, where everyone's feel-ings would be hurt and no one could profit. Indeed, it must have required the tact of a diplomat—and Eugenie was already becom-ing equal to that. The Andersons did not respond kindly at first to the bombshell that their father had married his nurse-housekeeper in secret. Their first actions were to ensure that A. P.'s will would secure for the four children their full inheritance of Tower View, its land, and all of A. P.'s assets. Managing that, they set up a gen-erous lifetime allowance for Vinnie and bought her a house in Red Wing. Vinnie had never wanted anything more—unless it was the acceptance and love that the Anderson siblings only very gradually extended.

Many say that America grew up over World War II, that any vestiges of being a young country or an upstart player on the international stage were over. The same could be said of Eugenie Anderson. In 1944, as the war moved toward its final year of resolution, Eugenie was thirty-five years old: middle-aged and never again "young." Her exposure to international affairs, preliminary education in government and the hopes for a United Nations, and awareness that her home life would never provide enough stimulation for her caused her to reach outward. In doing so, she was fully aware of the fact that she was deliberately walking into a male sphere of activity. She was not content with groups proscribed for women: the League of Women Voters, home front support of the soldiers, committees and domestic organizations such as nursery schools and PTAs. Although she recognized and respected their efforts and high value to many people, Eugenie was personally most interested in the wide world, not just her corner of it. And in order to be part of that world, even influence it, she had to step out of the kitchen and join the men.

Two
JOINING the PARTY

Although she could not have known it at the time, in
casting her lot with the Minnesota Democratic-Farmer-Labor
group, Eugenie Anderson did more than simply join a party.
She became a charter member of a dynasty, one of a hard core
of twenty-five or more dedicated, talented, young liberals, many
of whom were to play an important role on the national scene.

PEGGY LAMSON, *FEW ARE CHOSEN*

IN 1944, WORLD WAR II WAS STILL RAGING. PLENTY OF women had jobs in factories and businesses that were drained of their male workforce. Volunteerism was practically universal; everyone pitched in. But Eugenie had had enough of rolling bandages and of addressing other women circled around teacups in church basements and school cafeterias, asking for their spare change to support the war bond campaign. She knew that partisan politics, from the grassroots up to the national parties, was the only way for her to pursue her larger objectives—and that meant leaving the women's tearoom and walking across to the door of the men's club. "And it was in 1944 that I had reached the decision, especially after attending my first national convention of the League of Women Voters . . . that I should become partisan, that I should join a political party. I felt that in Minnesota that the Republican party was divided into an isolationist wing . . . but by that time I was more sympathetic with Roosevelt and the Democratic national administration."[1]

Eugenie's political plunge began with a spontaneous decision, with her brother-in-law Ray Hedin, to drive up to Minneapolis and "go and see this man Humphrey and find out what we should do." One seemingly off-the-cuff and informational meeting led to a life-time political alliance and deep friendship. Hubert Humphrey, a Macalester professor and Minneapolis mayoral candidate who had lost the previous year's election, was firing up a new campaign—not just for mayor, but for merging disparate factions and rede-signing the whole structure of the Democratic-Farmer-Labor Party in Minnesota. Eugenie responded immediately to Humphrey's well-known charisma and enthusiastic, folksy approach, and she listened carefully to his advice for taking those first steps, which encouraged grassroots involvement and organization: Go to meet-ings. Bring your friends.[2]

The first precinct caucus that Eugenie attended, in early 1944, changed her life. She followed Humphrey's advice and got herself elected as a delegate to her county convention, to the amusement of the elderly Irish county chairman, lawyer Frank O'Gorman, who had assumed that a Tower View Anderson would naturally be a staunch Republican: "He was very surprised and I think delighted, not only by the fact that I was an active woman but I represented a new element in the party that he was glad to welcome." Due to Eugenie's diligence, education, and willingness to show up and be heard, she was subsequently elected the chair of the First Con-gressional District at (coincidentally) the first district convention that she had ever attended. Everyone was shocked that a woman had achieved that position at the district level. Simultaneously, the Minnesota Democratic and Farmer-Labor parties were in the process of fusing to strengthen their positions against the Repub-licans and shore up President Roosevelt's bid for another term. Hubert H. Humphrey's keynote speech at the fusion convention was the first time Eugenie had ever heard the professor orate. She stated: "I remember saying to Frank O'Gorman . . . 'I believe that young man will be President some day.' And I think many others felt the same way." She also noted, "I think Humphrey was quite surprised to see me there because he remembered that just a few months before I had been [to see him] to ask about what to do."[3]

Eugenie Anderson's foot was in the door. The newly formed Democratic-Farmer-Labor (DFL) Party was gratified when its support helped elect F. D. Roosevelt to another four years in November 1944. Eugenie became better acquainted with Hubert Humphrey and his idealistic, smart young set of friends, including Evron Kirkpatrick, a political science teacher at the University of Minnesota; Arthur Naftalin, a journalist for the *Minneapolis Tribune*; and Max Kampelman, who studied and taught history and politics. Eugenie Anderson fit right in. In a 2018 interview, Arvonne Fraser, lifelong DFL powerhouse and one of its early pillars, said: "Genie was symbolic of the kind of person Humphrey and [later, Orville] Freeman especially wanted to attract to the Party and keep in the Party. . . . She was venerated by these men. She was the symbol of *exactly* what they wanted."[4]

During long car rides to campaign events and political meetings, and at the meetings themselves, Eugenie Anderson absorbed the Humphreyites' philosophies of the Minnesota parties and their evolutions. Her own views complemented the fascination that these men had for zealously weaving politics into every fiber of life—and she engaged in the heated conversations over the threat that they all saw in the infiltration of the Communists among the Farmer-Laborites and thus the Democrats. Anderson not only supplied an upper-middle-class, feminine perspective and example for this group's nascent image, but she also contributed vast amounts of her own (and John's) knowledge of political and human history, philosophy, and rhetoric. Much of that knowledge, based on study of totalitarian systems, fascism, Nazis, and spectrums that led to the extremism of Communist systems, provided the background for her intense condemnation of Communism in any sphere of politics, local to global. "Our . . . most able advocate was Eugenie Anderson," Max Kampelman wrote. He continued: "Unlike most

of us, she came from a family of means and a background of traditional civic gentility. Eugenie was well educated, intelligent, and
immensely effective, a woman of great dignity, beauty, and com-
manding presence. She provided an aura of respectability in a way
that no one else among us could. . . . But she also brought a wise and
independent and tough political instinct to our struggle. Her gentle
demeanor, which was real, cloaked an equally real spirit that was
determined and unyielding."[5]

After President Roosevelt's fourth victory, Eugenie's rush of
political involvement tapered off for a time while the war moved
through its final and agonizing stages. May 8, 1945, saw the end of
combat in Europe. A month later, Anderson was pleased to con-
gratulate Humphrey for his victory in the hard-fought Minneapolis mayoral election. The atomic bombs dropped on Nagasaki and
Hiroshima in August were deeply and fundamentally upsetting to
Eugenie and all of the Andersons, and these events were lamented
and discussed for decades to come. Betty Friedan noted the devastation and repercussions of this time: "There was, just before the
feminine mystique took hold in America, a war, which followed a
depression and ended with the explosion of an atom bomb. After
the loneliness of war and the unspeakableness of the bomb, against
the frightening uncertainty, the cold immensity of the changing
world, women as well as men sought the comforting reality of
home and children."[6]

A major difference in Eugenie's philosophy regarding the wom-
en's movement, the necessity of it, and her place in it, is evident
when considering the text of Friedan's *The Feminine Mystique*,
which had such an enormous impact on women and politics later
on. The book specifically addresses the women and housewives of
the immediate aftermath of World War II. Eugenie, if she read this
book when it was published in the mid-1960s, would not have seen
herself in the mirror Friedan held up: "The American spirit fell into
a strange sleep; men as well as women, scared liberals, disillusioned
radicals, conservatives bewildered and frustrated by change—the

whole nation stopped growing up. . . . Women went home again just as men shrugged off the bomb, forgot the concentration camps, condoned corruption, and fell into helpless conformity. . . . There was a kind of personal retreat, even on the part of the most far-sighted, the most spirited; we lowered our eyes from the horizon and steadily contemplated our own navels."[7]

"Scared liberals"? Head-in-the-sand middle class? No: there is little to no chance that Eugenie would have ever identified herself with such a brainwashed assessment of her sex. Why? Because she saw herself and her ambitions in politics as being outside of gender. So even while Eugenie distanced herself from feminism and from being lumped in with any subset of gender-segregated issues, she was also in the position that her secure financial background *allowed* her that differentiation.

Hans Anderson talked about his memories and what it was like as a child during and immediately following World War II, particularly as it involved his mother's growing political interest. He recalled candidly that while he tolerated school, had fun times with friends, and loved working on the Tower View farm with its manager, Ed Harliss, both his parents were virtually absent, occupied away from home. Nannies and housekeepers looked after the daytime needs of Johanna and Hans. Mary Moore Biederman was a constant presence, as well as their aunt Jean Anderson Chesley, next door in the big house. The primary memory he has was that Eugenie was "almost always gone." John spent every weekday morning and evening following his stock investments in the newspaper and consulting with his broker over the telephone. Most of the daytime hours were spent with Charles in their studios and workshops.

*   *   *

In 1946, Eugenie Anderson began to see real development of her career ambitions to move toward national involvement, by way of state politics. She not only joined Humphrey's circle; her mental archive of interdisciplinary knowledge and common-sense applications provided language and structure to the proposals and policies that Humphrey's group needed to formulate. Put more simply, she could articulate, and back up with facts, what she and the others were trying to say. Things did not go well for their agenda to oust the Communists in 1946, culminating in a crushing defeat at the state Democratic convention. Humphrey's biographer Carl Solberg provides a flavorful illustration of the scene:

> Although both Naftalin and Eugenie Anderson, delegate from Red Wing, warned of trouble, neither Humphrey nor his other friends were prepared for what happened next. As the party's most prominent officeholder, Humphrey was expected to deliver the keynote address. But when he arrived he was jeered at and spat upon. His wife was refused admission until Humphrey got his police driver to escort her in. His supporters had to muscle their way in. As Humphrey rose to speak, there were cries of "fascist" and "warmonger." A beefy sergeant at arms shouted him down, "Sit down, you son of a bitch, or I'll knock you down." He was not allowed to finish his speech. . . . The Humphreyites were flattened.[8]

Like any politician, Anderson didn't like to lose. The fact that her first ideological enemies were affiliated with Communists planted a bitter seed in her mind that she would feed and water for decades to come, right up to the Vietnam War and its demoralizing end. The tactics of the Communist members (both those who claimed it and those who were Communist in secret) among the Farmer-Laborites were at the very least offensive to her, and at the most, anti-American to the point of being criminal. "The methods they used, the way they marched up and down the aisle, and kept their eye on everybody, and the way they vilified Humphrey's character, said the most outrageous things against him, against you, against me, against all of us. . . . It woke me up. It woke Humphrey up," she said to colleague Arthur Naftalin. She also stated in her reminiscences:

> [The Communists] were able to confuse the convention with all kinds of phony issues. They accused us of being red baiters and they used outrageously dictatorial tactics. . . . It was an education which

I think had an effect on the rest of my life because unless you have actually been in an organizational struggle with Communists it's difficult to appreciate the kind of tactics and methods which they use—character assassination and lies and distortions. . . . And this made a very strong effect on me. I can remember when I came home and tried to tell my family about it that I cried. I hadn't realized how it had affected me although—and I don't cry easily—this was a really bruising, searing experience.[9]

"We had lost control," agreed Humphrey, "but we had two able people in important positions." Humphrey was referring to Orville Freeman and Eugenie Anderson, who were allowed by the victorious left-wingers to fill the roles of DFL Party state secretary and vice chairwoman, respectively. Humphrey wrote: "The left figured that they could overwhelm [Eugenie], but along with that femininity was a firm, tough-minded quality they couldn't handle."[10]

Humphrey and all of his supporters were bruised, but not terminally beaten. A month after the crushing convention, Anderson read an article by James Loeb in her copy of *The New Republic* in which the Washington insider (associated with Eleanor Roosevelt and her crusaders) sent out the "battle cry" to all liberals and progressives who were opposed to Communism: "mobilize or the American Left would be lost to Communism." It set Eugenie on fire, as well as colleagues Naftalin, Kirkpatrick, and Kampelman. Here in James Loeb's well-connected example, they had national corroboration for the necessity of an irreversible split with Communists that they felt was imperative for both Minnesota and the Democratic Party of the United States. Up until this point, Anderson and Naftalin had not been able to persuade Humphrey to begin the process of breaking up with old friends with Communist connections. Eugenie invited Loeb to meet with Humphrey and their group in Minnesota, and piece by political piece, Humphrey gradually severed any Communist ties. "Even after his break . . . Humphrey was so loath to cut loose that, as Eugenie Anderson said later, 'we seemed to be fighting for his soul.'"[11]

The networking increased between Humphrey's people and the path that Anderson and Naftalin had opened to Washington and Mrs. Roosevelt via Loeb. A few months after the lunch with James Loeb, on January 5, 1947, the *New York Times* ran an article about the founding of a new organization called Americans for Democratic Action (ADA). The heavyweight group included Hubert Humphrey, mayor of Minneapolis, on its prestigious organizing committee. Names listed under the Committee of the Whole included Eugenie Anderson, Arthur Naftalin, James Loeb, Mrs. Franklin D. Roosevelt, and Franklin D. Roosevelt Jr.

Eugenie kept a print copy of her December 1947 constitution for the Minnesota chapter of the ADA. On its first page under the name and address of the organization, it lists:

MINNESOTA OFFICERS

HUBERT H. HUMPHREY
President

EUGENIE ANDERSON
Chairman

SENATOR EDWARD HAGEN
Vice-Chairman

ORVILLE FREEMAN
Secretary

EUGENE MCCARTHY
Treasurer

Except for Edward Hagen (who died in November 1950), the leaders of this ADA chapter were all destined for significant political involvement at the national level. Under GENERAL PURPOSE, the constitution states: "In this spirit and within the framework of the democratic institutions, we invite all progressives in the State of Minnesota to join with us in creating a political and educational movement which affirms the democratic values of truth, justice, and freedom. Such a positive program is the only alternative to the totalitarian ideologies of both fascism and communism."[12]

As the ADA and its Minnesota chapter kept their eyes on the upcoming election year, Humphrey rallied young people at universities around Minnesota to reinforce their numbers. The Minnesota Young DFL was recognized by national Democratic clubs at the end of 1947, and it included such student members as Walter "Fritz" Mondale and Don Fraser, who were recruited by Orville Freeman. Finger pointing, jockeying, and mutual accusations of railroading went on for months in Minnesota. The Humphreyites accused the left-wingers of being Soviet apologists and dangerous to the United States' foreign policy in the escalating Cold War. Those on the "Popular Front" Left countered that the Americans for Democratic Action were "unsavory . . . created nationally to serve as liberal window dressing for the Wall Streeters and militarists behind Truman." Arthur Naftalin later recalled, in a 1984 interview: "The left-wing was Communist-oriented—it really was. This is a statement of historical fact, not something someone is thinking up to smear someone with." Eugenie reminisced that "there were endless meetings and it seemed as if all the big issues on which we had to stand and fight were nearly all related to international policy . . . we were not just seeing Communists under the bed . . . this was not a false issue."[13]

Throughout the intense activity with the ADA and the Humphreyites, the question of balancing work and home, for Eugenie, became not so much an attempt as a surrender. Knowing she couldn't have both, she chose work. Humphrey's biographer stated that "Eugenie Anderson, taking telephoned field reports and penciling her charts at ADA headquarters, all but abandoned her Red Wing home." Arvonne Fraser was a young receptionist in Humphrey's office at the time. She recalled Eugenie coming and going from Red Wing constantly, that "she had a reputation of being extremely smart, intelligent . . . a 'tough cookie.' . . . She was *the* Lady, dressed up, always with a hat." In our interview, Arvonne also described a pivotal memory she had of Eugenie Anderson. The two women were on their way to a meeting, Arvonne driving, going down Hennepin Avenue. As they drove, Eugenie told Arvonne about a dream she had had about getting into the driver's seat of a car—that "in the dream, her hands were cut off. So that meant she couldn't drive. So that she would be *stuck* in Red Wing." Arvonne made it clear, several times in our interview, that this was her most poignant memory of Eugenie. The rather brutal, visceral imagery of the dream was a powerful insight to Eugenie's need for both physical and intellectual freedom and involvement outside of Tower View and domesticity. Eugenie's children were the foundation of her empathy and outreach for human rights, but she believed that her work was important, and that if the goals of the ADA and Hubert Humphrey's increasing power could bring positive action to Washington and thence to the United Nations, all children—not just hers—would benefit. She truly saw her children as citizens of the world and felt that her absence at home (translating as their sacrifice) was necessary and part of what was required for the greater good. Quite a few voices in twenty-first-century child psychology argue that mothers working outside of the home are a positive influence and a critical role model example to both young girls and young boys. Ahead of her time in so many ways, this was no doubt one of Anderson's beliefs seventy years ago, and certainly one of her hopes. On the other hand, Eugenie had a strong traditional streak when it came to child rearing, and she was a mother with authority and high standards. Both Johanna and Hans knew that they, as children, were expected to learn and exhibit proper behavior and obedience to their parents and to any caregiver in charge at any given moment. They got mixed signals from both their mother and their father: attitudes that exalted their importance on a philosophical level as well as others that could leave them under strict judgment, or overlooked, in everyday life.[14]

A harsher light on Tower View in 1947 would also reveal continuing difficulty with alcoholism. Hans Anderson's recollection of John at home in the mid- to late 1940s is as follows:

He was very busy working with my Uncle Charles [Biederman] down in their shop. Because he made the constructions that Charles designed. And he was friendly enough with me, like at suppertime, but then he was drinking by then and he would fall asleep at the table, and he'd wake up about 8 o'clock—then he'd work at his desk for a long time. But he didn't do much with me. . . . He wasn't unkind. I thought he was kind of stern, but he never inquired about any friends I had at Burnside [School], and I was always afraid to bring friends home. One, because it was such a strange place, but two, he was so awkward and distant and uncomfortable around other kids, if they weren't in the family.[15]

Hans also recalls the frenetic atmosphere of the artists at work:

I remember the two of them in the shop; they had quite a good radio there, and they played classical music. And I can remember John spray painting these constructions; he wore a big mask, and he had a spray area over on the side in the far corner with a big fan that blew the [fumes] . . . and he was really good . . . he used lacquer. And it had this very distinctive smell, and I can remember that. And they both smoked: Charles smoked cigars and John smoked cigarettes, constantly. And John also used these Benzedrines, which is a stimulant-like amphetamine, Benzedrine inhalers that were marketed for congested nose and sinus, and you'd stick it up your nose and press the other side and breathe in, and you'd get this stuff—it was like snorting cocaine! And he used them constantly! Plus cigarettes, Benzedrine inhalers, and tons of coffee. They were just . . . intoxicated with this stuff. And then at the end of the day, they would drink.[16]

So while John and Charles were collaborating on groundbreaking art, utilizing materials they could get now that the war was over (fine wood, plastics, metals, and aluminum), they were so intensely involved with their work and its potential that both men started earning the reputations of being isolated and exclusive, and in John's case, inhospitable and antisocial. This remove applied to their own families as well as their extended rings of friends and community. Combined with addictive habits, dysfunction and suffering were inevitable. Eugenie had a number of reasons for keeping

John's drinking out of the public eye. For her work, it was essential that she retain a spotless reputation: no one talked about alcoholism or publicly admitted that a family member drank too much or that anyone was tainted by affiliation. As a woman in a man's working environment, it was crucial for her to appear completely in control of herself and her home base. It may have seemed to Eugenie, as it did indeed to society then, that women, especially working women, were responsible for the domestic happiness and contentment of their husbands. If those husbands were unsatisfied to the point of drinking, well, it was the wife's fault because she hadn't done her job. A traditional housewife *might* be allowed some sympathy if her husband drank; after all, she was fulfilling her feminine duty, and Man was the ultimate alpha dog. But a wife who purposely sought work outside of the home was defying her feminine duty and abandoning her husband (as well as any children), so she garnered far less forgiveness if alcoholism overtook the home. Eugenie knew that these pervasive beliefs existed. She had no intention of falling victim to any hint of hurtful gossip. Friedan attested to the insidious nature of the attitudes: "At dinner parties, the nursery school affair, the PTA open house, a woman who is more than just a housewife can expect a few barbs from her suburban neighbors . . . she can no longer share with other wives that cozy 'we're all in the same boat' illusion; her very presence rocks that boat. And she can expect her home, her husband, and her children to be scrutinized with more than the usual curiosity for the slightest sign of a 'problem.'"[17]

True also was the fact that John, as well as Eugenie, knew that his ambitions and his health stood a better chance of success if he and Eugenie presented a united public face, with no indications that they had anything but a harmonious marriage. John struggled with nebulous plans for his artwork and his developing talent in photography. Even though he did not have the tools or the strength to fight the disease of his alcoholism, and even though he and Eugenie often engaged in verbal battles, the fighting was never physical, abusive, or irreversibly damaging. And they held on to an overriding love for each other that—despite the roller coaster—always won out. The primary person with whom Eugenie shared her frustration was her sister Mary. No one could understand better the temperament and stubbornness of an artist like John. Eugenie may have even found some ironic comfort in comparing her exasperation with John to Mary's greater challenges with Charles's gigantic, loud, confrontational personality. At least John was reserved, dignified—both naturally and publicly—and respectable. Eugenie could never have gotten away with a political (especially diplomatic) career married to someone like Charles, who would unapologetically insult anyone to their face, deride people and movements for their stupidity, and publish inflammatory literature. Eugenie knew exactly how valuable John's good character and reputation were to her aspirations. While she accepted that marriage meant compromise, the bottom line, beyond politics, was that she loved him deeply.

Flora Belle Moore, Eugenie's mother, died on April 12, 1947. The first and foremost female role model of Eugenie's upbringing, Flora had been a quiet, conformist, accommodating woman with no ambitions outside her home, her church, and her duty as a preacher's wife. And yet, Eugenie would have known a thousand little details about her mother that attributed much more to Flora than just a life of servitude. Details and memories that shaped Eugenie herself as a mother—and a woman. An individual.

*　*　*

Knowing history shapes our sense of the possible. Leaving women out of political science and political history let students falsely believe that political woman did not exist, that politics was something properly reserved to men, and that women who tried to participate were "idiosyncratic individuals" rather than engaged and effective political actors who faced a lot of resistance.

JO FREEMAN, *WE WILL BE HEARD*

In 1948, it was plain to the DFL that Eugenie Anderson was far too valuable to be left out of any conversation. As chairman of the ADA (not merely the token sidekick "chairwoman"), she was an active participant in running the show. As the presidential election moved closer, the Minnesota chapter of the ADA, in concurrence with its national organization, started pushing civil rights agendas. The *Minneapolis Star* reported on February 6, 1948: "Civil Rights Probe Asked by State ADA." The article briefly explained that in a letter written by Eugenie Anderson to Minnesota governor Luther W. Youngdahl, the Minnesota ADA called for their state to mimic federal (meaning Truman's) efforts to examine civil rights. A week later, the *St. Paul Pioneer Press* ran a large two-page spread called "News about WOMEN," which offered photos and captions about eight specific "WOMEN IN POLITICS." The main article asserted: "It is generally conceded that women are expected to do much of the organizational or 'foot work' during election years. This lot falls to them because they have more time to devote to detail and their dogged willingness to serve equips them for this branch of campaign work. However, nowhere in the nation is femininity given such recognition in official party circles as in Minnesota." Also noted is that "in the First Congressional district the Democratic-Farmer-Labor people gave heretofore unheard of commendation to women by selecting Mrs. Eugenie Anderson as Red Wing district chairMAN." Anderson's photograph shows her seated at the piano playing Bach.

A great part of Anderson's work continued to be, in addition to pushing civil rights legislation, the massive effort to wrest the DFL party away from any and all Communists. On February 18, 1948, a writer for the *Minneapolis Star* analyzed the DFL infighting, clearly supporting the Humphreyites: "But the Communists don't tire. They are on deck for every meeting. . . . Many of these Communists have been trained in the east and sent out to Minnesota to infiltrate labor unions, DFL organizations, student groups. They must be bringing joy to their top bosses in the Kremlin, for they have been pretty successful—so far." In April 1948, the *ADA World* newspaper published a handy little illustrated guide titled "HOW THE RED MINORITY DOES IT," printing out seating charts

and warnings of disruptive audience tactics used by the Communists. "This is how the commie-czars take possession of a public
meeting. A well-organized minority of stooges . . . are located at
points of strategic importance about the lecture hall. . . . The tech-
nique of capturing public meetings included the use of Communist
goon squads whose business it is to do whatever 'rough stuff' the
occasion calls for." This kind of language echoed how Eugenie also
described Communists: goons and thugs, bullies and stooges.[18]

Critics of the ADA in 1948 saw the group's methods to assume control of the Democratic Party in Minnesota as little better than the
Communists' tactics. Political historian Jennifer Delton acknowledged parallels between both left-wing and right-wing zealotry,
noting that both groups fighting for control were small and "hyper-
disciplined," and they strove to keep their decision-making bases
tightly guarded. Delton wrote: "[The ADA] labored over deciding
who was 'okay' and who was 'commie-line,' sifting through statio-
nery headings and party listings for signs of an individual's past
support of left-wingers." Delton also asserted that "Naftalin, Freeman, and their minions doing the aggressive organizational work"
were cast in the roles of "bad cop," while Humphrey, the public face
and most frequent spokesperson, was "mopping up behind them,
assuaging the hurt feelings and rebuilding consensus." If Eugenie
had seen herself labeled a "minion" in Delton's book, she would
have been highly indignant. But Delton has convincing evidence
and the benefit of modern hindsight and fact-gathering efficiency.
The ADA was scrambling, as hard, and with all the weapons they
could find, not unlike the left-wingers.[19]

In May 1948, the Humphrey contingent managed to finally
oust the Communists from having any voice in the Minnesota
Democratic-Farmer-Labor Party by being better organized and
with greater numbers, and it voted them out at the state Democratic convention in the small northern town of Brainerd. Hubert
Humphrey wrote: "So intense, so hostile was our battle, that we
could have been at the bottom of a coal mine. The outside world

didn't exist as we fought and ultimately, inevitably, broke apart."
Humphrey's forces prevailed, while the left-wingers and Communists walked across the street to another hotel, where their members would begin reorganizing, many attaching themselves to a
new Progressive Party. Carl Solberg summarized: "From this fight
the Humphreyites emerged invulnerable to the charge that being
liberals they must be soft on communism. Their credentials were
proved. They were militants who succeeded in institutionalizing
their militancy."[20]

Bursting with energy from the victorious party convention and
renewed political ambitions, Humphrey even investigated the possibility of getting himself into the running as Truman's vice presidential pick: "He persuaded three of his ADA friends—[James]
Loeb, Joe Rauh, and Eugenie Anderson—to journey to Hyde Park
and ask her [Eleanor Roosevelt] whether it would be wise for him
to run as vice president even if he got shellacked." Mrs. Roosevelt,
confident that Hubert Humphrey's star was on the rise, advised
him to stay open to a vice presidential invitation if the opportunity
arose. In 1948, it did not.[21]

Humphrey was not the only member of the ADA making strides.
Another important outcome of the Democratic state convention
in Brainerd, for Eugenie Anderson, was her election as Democratic
national committeewoman and a delegate-at-large to the national
convention scheduled for August in Philadelphia. On June 20, 1948,
the *Minneapolis Tribune* headlined a full-page article: WOMEN PRO-
TEST POLITICAL BRUSH-OFF, subheaded "Being Delegates, Ringing
Doorbells Not Enough." Anderson was featured along with several
other women from all parties. Under her photograph, the caption
read: "While she has no illusions about the job, which in any party
is traditionally regarded as 'honorary,' she says that it can be a good
deal more than that, depending on the woman who holds it." Here,
Eugenie asserted herself. She was telling readers that if a woman
wanted involvement, she would get it—if she worked for it and
insisted upon it.

When the Minnesota delegation arrived at the national convention in Philadelphia, they were not prepared. Over the previous two months, having talked and worked through dozens of critical issues and flip-flopped on the best presidential hopeful to support those issues (someone with any actual prayer of getting elected), the ADA and fellow DFLers had, only the night before, settled on President Harry Truman as their pick. Minnesota came in committed to a civil rights plank. Eugenie later stated, "all during that campaign of '46 to '48 we were never just only anti-Communist. . . . We didn't ever become just a negative or an anti-group. If we had, I don't think that we would have won, nor would we have deserved to win. It was a pro-human rights, pro-civil rights, pro-democracy with a small 'd' that we constantly emphasized."[22]

Truman biographer David McCullough described the mood in Philadelphia at the opening of the convention: "Attendance was below expectations. . . . 'You could cut the gloom with a corn knife. . . . The very air smelled of defeat.' The crowd expected for the opening day at Convention Hall failed to materialize. The galleries were largely empty." The first and second days showed some improvement out of the lassitude, but it was not until Hubert Humphrey and his minority civil rights plank took the stage that any significant fever gripped the crowd.[23]

Humphrey, Anderson, and their contingent had stayed up all night before Humphrey was set to deliver that speech. Author Peggy Lamson noted, "Through it all Eugenie Anderson had been in a top strategy position, working as hard and determinedly as any of her male colleagues." Lamson also quoted Orville Freeman, who had spoken of Eugenie's involvement: "Not many women are emotionally constituted to be on the prime firing line and to be totally effective. But Eugenie is. She held her own very well in the smoke-filled rooms, she kept cool and she also remained a lady."[24]

Humphrey was poised to push for stronger language on civil rights, to push for changes that could and *would* anger and alienate Southern Democrats, to push for an agenda that was brazen and risky and prescient—but if he delivered the speech right, not only would the Democratic Party have an opportunity to take a giant step toward historic civil rights legislation, but Humphrey could make a national name for himself. The fact is that Eugenie Anderson drafted, and persisted in demanding upon, the final words in Humphrey's fiery speech that compelled the Democrats to embrace more clearly defined civil rights and simultaneously nominate Harry Truman. Michael Schumacher states in his book *The Contest*, "The consensus, then and in years to come, was that it was one of the greatest speeches in American history." The most famous and frequently cited lines of the speech are pure Humphrey:

> My friends, to those who say that we are rushing this issue of civil rights, I say to them we are 172 years late. To those who say that this civil-rights program is an infringement on states' rights, I say this: The time has arrived in America for the Democratic Party to get out of the shadow of states' rights and to walk forthrightly into the bright sunshine of human rights. People—human beings—this is the issue of the 20th century. People of all kinds—all sorts of people— and these people are looking to America for leadership, and they're looking to America for precept and example.

In closing, Humphrey delivered the lines drafted by Eugenie Anderson: "I ask this convention to say in unmistakable terms that we proudly hail, and we courageously support, our President and leader Harry Truman in his great fight for civil rights in America!"[25]

"Eugenie is really a very sharp gal politically," said James Loeb. "It was her stroke of genius that made victory possible, because she suggested that our minority plank include specific language mentioning Truman's Civil Rights Commission. The inclusion of Truman's name made it impossible for some delegates to vote against us." McCullough asserted that "Hubert Humphrey had done more to reelect Truman than would anyone at the convention other than Truman himself."[26]

Eugenie Anderson, ladylike, yet steely and determined, never let her gender stop her from investigation, inquiry, and proposed

Campaigning in Winona in October 1948, President Harry S. Truman smiles at his Minnesota supporters: (L to R) delegate Lamoine Dowling; future governor Orville Freeman; and Democratic committeewoman Eugenie Anderson. *Eugenie M. Anderson papers, box 19.*

implementation of her political beliefs. She wanted to join the men's club, so she simply stepped in to be admitted. Of course, the reality of events and sociology was never so simple as all that, and through the middle of the twentieth century, her experience unfolded with inevitable limitations and challenges. No real women's movement or advances for significant numbers of women would begin for another twenty years. "Now that we've marveled at the rapidity of the change," wrote Gail Collins of the mass women's movements in the late 1960s and early 1970s, "we have to acknowledge that it didn't really happen overnight. Women's lives had been evolving throughout the century." There were many unsung, influential women of the postwar 1940s who worked in political offices around the country and surpassed the envelope-licking, door-knocking stereotype of the ladies' brigades. Eugenie was one of the strongest, and she would become one of the most visible. She took her work seriously, sacrificed an enormous amount of her unpaid time to efforts on behalf of the Democratic Party, and deliberately ignored or overlooked entrenched sexism, choosing instead to champion civil rights and international human rights as "greater" agendas that she felt would address women's disadvantages within their scope. Eugenie became an example of sheer stamina and focus, not spreading herself thin over dozens of unrelated committees and organizations, but dedicating her time, talents, and uniquely charismatic voice to one objective: getting her candidates into office and into the seats of power that would manipulate the future of America. And in doing so, she moved herself into a position of consideration as well—with the trust and approval of Hubert Humphrey, the DFL, and President Harry Truman.[27]

Three
REPRESENTING AMERICA

I am bursting with pride over the wonderful reception
you are receiving. You deserve every bit of it.
Your appointment as Ambassador to Denmark is an honor
not only to yourself but to your friends and associates also.
You see we just sort of bask in your sunlight and glory
in your achievement. Good luck!

HUBERT H. HUMPHREY, NOVEMBER 2, 1949

Because [Eugenie] had always, as she says, worked in politics
"at the man level of the party," she felt no anxiety
about becoming a woman ambassador.

PEGGY LAMSON, *FEW ARE CHOSEN*

THE PRESS PHOTOS OF PRESIDENT HARRY TRUMAN flourishing the premature "Dewey Defeats Truman" headline on the *Chicago Daily Tribune* have become iconic. The close election and unexpected victory of 1948 created a prolonged playing field for the Democrats, and historians agree that Humphrey's civil rights speech at the 1948 Democratic Convention, cementing the link to Truman and his potential, was a major component in bringing about that victory. "That was the essence of that breakthrough there," said Walter Mondale. And of Eugenie Anderson, Mondale agreed that "Humphrey did it, but she was encouraging him to."[1]

The dust wouldn't settle for months. Washington kicked into high gear. The Democrats reveled in the *postwar new-New Deal*

Marshall Plan United Nations sky-is-the-limit future. And immediately, all sorts of Democratic politicians and political supporters around the country stepped in line to be considered for recognition from the White House. Eugenie Anderson maintained that the circulation of her name was a surprising honor, one that she never expected. Whether the "surprise" aspect of it was true or not, the mutual respect she engendered in both President Truman and India Edwards, the vice chairman of the Democratic National Committee, brought Eugenie's name to Washington. She reminisced:

> I met [President Truman] during the campaign for the presidency in '48, because of course I was the national committeewoman and I rode with him on the campaign train across the state. . . . I should say that after the '48 election in the fall I was very tired. I had been working extremely hard from '46 through '48. And I also felt that I had been sort of neglecting my family, I had been away so much. . . . I didn't think there would be very much activity and I was look[ing] forward to a sort of a rest.
>
> My father died the 4th of January 1949. . . . I was just leaving the house to go to my father's funeral . . . when I received a telephone call from India Edwards. She was the vice-chairman of the Democratic National Committee and director of Women's Activities. . . . I believe that Mrs. Edwards was a selfless person, she didn't want anything for herself, but she wanted to see other women that she thought were qualified serve, have a chance to serve in important political offices and public office.[2]

India Edwards was a force to be reckoned with. By 1948, when Truman was elected, she was fifty-three years old and had been widowed and divorced and married again. Her first husband had been killed in the first world war. During the second world war, her only son was killed serving in the army air forces. At the time of India's third marriage, she was the society editor for the *Chicago Tribune*, and her husband, Herbert T. Edwards, was in the "non-theatrical moving pictures business"; more specifically, he produced films and newsreels for the government and the US Foreign Service. After volunteering for the Democratic Party in 1944,

India Edwards quickly rose in its ranks, her primary objective being the greater inclusion of women in positions of influence. She deliberately refused many offers of jobs and appointments for herself, seeing her own key ability as that of conduit for *all* women. Her voice found its best sounding board in Harry Truman. Edwards recalled: "If Mrs. Truman had not been the Boss in her husband's estimation, he might not have been so willing to give consideration to women whose names I presented as possible high officeholders."[3]

India Edwards recognized huge potential in Eugenie Anderson. Eugenie was connected, she was informed, she was attractive, and she was available. She was simply too valuable not to be snared, both for Truman's initiatives and for Edwards's. First, her connections: Eugenie's name was already known to heads of the Democratic Party through her work for the ADA and her acquaintanceship with Eleanor Roosevelt, not to mention her close friendship with the recently elected rising star Senator Hubert Humphrey. Second, her intellect: she was extremely well informed about political history as well as interdisciplinary current events and philosophies, and she had communication skills that could hone any speech or article down to its most persuasive core. Third, her appearance: Eugenie was universally attractive. Men found her, in person and in photographs, feminine far beyond the caricature female political battle-ax, and with a fair amount of fashionable sex appeal. (One could imagine Herbert Edwards, filmmaker and propagandist, and his wife, India, agreeing that Eugenie looked great on camera.) Women were appeased by her good taste in clothes and careful balance of modest business attire with feminine adornments. Eugenie could get away with an ostrich feather–tipped hat. It didn't hurt that Eugenie promoted herself as an *unwitting* representative for women, as if that part just happened by accident. Women in the greater public who were wary of militant feminists had nothing to fear from Mrs. Anderson. Fourth, and absolutely critical: Mr. John Anderson. Eugenie would never have been considered as an ambassador if her spouse, marriage, and family were not completely transparent in their safe respectability. Any woman in the running for representing Truman's administration had to have little to no risk for embarrassing the government, either politically or socially. India Edwards saw to that.

Eugenie recalled that when India first approached her with the possibility of an ambassadorship, Edwards said: "I think, of course, your husband would have to be willing to go with you." And also: "I don't know how John would feel about that, but why don't you talk it over with him." Edwards was realistic enough to limit the pool of women to irreproachable widows or, outside of that superior quality, those women whose husbands' careers would allow the spouses to accompany their wives into their placements, much like Britain's Prince Philip was doing with Princess Elizabeth around the commonwealth of the British Empire. As a married woman with school-age children, Eugenie needed not just John's approval but also his willing participation to make herself eligible for consideration.[4]

Anderson's character was, of course, the other necessary half of the equation. After Eugenie ran the marathon of helping both Truman and Humphrey get elected in 1948, quiet walks around the Tower View fields must have felt slow and isolated by comparison. When New Year's Day dawned in 1949, Eugenie was pondering her future. Three days later, her father died, and a week after that, India Edwards telephoned with the first inquiry about prestigious opportunities. It wasn't just John's involvement that mattered: Eugenie's fortitude and commitment had to be rock solid. The Rev. Ezekiel Moore's death put stress on that foundation. Her father had always been a venerated source of wisdom, reliability, faith, and strength. Having lost her mother two years before, Eugenie now found herself an orphan. The Moore siblings were scattered around the country, raising their own families, writing regularly among themselves but riddled with typical family resentments and disapprovals. Ezekiel's death meant that the geographic and spiritual center of the Moore family was gone:

THEY MUST BE JUST WILD ABOUT HARRY

Rep. Helen Gahagan Douglas to UN

Frieda Hennock, FCC

Georgia Clark U. S. Treasurer

Eleanor Roosevelt to UN

Georgia Lusk, War Claims Commission

Perle Mesta Minister to Luxembourg

Dorothy Kenyon to UN

Eugenie Anderson Denmark Minister

Ruth Bryan Rohde, UN

Virginia Gildersleeve to UN

December 8, 1949, *Daily Republican Eagle*, Red Wing, Minnesota. Caption reads: "With 10 or more topnotch appointments for women since 1945, President Truman makes feminine factor perhaps a bigger one in government life than ever before. Appointments range from U.S. treasurer and the diplomatic corps to various United Nations posts as delegates and alternates." *Eugenie M. Anderson papers, box 19.*

Eugenie was relegated to the fields of Tower View, planted more firmly where her in-laws set the tone. One Moore was still accessible, and closest, to Eugenie—her sister Mary Biederman. But Mary and Charles were trying to grow more autonomous after years of heavy reliance on John Anderson's patronage. Charles's art and his manifesto publication, *Art as the Evolution of Visual Knowledge*, while not yet widely known, were getting some attention and visibility. John's participation, and his own artistic endeavors, were seriously waning. He was turning more to other art forms at which he excelled: still and film photography. The brass ring of a diplomatic appointment could not have been proffered at a more serendipitous moment. Eugenie could escape the narrow scope of Tower View, start an adventure in Europe, and battle fresh Communists on the international front. John could start writing letters to Victor Hasselblad (Swedish inventor of new formats in photography) and formulate schemes to take his cameras on the road where he could expand his photographic pursuits. And best of all, they could set off together, once again resuscitating their marriage from perpetual strife. The children were young and resilient. Why *of course* it was assumed they would love to go, too.

News had leaked out in March 1949 that Eugenie was being considered for a top post in the Foreign Service. Her name was often paired with another front-runner for appointment, Perle Mesta, who was a Washington insider and all-out unapologetic busybody party hostess. The two women could not have been more different. Mesta liked to publicize her Oklahoma-widow-tell-'em-as-I-see-'em platitudes, shouting loudly for women's rights; Eugenie, while knowing women's issues could not be completely ignored, tried hard to keep them on the back burner. The *Minneapolis Star*, reporting March 17, 1949, on Anderson's potential post, stated:

> There's little about this pleasant, soft-spoken committeewoman to suggest the old feminist politician. She isn't a feminist.
>
> "That aggressive attitude won't get a woman any place," she says. . . .

She took her first leap from the political springboard in 1944 after brooding darkly over the isolationist policy in her own congressional district.

"I couldn't stand it," she said. "After all, I had two children of my own. My sister-in-law and I ran a nursery school during the war. And I thought of those children all the time. What kind of a world would they have to live in?"

The article highlighted everything about Eugenie that reaffirmed her traditional image and priorities as a wife and mother first, a woman with feminine (not feminist) interests second, and political ambitions third.[5]

Many insiders and colleagues were contacted to write President Truman in support of Eugenie's placement as a chief of mission in the Foreign Service. In Hubert Humphrey's letter of recommendation to secretary of state Dean Acheson, he wrote: "Mrs. Eugenie Anderson . . . is a profound student of international politics and diplomacy. I have met few people whom I would consider her equal." The personalities and strengths of Anderson and Mesta were compared and contrasted in the press, as well as behind closed doors at the State Department. The positions open were Luxembourg and Denmark, which offered a "first" for women at the ambassador rank. Previously, American diplomats there, including a woman, Ruth Bryan Owen in 1933, had served at the rank of minister. Truman was elevating the rank to Ambassador Extraordinary and Plenipotentiary.[6]

The Danes made no bones about the fact that they wanted Eugenie Anderson. She exemplified and complemented their national attitudes and cultural pride. Mesta they viewed as a lightweight, a figurehead. Finally, on June 16, it was publicized that Perle Mesta had been offered the ministry to Luxembourg, and she had accepted. Eugenie, however, still waited. It took Hubert Humphrey and Orville Freeman's intervention to notify the president that something had to be done, and that it behooved Truman, because of Minnesota's loyalty and support, to get it done. As

Eugenie recalled it, Humphrey and Freeman, agitated by the long delay, thought it would be "personally offensive to them if I were not appointed." Humphrey wrote Eugenie as he rallied support for his last-ditch effort: "This adds up to one thing, Eugenie. Keep your shirt on! Time is a great healer and I have a sneaking suspicion that everything is going to work out all right if we don't upset the apple cart. . . . There isn't one damn reason in the world why it shouldn't go through."[7]

Eugenie was invited to the White House in September. Accompanied by India Edwards, she went in through a side door but out through a front door after the meeting, where the press could be met and notified of the president's intentions to push Anderson's confirmation.

The official nomination occurred on October 12, 1949, and the Senate passed the confirmation the next day. Mrs. Eugenie M. Anderson became the first woman in US history to achieve the top rank of Ambassador Extraordinary and Plenipotentiary. Overnight, an unknown Minnesota Democrat grabbed national headlines. John and Eugenie not only had to turn their lives upside down and scramble to pack for an indefinite residence in a foreign country, but they had to do it in tandem with a lot of press attention and public interest, with big smiles on their stunned faces. Almost immediately, the ramifications of Eugenie's job became clear to John. It was no longer an enticing possibility; it was a done deal. John had mapped out plans in his mind for photographic adventures and experimentation, but as soon as the press arrived at the gates of Tower View, he realized that the camera would not be in his hands. It was in theirs.

The *New York Times* announcement of Eugenie's nomination read: "Woman Nominated as U.S. Ambassador: Minnesota Artist's Wife Named to Denmark—First of Sex Slated for Such a Rank." The first six paragraphs of the article fill in the factual details about Anderson without much bias or ambiguous language. But the final three paragraphs reinforce the intentional manipulation by both

Eugenie and the press of her own image within a prescribed sexist framework:

> In the recent convention of the American Federation of Labor, the women trade unionists met there separately for the first time and Mrs. Anderson addressed them. She told them that "politics was fun" although she defined it seriously, saying that, outside the home, there was no more satisfactory work for women.

In October 1949, Eugenie Anderson displays the certification of her appointment as chief of mission to Denmark, the first woman in American history to reach the rank of ambassador, with Senator Hubert H. Humphrey, John Anderson, and Democratic National Committee chairwoman India Edwards. *Anderson family collection.*

"Politics," she said, "is an exciting way for a woman to do her part in molding for her child a better democracy in which we all believe."

She also said women should be in politics to do their part in the world struggle against communism and because they always work for the welfare of families. She endorsed President Truman's social welfare programs.[8]

Three other women had been named to important diplomatic positions in the past. As previously mentioned, Ruth Bryan Owen (later Rohde) was appointed minister to Denmark by Franklin D. Roosevelt in 1933. Mrs. Florence (Daisy) Harriman served as minister to Norway from 1937 to 1941. And, of course, Perle Mesta had recently left to take up her post in Luxembourg. All three other women, at the time of their appointments, were widows. It was deemed appropriate for them to spend their time at a desk because they weren't depriving a husband or a family of domestic needs, nor would their dedication to their jobs suffer. But in addition to being a woman given, for the first time, the highest-ranking position in the Foreign Service, Eugenie was also the first woman diplomat who would need to select schools for her children—and maintain a healthy marriage with her husband.

Another main emphasis in the press about Eugenie's appointment focused on her "farm wife" obscurity. While Eugenie spent her time traveling between Minnesota and Washington; juggling meetings and training at the State Department; attending countless government, business, and social engagements; and making domestic arrangements for the long-term and long-distance move around the world (thus, counteracting any and all stereotypes about her being a simple farm wife), the newspapers featured photographs of her wearing a kitchen apron, cooking, and talking on an antique wooden telephone on the wall of her farmhouse. Eugenie had to pretend to be amused by the publicity, but it was difficult. She later argued: "I think the press thought that the big story here was 'Farm Housewife Becomes First Woman Ambassador.' Well, I was a housewife, I did live on a farm, of sorts. But I was not a farmer's wife. And I had not been a simple housewife for quite a few years. . . . I had to become involved in not only politics but political theory and international affairs and obviously I never would have been appointed as an ambassador if I had been only a housewife."[9]

Reporters also outlined her fashion style, wardrobe, and favorite designer, even going so far as to comment on her weight and dress size. The *Washington Daily News* printed: "The Andersons are going to be among the best-looking couples we've ever sent abroad. Eugenie is slender, trim, wears tailored suits beautifully, dresses her trim feet and ankles in excellent taste. . . . John Anderson is tall, handsome and blond and eludes all publicity as he remains in the background to encourage his wife in her political work." The article closed with condescending skepticism: "So, when the Goodhue County woman sits in the embassy office in Copenhagen and directs her 15-man staff in affairs of state, she'll be a far cry from her initial entrance into politics in 1944 . . . this young woman, born in a Methodist parsonage in Iowa, apparently has what it takes to make a success of either job. We'll see."

Journalists, encouraged by their editors, grabbed the opportunity to shape their stories around the unique and titillating situation that Eugenie and John presented: reverse gender roles on the international stage. A United Press story out of Washington headlined: "John is 'Nice Guy, But Not Talkative', Reporters Agree at Eugenie's Swearing-in."

> Into the next room went Mrs. Anderson to pose for newsreel cameras. John went to a neutral corner while the flash bulbs popped around his wife.
>
> A friend rushed up enthusiastically and reported: "Genie's sure photogenic today."
>
> John drew a breath and spoke.
>
> "Yeah," he said. . . .
>
> Reporters, seeing that the ice was broken swarmed in. He answered a half-dozen stock questions politely and briefly. Yes, he was an artist. Yes, he was proud of his wife. Yes, his father discovered how to puff up cereals and sell 'em to kiddies for breakfast.

December 9, 1949. Original caption supplied by International News Photos: "Mrs. Eugenie Anderson, of Red Wing, Minnesota, America's first woman ambassador, is shown aboard the S.S. *Jutlandia* on which she sailed today for Copenhagen, Denmark, to take over her new duties. With her are her husband John, daughter Johanna, 15, and son Hans, 11. Mrs. Anderson took along three rooms of furniture, eleven trunks and fifteen suitcases. In a farewell speech, at a luncheon in her honor yesterday, the lady ambassador said her appointment was a symbol of President Truman's faith in the abilities of women in public life." *Photo by Hans Reinhart, International News Photos, author's collection.*

Then John eased away.

Up front, photographers had finished shooting pictures of the glamorous new ambassador with the chic dress and hat, and the flashing smile.[10]

Eugenie's actions, choices, and words were scrutinized daily, not just because she was the first woman at the full ambassador rank, but because her husband was the first male spouse on an ambassador's coattails. They were already at the mercy of some writers' jibes and insinuations; any small misstep would only make the jokes worse. John Anderson did his best to keep out of the limelight, depriving the press of any fodder for ridicule or words that could be misquoted.

The Anderson family sailed out of New York on December 9, 1949, bound for Copenhagen. The *New York Times* reported: "Attractively dressed in a red cloth suit trimmed with black Persian lamb, Mrs. Anderson was greeted aboard the Jutlandia by Capt. C. M. Kondrup, skipper of the vessel." When they arrived in Denmark eleven days later, the *Times* continued: "The former Red Wing (Minn.) housewife spent fifteen minutes talking to reporters and posing for photographs. Mrs. Anderson was plainly pleased at the enthusiastic welcome, but her husband, John, was bewildered. 'This is a most extraordinary experience,' he said. Mrs. Anderson was first down the gangplank. Then came her 15-year-old daughter, Johanna, and her 11-year-old son, Hans. Perhaps steeling himself for the life of ambassadorial husband, Mr. Anderson came last."[11]

Right out of the gate—at the foot of the ship that delivered them to Denmark—the press made it very clear that they would have a lot to write about in terms of John's position as secondary to his wife. John had anticipated the confounding aspect of this reception. The night before, he had posted a letter to his brother-in-law Frank Chesley, in which he wrote: "Arrive in the morning: brrrrrr. Not the weather, but what is in store for this little bunch of amateurs according to my pick up from several of the passengers, and sly sort of remarks by the Captain." Both John and Eugenie, because of the newness of being in the Foreign Service, and also because the amount of time that they had had to prepare was so inadequate, confessed that they felt like amateurs. Eugenie wrote home: "You have probably read about our overpowering reception by the press and the public the day of our arrival—I've never seen such a battery of photographers and newspaper people . . . all of which made the whole morning quite bewildering. . . . [William] Roll, the Press Secretary, is delighted not only with my press (he says he has never seen anything like it) but also with my viewpoint." To the public, of course, Eugenie always presented herself as completely self-assured and open to the attention of the press and photographers. A *St. Paul Pioneer Press* headline read: "Lady Ambassador Poised— No Jitters for Eugenie."[12]

Only days after taking up residence in the embassy, Eugenie began a ritual of writing long, detailed letters to the extended family back home. The process allowed her to kill several birds with one stone: (1) Sending her thoughts in a newsletter format that would be circulated among all family members and a select few friends would save her from writing multiple personal letters. (2) Shipping her private thoughts over the sea back home meant that they were safely away from any unsympathetic eyes at the embassy or among colleagues. (3) Instructing that all the letters would find their final destination with Mary Biederman would keep them filed and organized until Eugenie returned home. And (4) writing and preserving weekly notes on her activities and impressions in the form of these letters gave her a solid foundation if she chose to write more formal memoirs at a later date. Eugenie incorporated both her private audience and her eventual plans for more public writing into these newsletters. While they do not allow for an entirely unvarnished version of Eugenie's thoughts, the letters, styled like a journal, do provide critical observations and opinions that would not otherwise be available.

By the close of the year 1949, the Andersons were probably hoping that the novelty of their diplomatic debut was winding down.

They would be disappointed. If anything, Eugenie's image and persona were only becoming more popular, in both Danish and American newspapers. Ambassador Anderson had presented her credentials to King Frederick IX and Queen Ingrid just one day after setting foot in Copenhagen, her clothing and jewelry inspected by the press and the thousands of spectators lining the streets that led the royal coach with four black horses across town to Christiansborg Palace. In a letter from Minnesota, Frank Chesley asked John: "Was Hans really sitting in a convertible shouting 'Mule Team' when Eugenie rounded the corner in the coach when she went to see the king? That's what the papers said." Cute comparisons between the modern, youthful Americans and the more cultured Europeans only stoked the fires of interest in the new ambassador. Eugenie seemed to have a handle on all that was attractive and acceptable for a woman, far beyond that which was merely allowed. She was patient, and she was smart. She knew that in order to find the best outlets to advance Truman's foreign policy agendas—NATO, the Marshall Plan, etc.—she would have to forbear and placate the more superficial demands of the press first. Only after she had proven herself to be a good sport and a reliably accommodating female would she find journalists and editors willing to report on the more serious political subjects and democratic goals that she was actually in residence to support.[13]

A biographer of ambassador Clare Booth Luce, one of Eugenie's postwar diplomatic peers, noted: "In the WWII era, if you were one of the boys, you had to 'enjoy being a girl,' because there was 'nothing like a dame.' . . . This has been called the Feminine Mystique, and the generals would not have liked Clare [Booth Luce] at all if she didn't exude it unstintingly." The book also claims: "A celebrity ambassador can draw more attention than a diplomat should, but she can also publicize certain national interests far better than a faceless functionary." Yes, Eugenie and John Anderson were amateurs and unprepared for the posh world of diplomacy, let alone celebrity, but at the same time, Eugenie's deep intelligence and pragmatism never steered her wrong. In order to keep her place at the men's table, she found it fundamentally necessary *not* to be one of the boys, but to look like she "enjoyed being a girl." At the same time, she had to be extremely careful not to cross any lines and disqualify herself from being taken seriously. Many would find it a lose-lose situation. Eugenie Anderson walked the tightrope and earned respect within the rigid sexist framework she could not, and had never set out to, change.[14]

Eugenie remembered that "it was amazing for me to discover that most people seemed to regard an ambassador as an aloof and superior being, simply by virtue of being an ambassador." Adding another layer to that, historian Philip Nash believed that "[Anderson's] identity and behavior produced a level of fame unheard of for ambassadors." One of the ways Eugenie deflected the overwhelming attention on herself as a female diplomat was to expand the scope of her diplomacy to involve all the Danish people, in addition to the small group of foreign dignitaries housed in Copenhagen. She very astutely redirected the emphasis from her gender to her goals. Knowing the strength of the Social Democratic Party in Denmark, and knowing the realistic expectations of the press everywhere, Eugenie put her own democratic beliefs into action and subtly defied the old-school ways of former ambassadors. She didn't invent this, of course. In truth, she was picking up where former minister to Denmark Ruth Bryan Owen had left off. Nash wrote: "After assuming her post in June 1933, Owen was not afraid, despite her amateur status, to innovate as chief of mission. Her new practice was what Eugenie Anderson would later call 'people's diplomacy.'"[15]

Before she could begin putting her methodology into concrete plans, Eugenie followed diplomatic protocol for introductions. Ten days after her arrival in Copenhagen, she wrote to family at home:

> Most of this past week I was making the routine "Diplomatic Calls" which a newcomer makes. First I call on all the other Ambassadors (4 others: British, French, Norwegian and Swedish). Then they all

return my calls. . . . I must say that I cannot imagine spending a
minute more with any of them, except the British, than is absolutely
required . . . they seem to range from incredible "dried prunes and
stuffed shirts" to rather ridiculous or pathetic people who mostly
seem to take themselves and their trade with a terrific sense of their
own importance. . . . I like the members of the Foreign Office I've
met so far much better than my "diplomatic colleagues."[16]

Perhaps it was her negative reaction to the antiquated chore-
ography of this social circle, or perhaps it was Eugenie's premed-
itated objective to initiate "people's diplomacy"; in any case, her
first foray as hostess into diplomatic society was not an exclusive,
ritzy reception or a cocktail party to which princes and dignitaries were invited, but a housewarming party for the Danish workers
who had refurbished the embassy residence before the Andersons
moved in. Eugenie outlined this plan to her deputy chief of mission, Edward Sparks, a career Foreign Service officer with his own
deeply ingrained agenda of rules and continuity for the embassy:
"When I announced this plan to my deputy chief of mission," Eugenie reminisced, "this old line career officer, he was horrified. I can
still remember his expression on his face, and when I told him of
this plan he looked at me just sadly and said, 'Oh, Mrs. Anderson,
I don't think you want to do that.' And I said, 'Yes, I think I do.'"[17]

Anderson and Sparks clashed from the outset: "I seriously considered asking for [Mr. Sparks's] immediate transfer, not only
because of these disagreements . . . but he was a difficult person for
me to work with because he had such a different approach to almost
everything from mine." Eugenie went on to state that Sparks must
have seen her as an ignorant newcomer with wrong ideas. What is
interesting to note is that she did *not* initially comment on whether
Sparks had any prejudice against her because she was a woman. She
deferred those suspicions until they had worked together longer.[18]

Eugenie prevailed, and the housewarming party plans materialized. When writing home with a summation of the hugely successful
party, Eugenie described the *skål*, a distinctive toast that was used

at gatherings of all Danish peoples: "This means that you quickly lift your glass, gesture it towards the other person, looking right into their eyes, then drink rather deeply and then look into their eyes again as you raise your glass to them a second time." There was a downside to excessive drinking, beyond having to have the necessary stomach for it and the unavoidable hangovers. While alcohol might have served to heighten any party's joviality, it could also reveal issues and feelings that were normally kept in check. Edward Sparks unveiled his disapproval of Ambassador Anderson after getting drunk at a dinner following one of Eugenie's speeches. Eugenie recalled: "I questioned him as we were dancing as to what he thought about my speech, and he went into such detail as to all the things that were wrong that I was sure he had been quite bothered about it, also the fact that I had not talked to him about it." The situation had many layers: a power struggle between a chief of mission and a deputy, the behavior-altering effects of alcohol, and the fact that the woman in charge was not just expected to listen and endure but to do that while dancing. Eugenie noted: "I hope that he [Sparks] is not going to be so bothered about his having had so much to drink and more or less blowing off, that this will affect our future work, but it may. . . . I also feel quite sorry for him in this position, as I can understand fully how difficult it is for him, who has spent years reaching his present position, then having acted as Chief of Mission here for 9 months to be displaced by a political appointee and a woman at that."[19]

That basic element of being a woman affected everything Eugenie did, and said, and tried to accomplish, whether she wished to deal with it or not. Any reader can see an increasing sense of frustration as the months went by in Copenhagen and Eugenie reported back to Minnesota in her journal-style family newsletters. In spite of her primary wish to focus on Truman's foreign policy, she was more often called upon to give speeches and comment on other issues centered on women. On March 12, 1950, she wrote: "I should be working on a speech today so this cannot be a very long letter.

Ambassador Anderson visits farms and schools in rural Denmark, 1951.
Photo by John P. Anderson, Anderson family collection.

I am to speak this coming Saturday night . . . on 'The American Woman in Public Life Today.' This should be, I suppose, an easy enough subject, but actually I find that I have needed to do quite a bit of studying in order to have a good factual background, and also in order to try to present a rounded picture." In other words, Eugenie knew precisely the differences between presenting *herself* as a woman and representing or explaining *all* women as a political entity—and she indicated that she would rather the two circumstances had actually very little to do with each other. Eugenie also felt this differentiation when it came to her family life. She knew that as a full-time working mother in a traditionally male position, she was the exception to the rule in most women's experiences. That circumstance was not something for which she could turn to books or studying for help; not because women had not been working among men throughout history, but because very little had ever been recorded, affirmed, or established about those patterns or relationships. Eugenie felt an increasing sense of isolation, and while she worked very hard to stay on top of both her family and work environments, there were only so many hours in the day, and only so many other women she could talk to.

Above all, Eugenie continued to insist that women's issues were, if not less important, at least less worthy of immediate action than efforts on behalf of all citizens' rights. As a woman diplomat, she was required, time and again, to give speeches on the condition of women in politics. A good insight to her frustration with this, and her unvarying response, is revealed in a family letter where she discusses a speech to the National Council of Danish Women: "I talked again about American women in public life, much as I disliked giving the same speech again.... But it was what the organization wanted to hear . . . one of the things I emphasized about American women was that those in public life were more concerned with their responsibilities as citizens than with their rights as women."[20]

Even while Eugenie treaded the waters of multiple duties—being a woman diplomat, talking about being a woman diplomat, representing American women, representing America—the press continued its preoccupation with her fashionable image as a woman in charge, reporting frequently on the details of everything she wore. Sometimes this worked to her advantage, since it kept her person and therefore her American interests in the public eye. More often, however, it emphasized her femininity to a distracting degree. In April 1950, Eugenie was photographed in a blue silk suit that had a waist-length cape built into the jacket, a new silhouette for women's suits in 1950. "One of the pictures was taken in such a way as to make me look quite pregnant," Eugenie wrote home, going on to explain that her embassy press officer, cultural attaché William Roll, then had to field several phone calls from newspapers wondering if Mrs. Ambassador was "expecting": "It would have been very funny—was anyway I suppose—if it hadn't been so revealing of how the press would dearly love such a story, and how miserable one could be, having a baby under such a spotlight. I really shudder to think of it. . . . Reuters (London news agency) called Mr. Roll about it, and he refused to really believe him and sent a man out to the reception Friday to see for himself. I wore no cape on Friday, but one of my most slenderizing dresses just in case there were any doubts!"[21]

Another large part of Mrs. Ambassador's appeal in newspapers and photographs was her enigmatic, handsome husband. Most likely, if John Anderson had been in any way unattractive (short, portly, bald . . .) or even if he was just plain boring, there may have been significantly less attention paid to him and to the reverse gender roles that Eugenie and John were compelled to fulfill. But the fact that John had a handsome face and figure, tall stature, artistic interests, and intellectual depth heightened the interest in the chief of mission and her spouse both as individuals and as a couple. After only a few weeks in Copenhagen, John wrote home that he hoped the novelty would wear off: "I hate this business of being recognized everywhere I go, and how it completely gums up the possibility of examining the place leisurely, scouting equipment stores, etc. This is bound to stop within another month I should think, people can't be so dumb as to keep it up past two or three months."[22]

During the first few months of the appointment, John managed a sense of humor when writing home to family:

> It's like a cockeyed movie at night for a formal dinner . . . the time of departure is always set for a certain minute; E rustles down the stairs complaining about the length of the skirt, I try to keep from stepping on it and yet make the same speed. . . . Hjarmind is opening the car door, salutes E as she gets in, he with a big grin on (seems to like the procedure so well that we have not said anything; he has a very good sense of humor, knows that we don't give a hoot, and does it so naturally that I think this item is better left alone) and then salutes me as I get in.[23]

In February 1950, only two months after arriving in Copenhagen, John flew back to the United States, where his presence was required in California for legal issues with stocks and finances. While it gave him a respite from being "Mr. Ambassador," John's absence left Eugenie with the impossible task of balancing every aspect of embassy life: domestic responsibilities, children, house staff, office staff, social obligations, personal care, and public relations. She had tremendous support from William Roll, her press officer, but even so, the pressures to make the appearance of seamless effort were unachievable. Eugenie wrote of the problems in drafts of her own (never published) memoir, "Mrs. Ambassador": "Meanwhile at Rydhave we are undergoing various family adjustments. Hans' 12th birthday is not a happy one. He is a homesick boy, who does not even welcome his new puppy, but longs for 'Lassie,' left behind. The children are having problems at school, where there are sharp educational differences from home. I am trying to solve new problems as a 'career mother.'"[24]

Historically, at this time, when more women were entering the workforce, and some were gaining respect at upper-level management jobs and higher-profile positions, most women at top levels did not, simultaneously, have very young or school-age children. Eugenie refused to alter the State Department expectations of her career, as well as her own standards and goals for that work, even though she was a woman and a mother. She recorded some thoughts about this, in regard to work and career, much more openly than she did as it pertained to her marriage and children. John being so intensely private, it would have been unthinkable for Eugenie to speak or write about the stress on their relationship and family, not to mention the negative public reaction she would have received for any kind of personal complaint. Eugenie kept her acknowledgments general and carefully worded to avoid accusations of weakness or whining: "I was prepared to encounter some resistance, passive or otherwise, from my staff on two counts: first, because I was a woman, and most men are not notably enthusiastic about having women in positions of authority over them or even on the same level. . . . In the field of diplomacy, however, women in positions of authority were considerably fewer than in politics or business, so I would not have been surprised to encounter problems on this score, but hoped to overcome them if they did arise."[25]

If current work and family were not enough politics for Eugenie to juggle, communication from the Democrats back in the United States also added to the list of choices and decisions that she needed to address for serious consideration of her future in politics. The folks from home—Democrats, Humphreyites, and DFLers—continued to solicit Eugenie's advice and opinions on the party and the ADA, although they were longer on questions than they were on information. Overwhelmed with her duties in Denmark, Eugenie had scant time to keep up with Minnesota and Washington party politics, so Eugenie denied any notions of running for office while she was abroad. But that didn't stop the party from asking. Speaking for Hubert Humphrey and "a couple score people" in his organization, Arthur Schlesinger Jr., cofounder of the ADA and close adviser to Eugenie, Hubert Humphrey, Eleanor Roosevelt, and many others, wrote Eugenie when she had been in Copenhagen scarcely six months. "The deal's this: You've got to run for the U.S. Senate," urged Schlesinger:

> We need you in the Senate, Eugenie! Imagine a combination of HH and you; boy there's power! A "yes" from you and immediately we make strategy. . . . This would electrify the nation; it would help our cause, too, in the July national convention. . . . Do give this urgent appeal some kindly attention, Eugenie. It makes such good sense to me that I feel it would be a tragic mistake not to move forthrightly on it. . . .
>
> P.P.S. You no doubt know that you're slated for TIME's cover in June. They've had their boys around after all the information they can get . . . the TIME organization keeps telling him that all they've got is "fluff," which means that all they can find is good things about you. I told Jay [Edgerton] he was bound to be disappointed if he wanted anything else, because Eugenie Anderson, I told him, is just too good to believe, believe me![26]

The TIME cover portrait was painted by a popular illustrator but never made the cut, and neither did Eugenie agree to cut short her posting in Denmark to run in Minnesota for Senate. While Humphrey and others like Schlesinger were positioning Democrats to their best advantages in the United States, Eugenie Anderson chose to concentrate on the work at hand across the ocean, devoting her time and energy to doing what she had promised President Truman she would do: support the foreign policy of the United States and reassure the Danes and their European allies that they were safe with the Americans, NATO, and the Marshall Plan.

One of her prime opportunities to show the Danish people what she was all about occurred on Mother's Day, May 14, 1950. Eugenie accomplished a great number of things when Danish radio broadcast her Mother's Day speech, which she taped the day before, delivering the entire text in the Danish language. Eugenie had been studying Danish since her arrival, practicing every weekday morning with a tutor. While she was not at all fluent in so short a time, she was more than capable of reading her speech in the correct accent and vernacular particular to the general Danish public. Eugenie referred to the scheduling of her speech on Mother's Day, initially, as "amusing." It is safe to say that *amusing* was often Eugenie's code word for *irritating*. By couching her annoyance (even sometimes anger) in a benign term that made it look like she was laughing off something as unimportant, Eugenie covered stronger emotions or opinions that would have been criticized as the rantings of a female, and therefore weaker or insignificant. William Roll, Eugenie's public affairs officer, recognized, and convinced Eugenie, that designing the speech around Mother's Day was a good tactic to get the attention of the people as well as the press, and that it should highlight a nonpolitical approach. It was a common mind-set of the early 1950s, shaping women's words and objectives to try to push an agenda farther than it might go on less sanctioned ground. As Friedan put it in *The Feminine Mystique*: "If you write a political piece, they won't read it. You have to translate it into issues they can understand—romance, pregnancy, nursing, home furnishings, clothes. Run an article on the economy, or the race question, civil rights, and you'd think that women had never heard of them."[27]

Eugenie was willing to accept good timing and strategy, but she would not surrender her overriding goal to talk about her reasons and goals for being in Denmark. She stated: "I got in some important sentences, you know, I had to. I couldn't just talk about mothers." She also noted that "this was a sensation, the fact that—it was headlines in all the papers as I remember, that I spoke Danish." By speaking in the language of her host country, yielding to the advantages of placing the speech in a women's context, and furthermore accepting that placement gracefully, Eugenie was able to successfully reach thousands more than she might have with a detached political speech or article in English. Scholar Philip Nash agreed, especially in regard to utilizing Danish: "Anderson reached out in part by learning Danish—far more than [Ruth Bryan] Owen had. Not six months after arriving, she was able to deliver a speech in the language. Apart from her gender, nothing was noticed more by average Danes than her linguistic effort, which went far beyond the (at most token) instruction foreign envoys usually underwent."[28]

Eugenie felt a great responsibility as a representative of America and as a liaison for the Danes. Her Mother's Day speech followed closely on the heels of a national celebration marking the five-year anniversary of the end of World War II. After attending some events of that day, and putting down her thoughts on the brave individuals of the Danish resistance movement, Eugenie wrote home: "The confidence which these people expressed about being in the Atlantic Pact and knowing that they could never be occupied again without great nations coming to their aid, makes one feel very anxious that we really understand the commitments we have made—and what they mean to so many people."[29]

One of the strongest global voices for the United Nations and the North Atlantic Treaty was another American woman, Eleanor

Roosevelt. Mrs. Roosevelt, on a diplomatic tour of several European stops, spent five days in Denmark in June 1950, staying at Rydhave, the embassy residence, with Eugenie and John and the family. One day, the Roosevelt contingent and the Andersons traveled to Helsingør, where they attended a performance of *Hamlet* staged open-air at Kronborg Castle (the actual setting of Shakespeare's original play), including intermission coffee and sherry with the lead actor, Michael Redgrave, and some of the other Old Vic Players in the Knight's Hall. A third day of social engagements and appearances included tea with Professor Niels and Margrethe Bohr, during which Professor Bohr spoke at length with Mrs. Roosevelt about his published open letter to the United Nations, a lengthy treatise urging total openness between countries to offset the threat of human extinction by atomic warfare. Neither Eleanor nor Eugenie entirely agreed with Bohr, but they both appreciated his commitment, deep intelligence, and compassionate goals for government and humanity. After Mrs. Roosevelt's departure from Copenhagen, the official thank-yous and courtesies were exchanged by mail. Eugenie's letter to Mrs. Roosevelt stated: "Your being in Copenhagen was of real value for our interests here. Everything that you did and said while you were here reinforced the most essential aspects of American foreign policy, and I was particularly pleased that the Prime Minister had the opportunity of talking with you at some length. He has told me how much it meant to him."[30]

How extraordinary it must have felt for Eugenie, for only a few days, not only to be the woman in charge, but to be bolstered and accredited by an even more well-known and highly respected woman in the same field. The world was very slowly getting used to women in politics, but there was rarely more than one woman at the top levels in the same room at the same time. In this case, both women spent all of their time and energy supporting the international goals of the United Nations while enjoying a spike in their own visibility and popularity, which in turn served to help their messages. They did not have to discuss gardening or parties, nor

June 19, 1950. Original caption supplied by the New York bureau of Acme
Photos: "Holding a bouquet, Mrs. Eleanor Roosevelt, currently touring
Europe, is greeted by U.S. Ambassador to Denmark, Mrs. Eugenie Anderson
(left) upon her arrival at Kastrup Air Field at Copenhagen. Mrs. Roosevelt
had flown from Finland. In right background is Danish Foreign Minister
Gustav Rasmussen." *Acme Photo, author's collection.*

pander to gossip columnists looking for details about their clothes; Mrs. Roosevelt brought dignity and prewar continuity to Rydhave. It was as if a former US president were visiting Mrs. Anderson, and the two women together exemplified the fact that work could be done, and done well, even if the feminine gender controlled the atmosphere and the focus of the room.

Three weeks after the Roosevelt visit, Eugenie carried her growing popularity and reputation to the Rebild Festival in Jutland on the northern coast of Denmark. Since 1912, the Danish-American Society had organized a festival in the Rebild National Park on July 4 to celebrate American Independence Day and immigration between the countries. The American ambassador was always invited to speak, and Eugenie had spent a great deal of time perfecting her speech in Danish, which she would deliver in person (versus prerecorded) to an audience of perhaps ten thousand people. That, however, was not a good estimate: she faced a crowd of thirty thousand, in addition to many thousands listening over state radio. "I was nervous of course, but no one could tell it, and my preparation stood me in good stead, for the speech went really well," Eugenie later wrote home. The speech finally allowed Eugenie to reach the maximum number of people at one time. More importantly, it allowed her to shape and distill the subject matter and tenor of her words: she was not constrained to highlight women for Mother's Day, preach to a choir of Democrats, or introduce the next speaker.[31]

The 1950 speech at the Rebild Festival reinforced Eugenie's influence and outlined her own priorities and goals, and while one could argue that those goals were simply the objectives or propaganda of the Truman administration, they were, in fact, Eugenie's true beliefs. She addressed the Danes as respected allies in the North Atlantic Treaty, acknowledged that the United States must change with the times along with the rest of the world, and spoke passionately about interdependence and national survival. She closed the speech with these words: "It is my sincere hope that the mutual recognition of the new unity of interests between our two countries will deepen and increasingly strengthen the precious bonds which already exist through our common humanistic and democratic ideals." In later reminiscences, Eugenie recalled: "For a moment when I stopped speaking, there was a moment of silence and I thought nobody had understood a word. And then the applause was really deafening. It was just thunderous, in fact. Afterwards my public affairs officer [William Roll] told me that he was worried because he said, 'You got more applause than the King.' He said, 'That's not good.' But he was sort of joking."[32]

The press responded enthusiastically, and both Danish and American papers carried stories and photographs of Eugenie and her message from Rebild. While the coverage of her "first woman" status and image did not slow down, at least now it was tempered with news that accented what Eugenie wanted to say—not just what others wanted to hear her say about being a woman. Eugenie was fully aware that a large part of her positive and popular reputation was based on her gender. She was not naive or ignorant of the fickle nature of public perception. Eugenie also understood that the network of international journalism, which could either support or undermine her efforts, was a key component of democracy as a whole. In one chapter she drafted for her memoirs, she clarified the relationship between restriction of the press and control over freedom: "One must realize that one of the greatest dangers to democracy today lies in precisely the possibility of the unscrupulous manipulation and control of mass opinion. We have all seen instances both in our own country and abroad of how the public has been seduced and betrayed by demagogues and dictators."[33]

One of—if not *the*—highest-profile leaders of government in the free world, former British prime minister Winston Churchill, visited Copenhagen in mid-October 1950. Eugenie wrote of his reception by the Danes in the following excerpts of her family newsletter:

> When Churchill came out on the Town Hall balcony the immense crowd became quiet and then applauded wildly. It was surely both an interesting, and almost frightening thing to witness. While this

was a good-natured, not fanatical crowd, one could see what could so easily happen to a crowd in the hands of a demagogue or a dictator. Churchill stood in the floodlights, giving the V-sign over and over, with the roof above him lighted with torches and the Square below alive with many Danish and English flags as well as the people— quite a pageant in all.[34]

Ambassador Anderson hosted a dinner at the American Embassy with Churchill as guest of honor. Eugenie recalled that Churchill "took pleasure, and obvious pride, in reminding me that he was half American and at dinner when I was toasting him . . . he said happily, 'You know we have a lot in common.' . . . It was impossible not to like him and to think 'What an old boy he still is!' . . . Churchill obviously enjoyed the limelight, and is a marvelous actor."[35]

Other visiting government officials also fit the description of "old boy." Soon after Churchill had come and gone, the Andersons hosted three American congressmen at Rydhave: Representative Richard Chatham of North Carolina, Representative Laurie Calvin Battle of Alabama, and Representative Ovie Clark (O. C.) Fisher of Texas. Eugenie was the only woman in attendance at the welcome luncheon, and from there, she invited the men to accompany her to the embassy for a briefing session. Eugenie recalled that "one of them gaily replied, 'Oh, Mrs. Ambassador, the two curses of our trip are briefing sessions and European toilet paper!'" Highly embarrassed, both for herself and her staff, Eugenie redirected the conversation, but throughout their visit she endured the fact that "this same Congressman was always talking about how proud he was that we had such a *pretty* Ambassador here." The ingrained sexist attitude of this US Representative was, of course, not unusual in post–World War II diplomatic circles; in fact, it was the presiding mind-set. Even though Eugenie would have been perpetually attuned to sensing preconceived notions that questioned her abilities, opinions, and rights, she found it hardest to deal with the prejudices when they were spoken out loud, either directly or in supposed humor. When she wrote of these occasions, her code word, *amusing*, often popped out. As ambassador, she was expected to return good humor after bad, no matter the circumstances.[36]

Women were so rare in top-level Foreign Service positions that those among the first, like Eugenie, had to tread the waters expertly enough to avoid offending anyone even if it meant swallowing their dignity again and again. Philip Nash wrote: "We should not underestimate what these women were up against. As formal, accredited diplomats, they did not encounter the obstructions women of the earlier, informal diplomacy had faced. Nevertheless, other obstacles remained, and the female chiefs had to combat or evade the career men's attempts to usurp their authority, dictate the terms of their ambassadorships, or confine them to prescribed roles. They ran their embassies lacking the traditional spouse and while coping with double standards, sexist press coverage, and protocol complexities—often in the face of male indifference or hostility."[37]

Ambassador Anderson and secretary Vivian Meisen catch a ride on a diplomatic mail transport flight between European countries in 1951. *Photo by John P. Anderson, Anderson family collection.*

The visit of the US congressmen coincided with a time when John Anderson was absent from the embassy. Whether or not John's presence would have altered the men's comments or posturing, no doubt Eugenie was missing his support. Both of the Andersons struggled with John's ongoing role in Denmark. John found it intolerable to attend every formal dinner, every cocktail party, every public appearance, where he was scrutinized, belittled, or, just as demeaning, gushed over. On his behalf, Eugenie was genuinely sympathetic and understood that John needed anonymity and freedom in between bouts of spousal support and unpaid diplomatic service. Both of them constantly walked the line between maintaining their own convictions, setting an example for how they wished to be understood as a married couple with both similar and independent interests, while paying heed to others' expectations for how a husband and wife *ought* to be seen. Before their arrival in Denmark, the State Department had not given them precise clarity on John's rank or level of involvement. And after joining the community in Copenhagen and abroad, there was no set template from event to event that helped John become accustomed to what was expected of him.

Customarily, wives of ambassadors were given the same diplomatic rank as their husbands, to streamline events and protocol. But the Danes gave John Anderson the lower rank of "distinguished foreign visitor," which, as Eugenie put it, "if you know anything about protocol you know means nothing at all." The Andersons spent some time weighing the decision but ultimately decided not to make an issue of it, wanting to avoid repercussions among other dignitaries, embassies, and especially the press.[38]

In the fall of 1950, just before John left on a driving trip to Germany and France (thus missing the visit of the US congressmen described above), Eugenie made a very uncharacteristic public stand at a Danish Ministry of Foreign Affairs dinner. With a dining room full of dignitaries (and behind-the-scenes orchestration of the French ambassador), John and several other people without rank were seated out in the hallway. Eugenie described her reaction in her letter home:

> So I said in a clear *and* firm voice to the French Ambassador, "I think we need another place at this table, Mr. Ambassador," and remained standing while he motioned to the waiter to set another place. This took one or two minutes, so that everyone in the dining room became fully aware of what was going on and Prince Viggo said "Sit down, Mrs. Anderson," but I waited, again saying deliberately so that everyone could hear me, "I want to be sure that everyone is seated." And so we all were, but it was a miserable dinner so far as I was concerned and my only satisfaction was that at least I had not let them get by with it. John insisted that it did not bother him, but regardless it was an unpleasant thing. . . . I feel more and more as if it is impossible for me to attend many of these diplomatic functions and still do the things that I think are really important.[39]

The day after the dinner, Eugenie followed up with her protest and presented the difficult situation to the Danish foreign minister, who, mortified, raised John's rank to that of minister, just one step under ambassador but equivalent in matters of protocol.

John's feelings and actions remained, necessarily, private and controlled. Hans Anderson remembered going down to the harbor in Copenhagen with John to pick up their 1948 Chrysler Windsor, which had been shipped over from the states. John checked the car over before driving it, testing the oil pressure and the tires. Hans described in detail how John bent the tiny valve on one of the tires to release a little air, drawing it into his nose with a deep inhalation, saying: "Mmmmm. Minnesota air." Hans continued: "Which let me know that he was missing Minnesota and that being there in Denmark was probably just as hard for him as it was for me. Maybe harder."[40]

And so the end of October 1950 found Eugenie handling the embassy's office and residence, and the children's needs, while John took some time on a photographic road expedition, a respite from his increasingly frustrating position. The family faced a crisis when Hans, who had not yet acclimated to Denmark or school, was suffering from depression severe enough to warrant important decisions. Eugenie's answer was to enroll Hans in a boarding school in England. But when she sent a telegram to John in Paris with this information, John immediately got in the car and drove without stopping back to Copenhagen.

Perhaps because of the pressure Eugenie felt from all sides, and the hopelessness of balancing both work and family, she was unable to facilitate Hans's needs at the time. John knew instinctively that boarding school was a terrible idea; moreover, Eugenie's telegram must have struck him deeply, forcing him to see that there *was* a solution—and it was John himself. "He saved me," Hans asserted, proudly. "It gave him something to do that was important. In a very real and immediate sense for the family, and for me, and himself. And it gave him something to feel important about." Up until this season of his life, at age forty-three, John had felt a polarity with fatherhood. He strained against its responsibilities, its conventions, and the energy it took away from his creative work and ambitions. For many years, he had simply left the work and the decisions up to Eugenie and the women she hired to help. But behind it all, as with his love for Eugenie, was a fundamental devotion to both of his children that won out in a crisis. Hans believes that, beginning that fall, John came to better understand that his presence and involvement as a father brought him genuine happiness of a kind he had not known before. While the role reversal on the public side of the family remained complicated and unrewarding for John, in private it allowed him to see new talents in himself—teaching, playing, and simply spending time with his children.[41]

As December 1950 approached, John and Eugenie's decisions regarding their children went beyond that of a private matter of negotiation and personal feelings. The growing crisis between Communist Korean aggression (precursors to the Korean War) and the countries of NATO had a very close, real impact on the Andersons' residence in Denmark. Their physical proximity to

Communist-held air bases in Europe made them imminently vulnerable. In later years, when an interviewer asked Eugenie if Europeans, and Danes in particular, were fearful of a full-scale attack, Eugenie answered:

> Yes, they were, because they felt quite open to attack from the outside. They had no natural defenses. [Denmark] is a peninsula jutting up there in the North Sea at the gateway of the Baltic and they were just fifteen minutes by air from Soviet bases in Poland and in East Germany and they were really quite concerned. And they felt it was only the protection of NATO that gave them any hope at all that the Russians wouldn't dare to attack them. . . .
>
> It was difficult for me even personally because I had received instructions from the State Department to make plans to evacuate all Americans within twenty-four hours notice, and I think that this was not an easy assignment because they couldn't promise me any airplanes, they couldn't even promise me any boats and how would I get 600 or more Americans out within twenty-four hours. . . . I was quite concerned about the safety of my own children. I realized that if anything like that did happen, a sudden attack, that we would undoubtedly be the first ones to be captured and I didn't think it was quite fair to my children for them to have to go through this.[42]

Eugenie expressed candid worries in her family newsletter of December 3, 1950. She was frustrated with what she saw as a cautious approach by the US government, writing: "To be delaying any effective action in Korea while Truman and [British prime minister Clement] Atlee meet and the U.N. discusses—well, it begins to seem like sitting down to talk about how we should put out the fire while meanwhile the house burns down." At the end of the letter, she closed with: "Let us hope that the next week will not be as desperate as it looks now . . . one can only hope that in America, at least, people will see what must be done, and not be afraid to do it."[43]

Military action was officially implemented on December 16 when Truman signed a proclamation declaring a national state of emergency in order to repel Communist imperialism. Eugenie strongly approved of Truman's decision, as well as General Dwight

D. Eisenhower's appointment as supreme allied commander of NATO forces in Europe. Notes for her memoirs included: "The traditional Danish Christmas festivities are celebrated with fatalism heavy in the background. I have a sharpened awareness of Denmark's defenselessness and defeatism." She also provided a more personal illustration of the family's apprehensions. Describing the New Year's Eve telephone call between Copenhagen and Red Wing, Minnesota, she wrote: "Hans had disconcerted us by saying that his first words to his Uncle Frank would be, 'How would you like to be sitting here only 90 miles from the Russians right now? Just about as if they were over at Albert Lea?' His comment revealed to us that as usual, the parents' attempts to conceal their anxieties from their children had been futile."[44]

Eugenie was tough. She was a tough politician, a tough critic, and a tough authority figure. Even while she agonized over what was right for her children, knowing that there was no simple answer, morally or realistically, her default was to rely on faith, reason, and her deep reserve of educated knowledge. Both she and John spent many late nights in December 1950, changing their minds again and again over whether to put Hans and Johanna on a ship home. But ultimately, Eugenie could not do it, because she knew that such an action would publicly call into question everything she had ever said about the strength of the United States, its commitment to NATO and the United Nations, and the calm face of control that all citizens of the free world must present to Communist aggressors. She would not undermine her standing as a strong ambassador, even if it risked an appearance of being unfeminine or nonmaternal.

Immediate fears of war in their backyard eased somewhat, and the Andersons began their second year at the embassy with the opening of 1951. Eugenie was in charge of a diplomatic staff of 279 Americans, including twenty chief officers. She continued to study the Danish language; consumed dozens of newspapers and publications daily; wrote hundreds of pages of reports, correspondence, letters, and journal entries weekly; read countless books on history and current affairs; and delivered an average of two speeches per month, which she wrote and tailored to each separate occasion. Her male Foreign Service counterparts had wives to oversee all of the domestic arrangements of their residences and act as hostesses for events as small as afternoon teas to full-blown state dinners for kings, prime ministers, and dignitaries. Those duties fell to Eugenie as well. Her challenge was to cast the illusion that everything was under control, natural, and easy at home because she was a woman, and perfectly manageable at work because her gender should not be of consequence in that setting.

An example of this thankless situation occurred when Eugenie's predecessor, former US minister to Denmark Josiah Marvel, who was at this time acting as an attorney for the War Claims Commission, came for a few days' visit to Rydhave. In standard practice, Eugenie arranged a dinner for him at the embassy. Eugenie started off this story to her family by writing: "A very amusing thing about this evening was that I got home about 6:30 that evening and discovered that the flowers for the table were not at all nice. (I had ordered them but hadn't seen them nor arranged them.)" She went on to describe how mortified she was, especially when the wife of the British ambassador Lady Randall "asked John innocently, 'Does your wife always arrange the flowers?' Meanwhile looking just at these crude pink bunches." At a luncheon the next day, Lady Randall "asked me again in this same elaborately careless manner how I had time to do so much, and whether I even arranged the flowers for dinners etc." Forced to justify (if not apologize for) the "ghastly" flowers, Eugenie felt clearly shamed that she had allowed a less-than-perfect table to represent her.[45]

The following week, Eugenie discovered the poison that Josiah Marvel had left in his path after the dinner—character defamation and petty jealousy that made fretting over flowers pale in comparison. Marvel had spent his days in Copenhagen meeting as many officials and former acquaintances as possible, inflating his own current importance and insinuating that Ambassador Anderson was incompetent. Upon first meeting embassy deputy chief Harold Schantz, Marvel had asked him: "How are you getting along with your *Master*?" Several of the other men Marvel tried to draw into confidence found his comments "astounding" and "disgusting." Eugenie wrote that "Mr. Roll thought that some of his actions were so intentionally destructive (potentially so, at least) of my position here that I should protest to the State Department." She went on to say that she had no intention of reporting or discussing anything about Josiah Marvel to officials, that she would not "stoop to his level," and that she realized "that in his eyes, I am not only his successor, but also a competitor and even victor." One can only imagine what Marvel expected to get out of his agenda, or what disgusting slurs he made against Eugenie. And realistically, he could not have been the only such person in the Foreign Service to perpetuate sexual harassment against women at all levels.[46]

After more than a year at her post, professionally succeeding to a high degree, Eugenie remained, because of her gender, at the mercy of the press—as it continued to patronize and glorify her femininity. Americans saw in their newspapers "Ambassador Anderson Plans to Please Her Danish Guests," next to a photo of smiling Eugenie pouring tea out of a plain, dark teapot into a cup, ensconced in the kitchen with pans hanging on the walls. Concurrently, the Danish press ran a photo of Eugenie operating an electric mixer, captioned "Ambassador Fixes Food." Finally the *New York Times* reported on hard news, announcing, "U.S., Denmark Sign Pact on Greenland" on April 28, 1951. The article stated: "Although signed in Copenhagen today, the agreement will not go into effect until it is ratified by the Danish Parliament. Mrs. Eugenie Anderson, United States Ambassador to Denmark, and Ole Bjoern Kraft, Danish Foreign Minister, signed for their respective governments." While much of the following publicity for this joint defense pact highlighted the fact that Eugenie was the first woman to ever sign an international treaty on behalf of the United States, it must have been gratifying to read, at the outset, simply her name and her achievement, without any qualifier of her gender. General Eisenhower revisited Copenhagen the week after the treaty signing, accompanied by his wife, Mamie, and the press coverage fortunately applied more copy inches on the North Atlantic Pact and Eugenie's role in securing and signing the treaty than it did on her appearance or her hostessing flair.[47]

Eugenie made a journey back to the United States in October 1951. Despite continuing ADA and DFL efforts to entice her to run for Senate or governor in 1952, Anderson refused, and committed

In May 1952, Ambassador Anderson welcomes General Dwight D. Eisenhower, Supreme Commander of the North Atlantic Treaty Organization (NATO), in Copenhagen, Denmark, where he congratulated her on signing the Treaty of Friendship, Commerce and Navigation between the United States of America and the Kingdom of Denmark. *Anderson family collection.*

her trip to proceedings at the State Department, briefings in Washington, meetings with congressmen to discuss pending bills and trade embargoes that would affect Danish commerce, delivering speeches, including one to the Women's National Press Club, and visiting family and friends in Minnesota, where she had been absent for nineteen months.

Eugenie wrote many long letters to John back in Copenhagen while she moved between Washington, DC; New York; Minnesota; and the Midwest for five weeks that fall. These personal letters are much more revealing of her feelings about work pressures, outside opinions of her, and press realities than are the family newsletters that she mailed home (knowing those would be accessed by many and used later for reference). She made no bones about the repugnance of campaigning: "The more I see of political life, the more convinced I am that it would be impossible for me to ever run for political office. The pressures—even once one is elected—are so great that it is no wonder that so few people of real quality go into politics. . . . I really feel as if I have been talking so much I just get sick of hearing myself. If it is not the press, or the State Department then it's my friends plying me with questions."[48]

The friends, including India Edwards, Evron and Jeane Kirkpatrick, Max and Maggie Kampelman, Hubert and Muriel Humphrey, and Orville and Jane Freeman, were among those with whom Eugenie appreciated reconnecting, but they also pushed her nighttime socializing to two and three in the morning as they visited each other's residences and hotels after dinners and speeches with circulating groups of politicos and Washington insiders. Of the atmosphere, Eugenie wrote: "All the news I have been hearing about Congress is very depressing. You may not agree with Humphrey about some things but I think you would agree with his opposition to all the forces of corruption, special interests (really *big* steals) and greed. . . . There are good people here in Washington, I know, but the others certainly make the most noise!"[49]

John's letters to Eugenie at this same time illustrated, by their contrast to her letters, the depth of their role reversal. He wrote: "Each day I see Hans and Jo grow and develop, and try to grasp what goes on in them I am impressed with their basic health and mental vigor. . . . I keep thinking of the things I haven't done with Hans and Jo and it makes me feel very depressed many times, as it should; altho I should take my realization of that as a clue to do differently. . . . The household staff is having what amounts to a fall vacation since there is very little to do apart from basic things. On that score things will go smoothly and I am having no difficulties with details."[50]

Of course, John also wrote at great length about books he was reading, his political theories, the stock market, military history and current events, and photo equipment technicalities. Even apart, John and Eugenie carried on their dialogue through letters, in between phrases like "I worry about you Sweetheart" and "You must not neglect your health." The Denmark years put enormous stress on their marriage, but the experience also created the necessity for a supportive partnership they might not otherwise have developed. John confessed:

> It's just two weeks ago tonight that you left and will say it seems longer than that. This being a most unnatural environment to me and the whole business seemingly suspended in space makes for warped sensing of reality as I was used to it for the early part of my life. . . . It's all part of the madhouse of the present world and since it's all we've got there is nothing to do but play one's part. If I can accomplish something with the children for this early period of their lives that's a fine gain as far as I'm concerned.[51]

Everyone had their opinions of Eugenie as an ambassador/ mother, and whether or not *she* should be permitted to embody such madness, but John never saw it that way. He turned the tables and called it "the madhouse of the present world." It is clear that his commitment to their democratic motives and services was on the same plane as Eugenie's: that the gender of the official should not matter, and what counted was effort on behalf of global human rights. He didn't have to like waiting at the dentist for his children or editing the weekly grocery order, but he saw the big picture. John and Eugenie were mostly united in their objectives and sacrifices.

The Andersons' relationship with Eugenie's sister Mary and Charles Biederman suffered strain. The Biedermans were living at the Tower View farmhouse with their daughter, Anna, while the Andersons were abroad, and although Charles continued to use the labs and workshop facilities on the estate for his constructionist art, he had fallen out with some of the extended Anderson family, and his correspondence with John deteriorated to terse acknowledgments when John sent monthly checks. Eugenie and Mary, still very close and sympathetic with each other, were in a terrible situation with no easy resolution. When Eugenie traveled to Minnesota in October 1951, she wanted nothing more than to sleep in her own house, walk the meadows, and spend time with her sister and family. But she opted instead to stay at Elizabeth and Ray Hedin's house in Red Wing, where she would not have to deal with Charles's volatility and Mary's apologies and buffering. Eugenie wrote:

> Mary & I walked around the place & went down to the Indian Mound and all around. It was good in one way but it also made me terribly affected, and several times I could hardly keep from crying at the sight of things I have loved so much and feel so close to—and yet now so far removed from. I didn't cry but it was really a strain especially because everything in our house seems so different. Charles tried to be nice but the atmosphere was rather tense as long as he was in the room and I just felt sick at heart to see how things are between him and all the rest of us except Mary.[52]

Soon after Eugenie's return to Copenhagen in November 1951, the Humphreys came to Rydhave, and John and Eugenie hosted them at the embassy and guided them around the country for several days. Hubert mentioned in a personal letter to Eugenie that "I find that this trip of mine has been of great help to me. It really did something for my spirit and I believe that it greatly improved my understanding of our foreign policy and the problems that we face."[53]

The Andersons celebrated a third Christmas in their adopted home, and January 1952 brought a visit from Mrs. Edith Sampson, the first African American US delegate to the United Nations. She was a member of the UN's Social, Humanitarian & Cultural Committee, and her visit to Denmark came on the heels of a speech Eugenie had given to an educational society for workers at Hillerød, just north of Copenhagen. Lasting more than an hour and given in Danish, Eugenie's speech, titled "The Negro in America Today," outlined the positive initiatives and aspects of the United States' efforts to improve the lives of African Americans. While a speech to a relatively small audience might usually go unnoticed, the wider public was brought into the issue when Eugenie called out the Communists for using propaganda to vilify racist America. The *New York Times* picked up the story, "NEGRO GAINS IN U.S. CITED: Envoy Tells Danes of Progress and Scores False Red Role." The Associated Press article ran nationwide, with headlines like "Mrs. Anderson Slams Reds on Negro Issue," citing: "[Anderson] blamed Communist propaganda sources and added: 'From such a source, outraged cries and pious concern for the American Negro can only sound false and hypocritical.' She described the Soviet Union as 'a nation whose totalitarian government not only sanctions slavery but officially sponsors unbelievably terrible slave camps throughout its own land and satellites—thus enslaving a minimum of 10 million of its own people.'"[54]

Eugenie's job as ambassador was to shore up the reputation of the United States and shine light on its strengths and importance to European allies. In this case, her objective was to try to correct the "misinformed" ideas that many Europeans held about the position and lives of African Americans. One of the main objectives of Eugenie's political ambition—if not the most critical—was to fight Communism on behalf of democracy, anytime, anywhere, anyplace. Her speech conceded that she was "deeply and painfully conscious that such undemocratic practices as segregation and all forms of discrimination should have no place in any democracy." But she was

EUGENIE ANDERSON, U. S. Ambassador to Denmark

IS DIPLOMACY A WOMAN'S JOB?
(SEE "NATIONAL NEWS")

Quick magazine presents the question: "Is Diplomacy a Woman's Job?" "Mrs. Anderson, a housewife, has parties for Danish workers at the embassy. She talks with Danes—in their own language—on the street. She deals directly with farmers who protest the U.S. bans on importing cheese. Simple directness is her forte." *Eugenie M. Anderson papers, box 15.*

Wing, Minn., as the first U. S. woman ambassador to any country — Denmark. The same year he sent Washington's No. 1 hostess, Mrs. Perle Mesta, to Luxemburg as our minister.

Mrs. Anderson, a housewife, has parties for Danish workers at the embassy. She talks with Danes—in their own language—on the street. She deals directly with farmers who protest U. S. bans on importing cheese. Simple directness is her forte.

Eleanor Roosevelt

Mrs. Mesta, widow of an Oklahoma oil man, combined her social skill with a "common touch" in the Grand Duchy of Luxemburg. She visits the coffee houses to talk with the people, entertains any and all at the embassy. Says one Luxemburg official: local Red cells will keep melting away under her charm.

Tops in the U.N.

Mrs. Roosevelt is the center of U.N. attention. Once scorned by the Reds, she's now respected by them. Having felt the lash of her arguments, they now duck debating with her.

As for other countries, India's Madame Vijaya Pandit, as ambassador to Washington, was credited with winning U. S. grain for India. Chile's Ana Figueroa heads the U.N. Social Humanitarian and Cultural Committee. Brazil's Rosalinda de Larroigitti, Russia's Elizabieta Popova are U.N. standbys.

The top U. S. booster for more women diplomats is India Edwards, head of the women's division of the Democratic party. Says she: "The battle for a decent world is no different from the battle women have been waging at home for social improvement."

never willing to concede that the current US government had any immoral equivalent to the crimes intrinsic to Soviet Russia.

On the fluff side that January 1952, *Quick* magazine ran a full-page photo of Eugenie in her ostrich-tipped hat, captioned: "IS DIPLOMACY A WOMAN'S JOB?" Betty Friedan later summarized the historical marketing of these types of 1950s women's magazines in her 1973 reprint of *The Feminine Mystique*. She stated that in such publications "it was unquestioned gospel that women could identify with nothing beyond the home—not politics, not art, not science, not events large or small, war or peace, in the United States or the world, unless it could be approached through female experience as a wife or mother or translated into domestic detail!"[55]

To the ADA's repeated pleas, again in April 1952, that she leave Denmark to start a Senate campaign, Eugenie replied to Arthur Schlesinger: "I appreciate your thoughts about the possibility of my returning to run for the Senate in Minnesota, but I decided definitely sometime ago not to do this, and, in fact, have never seriously considered it. I think I can accomplish more at present by staying here." Six years later, she would look back on this decision not with regret, per se, but with frustration that a good chance for a career in the Senate may have happened in 1952. There is every reason to believe that had she been able to join Humphrey in Washington and fortify his presidential ambitions through the 1950s and '60s, Humphrey's future campaign snags might have untangled enough to alter history.[56]

In mid-July of 1952, when normally she would have been on a family holiday, Eugenie used vacation time to travel back to the United States for the Democratic National Convention in Chicago. India Edwards achieved her goal of incorporating more women into the Democratic Party process at the Chicago convention, bringing in 525 women delegates (as opposed to 380 at the Republican convention) and presenting, as the *New York Times* called it, an "all-star cast of women speakers," who, in addition to India Edwards and Eleanor Roosevelt, were each high-profile appointees of President

On July 22, 1952, Ambassador Anderson joined four other featured women speakers on "Ladies' Day" of the Democratic National Convention, coordinated by India Edwards, addressing the hall and a national television audience. *Associated Press Wirephoto, author's collection.*

Truman: Eugenie Anderson, ambassador to Denmark; Perle Mesta, minister to Luxembourg; and Georgia Neese Clark, treasurer of the United States. After the Tuesday "Ladies' Day" speeches on the second night of the convention, the *New York Times* ran individual photos of Roosevelt, Edwards, Anderson, Mesta, and Clark speaking at the podium and printed Eleanor Roosevelt's speech in its entirety. The *Los Angeles Times* ran similar photos but placed them over a grossly sexist opinion piece: "Television Viewers Get a Look at Democracy's Charming Six." Journalist Art Ryon joked crassly:

> Let's face it, the ladies just don't have the rostrum vigor of the men. . . . [Eleanor Roosevelt] . . . looks well, but—well, the lady has put on some weight. . . .
>
> Incidentally, from the viewer's viewpoint, the cameras are being kinder to the Democratic women than they were to Republican femmes who occupied the speaker's platform. That's because, at this conclave, a platform for TV cameras has been put up in the middle of the hall's floor to give a head-on view of all the speakers. Excess chins don't show up so much. . . .
>
> Mrs. Eugenie M. Anderson of Minnesota, U.S. Ambassador to Denmark, was a charmer. But there was a moment of awkward silence during her speech. She must've thought the Republicans were still in session. She quoted Abraham Lincoln!

The convention ended nominating Adlai Stevenson, governor of Illinois, for president, with John Sparkman as his vice presidential running mate. As the Democratic National Committee reconfigured to plot out their strategy for beating Republican general Dwight D. Eisenhower in the fall election, India Edwards wrote Eugenie, thanking her for her faithful attendance at the sessions and "magnificent" convention speech. She also admitted that "I do not feel that it would be wise for me to be [Democratic National] Chairman and Adlai truly does not want a woman." Indeed, in her memoir *Pulling No Punches*, Edwards elaborated that "Stevenson would have had trouble with the women libbers. . . . Adlai walked over to me and said quite seriously, 'India, what are you doing in politics with such an attractive man as a husband?' He thought only frustrated housewives or lonely spinsters could be interested in politics." Edwards's letter to Eugenie continued prophetically: "I am too realistic not to know that few men are willing to trust a woman in such a spot even though her advice is sought and followed in the most important matters. Some day it will be different but today it is not. I think women like you will help to change this attitude of males, however."[57]

Adlai Stevenson's campaign efforts were not enough to overcome the popularity of General Eisenhower, who was voted in as president in November 1952. As Eugenie prepared for her resignation, like twenty-three other ambassadors would do when the administration changed from Democrat to Republican, India Edwards sent her gratitude for Eugenie's service. She wrote: "The job for all of us is even more challenging than it would have been had we won so we are counting on you to continue to give generously of your time, experience and talents in helping our Party to continue its work for a stronger America and a more peaceful world." Clearly, no matter what Eugenie's plans were for herself and her family, the Democrats had no intention of excusing her from political involvement.[58]

William Roll, Eugenie's embassy public affairs officer and good friend, spoke for many when he bid farewell: "Eugenie—I don't know what to say. My heart is acting very strange, and although I know so is the best [sic], i.e. that you are 'retiring'—for the time being—I just don't care to go back to my office any more. I know I shall have to, for a very brief spell, but I dread to think of the tremendous vacuum—not only for me—but for so many of us." Before she departed, King Frederick IX bestowed upon Eugenie the Grand Cross of the Order of the Dannebrog, the second-highest honor of Denmark, along with the insignia of the order dating to 1671, at Anderson's farewell audience at the royal residence Amalienborg. She was the first nonroyal woman in the country's history to receive the knighthood. And although under US law she would not have been permitted to receive a foreign decoration while she served in an official capacity, Denmark waited until the day after her official resignation so that she could be knighted without citizenship conflict.[59]

By February 8, 1953, the trunks and crates were packed, all the farewells were said, all official documents had been finalized, and all ceremonies had been concluded. Over the next few months, Eugenie began outlining material for a possible book that several different publishers had expressed interest in seeing. As far back as December 1949, before Eugenie had even commenced her post, Harold Strauss at Knopf had written to her: "The impression left thus far by press stories and feature articles is an enchanting one, and I suspect that you are going to find a rather special place in the American heart. I think a book of reminiscences by you would have enormous appeal to American women. I do not mean to suggest that the serious side of your mission should be neglected. There ought to be room for both aspects."[60]

Strauss—and his hopes for a lighter-weight book by a woman for a primarily female audience—would be denied. Establishing her outline in 1953, Eugenie wrote: "The fact of being a woman, however, is not central to my work." Other publishers, such as Lynn Carrick at J. B. Lippincott Company, also tried to solicit a more gender-angled story. Carrick explained: "But we do not have in mind an 'official' book so much as an informal account of your life in Denmark as an American wife and mother as well as an Ambassador." Any signed contract between Eugenie and Knopf, Lippincott, or, later, Random House did not materialize. While a partial outline and pieces of chapters are among the Eugenie M. Anderson papers at the Minnesota Historical Society, any further plans for a book stalled after Eugenie had returned to the states and resumed working on Democratic committees and lecture tours, and eventually considered running for public office. Negotiations for book deals may very likely have hinged on Eugenie's unwillingness to dilute her subject matter or shift the focus from her deep commitment to democratic ideals, foreign policy, and the goals of the United Nations to how

Eugenie brings her love of outdoor picnicking to Denmark, 1952. Showing her combining business with pleasure, this photo was snapped by her thirteen-year-old son. Embassy chauffeur Hjarmind in the background. *Photo by Hans P. Anderson, author's collection.*

she felt about being a woman in a man's world or balancing a day's work at the office against her children's needs. In the early 1950s, women's issues were seen as lesser issues, and Eugenie had no wish for her book to be shelved among celebrities or personalities like Perle Mesta when the publication that would serve her legacy—and her future career in politics—best would market her story next to serious politicians and figures. "The fact of being a woman is not central to my work," she proclaimed. She was right. But few others would see it that way.[61]

Four
REACHING for WASHINGTON

*I hate to admit it, but I now believe there was a great deal
of both classism and racism in the Democratic-Farmer-Labor
Party in those years. . . . League of Women Voters activists,
who might look like nice ladies but were tough politicians—
some going back to suffrage days and the origins of the League—
were courted by Freeman and Humphrey. . . . Politics is complex
and democracy imperfect but, as Winston Churchill
famously said, it's the best we've got.*

*Women candidates also walk a fine line. They can't appear
to be aggressive and yet have to portray themselves as substantial
enough to carry out the duties of the office they seek.*

ARVONNE FRASER, *SHE'S NO LADY*

IN MANY WAYS, 1958 WAS THE MOST PIVOTAL YEAR OF Eugenie Anderson's political career. Unfortunately, it was also the most devastating.

During the five years that followed Eugenie's historical ambassadorship, another Minnesota politician became a "first woman": in this case, a US representative to Congress. Coya Knutson of Oklee, Minnesota, Democrat from the Ninth Congressional District in the northwest corner of the state, was the first woman that the state of Minnesota had ever elected to serve in Washington. Knutson was folksy and ebullient, sang and played guitar at her own rallies, and held her unique ground just outside of the DFL nucleus powered by Hubert Humphrey and Orville Freeman. Being female and Democrat were just about the only commonalities between Coya

Knutson and Eugenie Anderson: to a large degree their political agendas, philosophies, and methods were completely different, and it is unlikely that they would have deliberately chosen to work together at any juncture. In truth, they never did. But a very cruel trick of circumstance put both their heads on the chopping block in May 1958, and ever after, Knutson and Anderson had to relinquish their dreams of establishing themselves long term among the congressmen in Washington.

As soon as Eugenie landed on American shores in June 1953, the *New York Times* declared: "Minnesota Ex-Envoy Boomed for Governor," above Eugenie's beaming face and name. No, no, she told reporters the following week at her homecoming celebration in Red Wing: it's just gossip. Hubert Humphrey chided her in a letter: "Now listen, Eugenie, don't you close that door on political activity too tight." Humphrey also pulled her into close involvement with Orville Freeman's gubernatorial campaign, from which Freeman came out victorious in 1954. "Wasn't it a great victory!" Humphrey wrote to Eugenie. "Orville will need your guidance, and do feel free to give it to him. I know he will want it." As early as November 1955, Humphrey was persistently priming Eugenie for a Senate run three years down the road. When Humphrey caught wind of any support for Eugenie around him, he never hesitated to employ it. "Mrs. Eugenie Anderson . . . would make an excellent partner for you in the Senate," wrote one Carleton College professor, "and this letter is sent with the hope that a movement can be launched to nominate Mrs. Anderson for the Senate campaign against Mr. [Edward] Thye when he comes up for reelection." Humphrey forwarded the letter to Eugenie and added his own two cents: "I thought you would be interested in the attached. I agree—and have so stated to Professor Qualey. Shall I drop Ed Thye a note and tell him to pack up and get ready to move, or would you rather do that yourself?" At this point, Eugenie was still far from committing herself to any serious plans. Governor Freeman had appointed her chairman of the State Fair Employment Practices Commission, and that work, along with lecture tours and support of other DFL and Democratic Party initiatives, kept her very busy. A week after receiving Humphrey's latest encouragement, above, Eugenie confessed to her son as she traveled to a meeting in Chicago: "I find these big [Democratic Party] shin-digs very boring now but yet I guess they are a necessary part of politics, and if one wants to be in a position to help decide the important things, you also have to go through with a lot of the superficial rituals."[1]

Coya Knutson had little patience herself for certain machinations of the Democratic Party. Her first experience with the DFL inner circle was at the 1948 state Democratic convention, when Knutson witnessed Hubert Humphrey, Orville Freeman, and Eugenie Anderson take back the majority by obliterating Communist participation. Two years later, Coya threw her name into the ring and ran for Congress in the ninth district. The *Minneapolis Tribune* always reached the widest market of Minnesotans, so of course Coya agreed when Barbara Flanagan telephoned for an interview. Gretchen Beito, the author of Knutson's biography *Coya Come Home*, wrote: "The questions had come so quickly that Coya barely had time to think. . . . She wanted to convey the image of a traditional and happy homelife. . . . All in all it was a good, safe, pleasant little story, Coya thought, and just the sort of Sunday feature folks liked to read." Like Eugenie, Coya was compelled to present herself as a contented homemaker with her priorities in order. It should be said that male politicians were also expected to appear domestically secure and traditional: a wife at home (or safely deceased—very rarely divorced), unquestionable heterosexual status, and no public hint of infidelity, although the "boys will be boys" allowance for private affairs was generally tolerated. But unlike female politicians, the men did not have to habitually justify their motives for putting themselves in the public spotlight. Any woman who wanted to be elected was required to offer overwhelming reasons for her wish to be of service outside the home. Knutson understood those requirements but always found them infuriating and a waste of good time: "Coya was irritated that it was only after her credentials as a homemaker had been established that Flanagan went on to write about Coya's legislative goals. Issues that were important to Coya—fair employment practices, state aid for education, and a school nurse program—were not mentioned until the closing paragraph."[2]

So things stood in the fall of 1955, as Eugenie contemplated her future and whether or not it could include a potential of one term, two terms, or indefinite years in the US Senate. Hubert Humphrey, established senator and one whom many considered a future president, was her strongest champion. Few people denied that Humphrey was anything but honest and a true believer in his agenda for civil rights and equality for all. Among those few doubters was Coya Knutson: "Coya felt that Humphrey was unwilling to hear the objections she thought should be raised on behalf of the farmers she represented, and that he had highhandedly dismissed her viewpoint. 'Shucks, I'm only a woman, and he figures women are not to be taken seriously.'"[3]

The 1956 Democratic National Convention proved to be a significant turning point for Humphrey. Maneuvers among the presidential and vice presidential wannabes, Adlai Stevenson, Estes Kefauver, Hubert Humphrey, and a young senator from Massachusetts, John F. Kennedy, kept the top men and their supporters in a constant frenzy of negotiation and "I will if you will" power plays. When Stevenson was finally cast as the presidential nominee, he shocked the crowd by throwing the convention open to allow delegates to pick the vice presidential nominee, rather than name the running mate himself. "Humphrey was devastated. His Minnesota friend Eric Sevareid, bumping into him directly after Stevenson's announcement, said: 'I've never seen him so upset.'" Through the night, Humphrey, Kefauver, and Kennedy each went through agonizing stages of strategy to recruit delegates' votes. Kennedy tried to entice Humphrey to conspire against Kefauver. Carl Solberg illustrated well the dramatic scene:

At this ghastly moment, as Humphrey watched his chances go down the drain, and feeling miserable about the whole fiasco, a young man ran up to him and, as if offering an audience with royalty, announced that Senator Kennedy would like Senator Humphrey to come to his hotel room and see him. Before Humphrey had time to explode at this affront, Orville Freeman bolted into the room and said melodramatically: "It's all over." It wasn't quite; there was no way out of the trap for Humphrey. Estes Kefauver burst in. "Hubert," he pleaded, "you've got to help me, you've GOT to help me." Kefauver was crying, Humphrey was crying. Everybody crowded around him. Eugenie Anderson said: "Leave Hubert alone. . . . He's got to make his own decision. Leave him alone."[4]

Not only was Eugenie upset on behalf of Humphrey, but she got her first glimpse of the Kennedy machine's way of conducting politics. Humphrey did what he had to do and backed Kefauver. His action halted the slide toward Kennedy. "Hubert Humphrey suffered heavier defeats in his life, but his wife said later, 'That was the worst, that was the bitterest defeat. He felt he had been made a fool of. He never would talk about it.'" Beito provided Coya's point of view: "Minnesota's vote broke the dam. Kefauver got the majority he needed. . . . With the announcement that Kefauver was the winner, pandemonium reigned in the Minnesota section. Coya [Knutson] threw her arms around an alternate delegate, crying, 'We saved the farm vote, thanks to Hubert's switching.'"[5]

Knutson was out there on the floor, set apart from the Humphrey inner circle. "Putting distance between me and the know-it-alls did my heart good," she said. Managing her own campaign for a second term with the bare minimum of DFL support, Knutson also suffered the handicap of a scandalous, disintegrating marriage. Coya's husband, Andy Knutson, back in Oklee, Minnesota, was a chronic alcoholic prone to embarrassing public displays. The couple was on the downward spiral of complete separation, but for appearance's sake, Coya was forced to stay legally married to Andy. Political friends and colleagues knew the truth. Beito wrote: "As her first term in the U.S. Congress ended, one thing was certain. Coya no longer thought that her image as a DFL member was important. She had let people know that she was on her own. . . . At an August DFL meeting, she met Muriel Humphrey in the hotel lobby, carrying a little ironing board under her arm. Coya envied Hubert—she wished that she too had someone to help her be at her best at all times and see her through the rough patches."[6]

That image of the ironing board echoes the ghastly flowers on Eugenie's embassy table in Copenhagen: all those behind-the-scenes duties, tasks, details, and necessities that combine to create the critical big picture of confidence and authority—a totality of details without which no politician can succeed. Coya Knutson prevailed in November 1956 and won reelection, as did President Eisenhower over the Stevenson-Kefauver ticket. Knutson's victory, and Humphrey's setback, sent both legislators into unforeseeable and irreversible circumstances. If Knutson had lost, she would not have been dragged into the "Coya Come Home" scandal that would soon destroy her entire political career. If Humphrey had won his party's endorsement, he might not have been forced to compromise his loyalties among other Democrats in the next few years. These were seemingly two separate situations, but together they led to a perfect storm that finished Eugenie's Senate hopes in 1958.

In former vice president Walter Mondale's memoir, *The Good Fight*, he reminisced on advice from fellow Minnesotan Hubert Humphrey during his own freshman time at the US Senate: "Humphrey had gone to Washington sixteen years earlier blazing away, giving speeches and telling his elders how to turn things around— and he advised me pointedly not to follow his example. Instead, he always emphasized the importance of relationships. . . . You learned quickly that your career depended on getting along with other members, especially the ones with seniority."[7]

The bitterness of Humphrey's 1956 defeat may have forced him to make concessions he never thought necessary in order to keep reaching for the presidency someday. While he would never *officially* turn his back on friends or burn bridges, his priorities resulted in dashed hopes for some who had counted on his valuable coattails. More specifically, as an example, Humphrey found it necessary to withhold any public endorsement of Eugenie Anderson.

Eugenie wasn't the only DFLer who contemplated Republican senator Edward Thye's seat. Everyone from Governor Freeman, lieutenant governor Karl Rolvaag, representative Eugene McCarthy, and state attorney general Miles Lord to lesser-knowns like Bob Short and Hjalmar Peterson were mentioned in the papers as potential Senate candidates. Katie Louchheim, India Edward's replacement as vice chair of the Democratic National Committee, wrote to Eugenie in May 1957: "I wanted you to know that I had a conversation with Orv at the dinner (I sat next to him). The impression I got was that if you were interested in the Senate race, there was plenty of support for your candidacy." In June, the *Minneapolis Tribune* asked: "'How About Eugenie?'—Some Democrats are trying to convince Mrs. Eugenie Anderson, Red Wing, that she is the logical DFLer, with the best chance of victory, to run for the senate. These Democrats point to Mrs. Anderson's personal and diplomatic stature to argue that she would attract a broad following of farmers, intellectuals, internationalists, women's organizations, southern Minnesotans and even Republicans." And in July, Humphrey wrote to Eugenie that "I am convinced that Gene [Eugene McCarthy] will not run for the Senate, even though from time to time he toys around with it." Hubert went on to say that Eugene's wife, Abigail, was unhappy with the family concessions necessary between Washington and Minnesota.[8]

In these early days, Humphrey, Freeman, and others respected and supported Eugenie's preference for a Senate run, versus a House of Representatives run against first district Republican bulwark August Andresen. She was repeatedly asked to consider the less prestigious arena, but she flatly refused, not because she scorned the idea of being in that pool of Congress, but because she could not face campaigning every two years, and her long-term goals of working in international and foreign policy were better suited to Senate committees than those of the House. And in the summer of 1957, all indications were that anyone eyeing Thye's Senate seat in Minnesota had a snowball's chance in hell of winning. Eisenhower's popularity and Republican trends at the polls were too strong. In Eugenie's reminiscences, she stated: "Indeed, I think one reason that people wanted me to run was because they thought, well, probably we can't win so let's let a woman try it." She was certainly not alone in thinking so. India Edwards once said: "If the party backs a woman you can be pretty sure they do it because they think it's a lost cause but they know they have to have some candidate."[9]

William Proxmire of Wisconsin proved a game changer, to the wild glee of the Democrats but to the detriment of Anderson. A Wisconsin special election on August 27, 1957, shocked the nation by voting in Proxmire, the first Democrat Wisconsin had sent to the US Senate since 1932. No one had thought it was possible, and it stoked up many dormant fires among Democrats in the Midwest. Suddenly, a bid for Senator Thye's seat was not just a token gesture—it was a bona fide threat with true potential. And faced with this golden opportunity, Humphrey conceded to his new reality in the top ranks and, as subtly and indiscernibly as possible, cut his formal ties with Eugenie Anderson's campaign. He could no longer afford to back her unconditionally when the Democratic Party would demand his alliance with a candidate—a man—who could conceivably win.

Just forty-eight hours after Proxmire's victory dominated nationwide news, the *Minneapolis Tribune* reported: "Elsewhere in today's Minneapolis Tribune is another trial heat which shows Mrs. Eugenie Anderson, Red Wing, running about as well as either Freeman or McCarthy against Thye. This is likely to give Mrs. Anderson and her champions a shot in the arm similar to McCarthy's." Anderson's most serious competition for the Senate nomination was Eugene McCarthy, a forty-two-year-old World War II veteran, academician-turned-politician who had served as Minnesota's

Fourth Congressional District representative in Washington for the previous ten years. He was serious, he was driven, he was Catholic, and he was a formidable opponent. Eugenie persevered with her ambitions, even though many DFLers, now drawn to McCarthy, continued to badger her, trying to convince her to switch to a House run against Andresen. Time and again, she rejected the proposals and clung tightly to her resolve to run for the Senate. In spite of the tougher new realities of the race that worked against her because she was a woman, she maintained that she would not yield to this daunting challenge. Not from the party leaders, nor from the voters. "When asked if she thought the women of Minnesota would be more likely or less likely to vote for a woman as senator, Mrs. Anderson said she wasn't even thinking about that aspect of the problem. She said she never thinks of political decisions as being either male or female in nature." Eugenie aspired to serve a democracy that lived up to its most basic tenet: that all men and women were equal in all things. True to her convictions, she stuck to that hope in the midst of a sea of contradicting voices and histories. She believed that if women and men continued to insist that gender should not influence democratic politics (with a small "d"), eventually, collectively, the mind-set could prevail. While Eugenie's hopes in this regard were unrealistic for the times, she did have other reasons for running. Her determination to stay in the race also reflected close to ten years of professed support—not just by Humphrey and the DFL top dogs, but by hundreds of network contacts she had made through the ADA, the State Department, and the Foreign Service. Since her earliest days on Truman's campaign in 1948 and even as the boat sailed for Denmark, all levels of people, by letter, by telegram, and in person shaking her hand, had crowed: *So when are we sending you to Washington?* Hundreds of supporters still wanted to know the answer, even if the stakes were higher and the field more crowded. Anderson herself may have had a "now or never" attitude. In October 1957, Eugenie became a grandmother when her daughter, Johanna, married to Dr. Som Nath Ghei, gave birth to her own first daughter. Eugenie was forty-eight years old, her hair had a liberal amount of gray, and her persona, while it could still be fashionable and appealing to a degree, would never again be youthful. Did she now regret missing her chances to run sooner? Possibly. But she never regretted completing her mission in Denmark and fulfilling her diplomatic duties—in fact, her reliability on the international front gave her stronger Senate credentials than a youthful change of heart would have. Eugenie banked on her strong, consistent character, high morals, and wide support network to override the fundamental fact she was not allowed to ignore: her gender.[10]

Anderson supplemented her Senate ambitions with a concurrent opportunity to address world human rights issues when she joined a group of international refugee analysts led by private industrialist Harold Zellerbach and Angier Biddle Duke, chairman of the International Rescue Committee. "I had only barely known Angie Duke before that time," said Eugenie, "but since the commission . . . [we] traveled together in Europe for about three weeks, visiting these refugee camps and studying the problem, we all became well acquainted and good friends." The work of the committee—visiting, evaluating, and providing information to the United Nations regarding eleven Western European refugee camps that housed two hundred thousand escapees fleeing persecution behind the Iron Curtain—put Eugenie's talents to their best use. In her element, Eugenie was perfectly at ease speaking with representatives of a dozen different European governments and contributing to written reports that laid out the evils of Communism and the totalitarianism that was resulting in a large wave of refugees. While the publicity she brought to the issue was of course important to Zellerbach and Duke's cause, it also benefitted Anderson, since news articles about her humanitarian goals and teamwork competence not only showed her to be a leader of Senate quality but also highlighted her actions and words rather than the abstract conditions of her feminine nature. "Let me know when you decide to run for the Senate," wrote Zellerbach, who added that "I would like to help be a 'Queen-maker.'"[11]

By December 1957, Humphrey was still in a quandary. His own political ambitions dictated that he back the Democrat most likely to win against Thye, and he was feeling intense pressure to side with Eugene McCarthy, who, in addition to being a man, also attracted a large number of Catholic voters. Still, Humphrey delayed.

Over the holidays, Eugenie invited Hubert and Muriel to Tower View, to join her and John for an intimate dinner with Professor Niels Bohr and his wife, who were visiting from Denmark. They spent hours discussing international politics, hopes, dreams, and aspirations for the world. Afterward, Eugenie wrote to Hubert: "I am most anxious to talk with you . . . Professor Bohr was very much impressed with you. It might also please you to know that John has now joined the ranks of my Humphrey Is The Only Man For President Club." Soon after the dinner, Humphrey became hard to get ahold of. Eugenie called and wrote several times, reaching out to mutual friends in Humphrey's circle, such as his close adviser Max Kampelman, but was unable to nail down a definitive meeting or phone call. Two days after Christmas, Kampelman reported: "I had an opportunity the other day to chat with Hubert at Lunch. During the course of many items we discussed the Senatorial picture. I gather from him that there is increased activity on your behalf." By the early days of 1958, it became clear why Humphrey had made himself unavailable: Eugene McCarthy was running. Anderson wrote to her friend Doris Heller: "At the present, Orv and Hubert are apparently keeping a 'hands-off' attitude, which is probably necessary although somewhat disappointing."[12]

Eugene McCarthy announced his official entry into the Senate race in January of 1958. McCarthy's biographer Dominic Sandbrook confirmed: "In truth, though, Humphrey had actually encouraged McCarthy to enter the race, urging him in January to 'give it all you got.'" The defection hit Eugenie hard, and she expressed her doubts and fears in a letter to her son Hans: "Any slight chance I may have had of getting the Party's endorsement for the Senate is now gone. It was probably gone before anyway, in view of McCarthy's decision but this surely settles it. . . . I will admit that right at the moment I am feeling somewhat disappointed. But then it is better to accept defeat now rather than at the end of five months more—at the state convention."[13]

The *Minneapolis Tribune* publicized the pressure on Eugenie to abandon her Senate hopes: "The DFL is faced with a man-sized job in taking over the Andresen [House] seat. And almost to a 'man,' they agree their best candidate would be a woman, Mrs. Eugenie Anderson. . . . Some of her intra-party opposition would deny her the senate nomination on grounds that she has never run for a lesser office. These people will have new ammunition if she refuses to listen to their demands that she make a 'team' try for Andresen's seat. Matter of fact, such a refusal probably would eliminate her from senatorial consideration."[14]

Humphrey finally managed to fit Eugenie into his schedule, after avoiding her for six weeks. On January 28, they met for another family-style get-together, with spouses. It is interesting that Hubert chose to include Muriel, which would minimize any opportunity for Eugenie to confront him tête-à-tête about the realities of his allegiances and real political motivations behind the upcoming Senate endorsements.

For another month, Eugenie sent out hundreds of letters gauging support, consulted with as many people as possible, changed her mind a dozen times, and nearly quit. She wrote to Max Kampelman that influential friends such as Geri Joseph and Arvonne Fraser were urging her to declare, in spite of notions that top DFL ranks were backing McCarthy: "They all say that there is . . . considerable 'rank and file' suspicion that McCarthy is going to be forced on them by the Party 'leadership.' . . . However, in addition to these questions of strategy, there is the more fundamental one of what I should do in the absence of any indication of continuing interest from Orv and Hubert. . . . In any event, I assume that neither

1958 campaign button.
Author's collection.

Orv nor Hubert are going to do anything whatsoever to oppose McCarthy . . . I cannot help but wonder if it is not completely ridiculous for me to even consider it further."[15]

But on February 24, Anderson announced her candidacy, with the full awareness that earning the DFL endorsement would probably be harder than actually winning the election. Now that both McCarthy and Anderson were officially in the race, Humphrey had to make some sort of declaration. Uncharacteristically, it was not a brave nor a loyal one: he claimed neutrality. To Eugenie, he explained that he could not in good conscience choose between two worthy, vital candidates who both deserved his loyalty; therefore, on public record, he would not endorse or state a preference for either of them. But "no comment" was as good as rejection, and Eugenie keenly felt the sting of it. Nevertheless, she resolved to separate her personal feelings from her professional good sense and maintained the close friendship with Hubert in spite of their diverging political commitments. "I had a letter from Sen. Humphrey a few days ago, Hans," she wrote to her son, "telling me that he would be very happy to serve as a reference for your Medical School Application, and saying that he would do anything he could to help you. Have you completed the form yet?" Mother. Politician. Eugenie's dual role was about to be confronted in a manner that she, let alone anyone else, would never have predicted.[16]

On Wednesday, May 7, 1958, the front-page layout of the *Minneapolis Star* included a small item, about an inch and a half square, headed "Coya's Husband Says 'Don't Run.'" By the next day, the full story assaulted Coya Knutson and took her down: "The delicate balance Coya had maintained in public between her domestic and political lives had been shattered. An eager press seized upon the message and the letter was immediately reprinted in newspapers and repeated on the radio and television newscasts across the nation. . . . *Fargo Forum* editor Lloyd Sveen used the phrase 'Coya, Come Home' in an article about Andy's open letter to Coya. The Associated Press picked it up. The catch phrase, 'Coya, Come Home,' was born."[17]

> Thursday, May 8, 1958
> *Minneapolis Star*
> INSIDE THE STAR : DFL 'STORMS'—Twin storms stirred Democratic-Farmer-Labor party ranks today. One centered around Rep. Coya Knutson whose husband issued a statement declaring he had asked her to retire from politics. The other whirled around the campaign for the DFL state convention endorsement for senator, with claims and denials clashing over delegate support for Mrs. Eugenie Anderson and Rep. Eugene McCarthy.

And on the *Minneapolis Tribune*'s front page, MATE URGES COYA NOT TO RUN AGAIN was printed directly against a column headed: BACKERS SEE QUICK VICTORY FOR MCCARTHY.

Coya Knutson's first instinct was to offer no comment. She took twenty-four hours just to catch her breath and steel herself for the inevitable fallout. Eugenie Anderson's first reaction, in all likelihood, was an intellectual rationale that this had nothing to do with her. Her fight was a campaign battle with Eugene McCarthy, and any tempest over Knutson and her embittered spouse could not possibly have any bearing on Anderson's candidacy. But it could— and it did.

Immediately after the "Coya Come Home" story caught fire, speculations began circulating that Andy Knutson had been coerced into striking the match (publishing his open letter) by taking bribes from Minnesota Republicans. They wanted Knutson's seat, and her wretched marriage provided an excellent means to question her character. However, the *Minneapolis Star* stated: "Some DFL party officers charged privately that Knutson's action was spurred by his wife's [DFL] political foes, angered at [William] Kjeldahl's maneuverings." Kjeldahl was Knutson's secretary, and not only was he implicated because he was seen by many Democrats as overstepping his bounds and being too manipulative of Knutson's legislative activities, but rumors frequently surfaced that he and Knutson had a sexual relationship. The whole business could not have been more salacious and absurd: a pathetic, drunken, unemployed husband who either (1) released his letter (on his own) to the press expecting his wife to pity him, quit her job, and go home; (2) was bribed by *Republicans* to advertise his letter and reap some financial reward; (3) was persuaded by *Democrats* that his wife was having an affair with her secretary and he could get her back with a public plea; or (4) was inspired by an unknown factor to trash his wife's life work and, as a side bonus, created a not-so-subtle public comparison between Knutson and Anderson. Salacious and absurd, yes. But such a smear campaign was deadly serious, and no one close to Coya or Eugenie was joking. Day after day, the papers jockeyed for interviews and opinions, following every movement of Knutson, Kjeldahl, and pathetic Andy back in Oklee. "Minnesota seldom gets as much publicity as it did last week when the call went out, 'Coya, come home!'" printed the *Austin Daily Herald* on May 13. It went on to say: "The question of whether Andrew or Coya is right has stirred up a subject for warm weather debate. Some will sympathize with Andrew while others will stoutly defend woman's right to a congressional career. . . . The ruckus may also have some effect on whether the DFL at its convention at Rochester, May 23-25, will endorse Eugene or Eugenie for nomination in the U.S. Senate race."[18]

Those throwing doubt against Anderson tried to make it sound like it was her own selfish choice to persevere, when she should have known that McCarthy would stand a better chance against

Thye, and she should withdraw for the good of the Democratic Party. Obviously, Eugenie strongly disagreed, and even in the storm of the "Coya Come Home" scandal, she kept herself as distant from the issue as possible.

Coya did not have that luxury. When the first shock of Andy's letter had worn off, Knutson came back fighting. In private, she admitted, "I could have lain down and died in shame," but publicly, she called a press conference to clarify her intentions: Yes, I'm still running for a third term, she confirmed. Yes, Bill Kjeldahl will continue as my congressional aide. My husband favors small-town life. I prefer public life. One journalist in particular showed solidarity with Knutson. Doris Fleeson, the first American woman to have a nationally syndicated political column, called a spade a spade and wrote this for the *Washington Evening Star*: "There are many better stories here than *l'affaire* Knutson and they are about much more prominent people, but it is not considered cricket to use them as a political weapon. The lesson is that, as a practical matter, women are held to a far higher standard of accountability in politics than men are. Women clearly cannot count on the club spirit for protection."[19]

Men kept the "club spirit" to themselves, and women politicians, stranded outside of it, were often accused of catfighting among themselves. Even if Eugenie Anderson had considered any sort of direct comment on Coya Knutson's situation, neither sisterhood nor mudslinging were political tools that Eugenie employed. Apparently, Coya kept her feelings about Eugenie unspoken as well: "It seemed the press was always trying to foment a feud between Eugenie and Coya, but they would not succeed. According to Coya, there was tacit agreement between the two women that 'I would keep my mouth shut and Anderson would keep still.'" It's hard to imagine what Knutson actually meant by that. That they would simply not comment on anything about each other? That they would not comment on political comparisons? That they would not comment on domestic comparisons? Regardless, they could only control the one-to-one relationship between themselves. Outside of that, they were powerless to control how the press, and the DFL, chose to depict and manipulate their similarities, differences, and usefulness in Washington. Brenda Ueland, well-known Minnesota writer and journalist, understood and described the harmful contradictions to which women were subjected, noting that "No newspaper in the United States would think there was news if a wife demanded her husband give up his political work. And no big newspaper would think there was even a sigh of news in a wife's jealous caterwauls against a man's secretary. Why, it is utterly inconceivable! A joke, a scream! It made us laugh—though wryly."[20]

Both Knutson and Anderson stayed the course at this point, and neither yet bowed to pressures from any angle.

Four days before the state Democratic convention that would finally determine the DFL endorsements, word circulated that lieutenant governor Karl Rolvaag was still a contender to run for the Senate, and that even Governor Freeman might be willing to offer himself as a candidate. Republicans like state treasurer Val Bjornson commented on what he called a puppet show: "Eugene dances against Eugenie while Karl stands ready in the wings. Hubert Humphrey and Orville Freeman are, of course, pulling the strings. Come next Sunday, the dance will end. Both Gene and Genie may well fall exhausted to the floor while Orville modestly 'bows to party pressure' to seek the senatorship, and Karl admits a willingness to run for governor."[21]

The circus metaphor dissolved and turned to war when the state Democratic convention began. As delegates convened in Rochester, Minnesota, on Friday, May 23, 1958, the Anderson and McCarthy camps staked out their territories in the hotel meeting rooms, suites, and lobbies of the Kahler Hotel. In a virtual tie, each of them went after the undeclared delegates, primarily from rural areas. After the first day, the front page of the *Minneapolis Star* characterized McCarthy as cool and confident; Anderson as tardy and feminine: "McCarthy, the amiable St. Paul DFL hero, was on

hand wooing the early birds. Mrs. Anderson, the former ambassador to Denmark, showed by mid-morning today to use her personal charm to win support." Even so, the paper disclosed that "the
endorsement committee . . . was believed to be slightly favorable
to Mrs. Anderson." Among further comparisons of the candidates'
strengths and weaknesses, the article reported: "Mrs. Anderson
is encountering some opposition simply on the grounds she is a
woman whose proper place is with her family, not in public office."
This was not a quote, and its source was not attributed directly to
McCarthy's people (some of whom were, in truth, active in that
assertion). However, the printed words served to act as a direct
correlation to Coya Knutson, placing the two women under the
same damning umbrella. Elsewhere in the melée at the convention,
Knutson waged her own battle with challenger Marvin Evenson.
Coya upheld "that the conflict in her life fueled her. 'I am sitting on
a powder keg, and working my fool head off.'"[22]

Another full day of frenzied activity on Saturday still showed
Anderson and McCarthy in a deadlock. Both anticipated a victorious outcome. Sunday's first ballot for endorsement put McCarthy
ahead, but short of the two-thirds required majority. The second
ballot put Eugene McCarthy over the top. "'This endorsement,'
McCarthy told the cheering, whistling delegates, 'gives me a license
to hunt Republicans all summer long.'"

> "He won," Eugenie recalled, "and I made almost immediately a . . .
> concession speech which was one of the more difficult speeches in
> my life because all my supporters were backstage crying. And I had
> to comfort them and tell them not to feel so badly and assure them
> that I didn't feel so badly. In fact, I don't think I did feel as badly as
> they did.
>
> INTERVIEWER: Why do you think you lost?
>
> ANDERSON: I think I lost in part because I was a woman. This was
> one of the arguments that the McCarthy people had used, that a
> woman could not be elected in Minnesota. I think myself that a
> woman could have been elected. . . . And then I think that I lost

DFL Endorses McCarthy

On May 26, 1958, the *Minneapolis Morning Tribune* headlines Anderson's loss to McCarthy. Eugene McCarthy at the podium; Eugenie Anderson stands between Orville Freeman and Hubert Humphrey; behind Freeman (left) in the background is Walter Mondale. *Eugenie M. Anderson papers, box 17.*

because I did not have the support of my natural allies and friends at the top levels in the party. This is a realistic way of looking at politics but it is true. And I decided from that time forward one should never engage in a political contest or nomination unless you know in advance that you're going to have the support of those really influential people . . . this is the nature of a political party. I was disillusioned—I think I was more realistic after that about politics and political leaders.[23]

Humphrey's neutrality and Knutson's scandal, the primary insurmountable challenges that rendered Eugenie unable to swing undeclared delegates, were both based on the condition of her being a woman. In a conversation with Walter Mondale about the 1958 convention, his initial recollection was that "the problem was that

McCarthy was a prominent, elegant Catholic candidate for Senator. And I think that that's what carried the day. They weren't thinking about Coya." When asked, "So you don't think that they were nervous about running a woman?" he replied: "No." But then he paused and said, "Well, they may have been. I don't have an answer." He laughed and added, "You know, we *have* been nervous all along!"[24]

Syndicated columnist Doris Fleeson summed up the Minnesota results with her unfailing logic and realism. The DFL needed McCarthy, a Catholic, to take his place on the chess board next to presidential hopeful Humphrey: "[McCarthy] and his friends must necessarily back Humphrey should the Senator decide as undoubtedly he will to enter Wisconsin against Kennedy." And there it was: Humphrey needed McCarthy's male advantage and his Catholic votes to beat John F. Kennedy for the Democratic endorsement in 1960. Hubert allowed this future necessity to trump his deep friendship and loyalty to Eugenie Anderson. Lacking a crystal ball to see into the future—to 1968—Humphrey could never have known that Eugene McCarthy would, at that most critical time, abandon Humphrey and fall neutral himself, contributing to the end of Humphrey's strongest presidential run. Eugenie reminisced: "It was interesting to me in 1968, just ten years later, when McCarthy opposed Humphrey in the presidential election. . . . Many of the people who had supported McCarthy back in '58 came to me and said, 'If only we had supported you in 1958, we wouldn't have had this awful situation.' But that's history."[25]

Coya Knutson rallied enough support to beat her DFL challenger in Rochester, but she lost the election to a Republican in November. The *Minneapolis Tribune* reported: "Privately, more than one DFL leader heaved a sigh of relief at Mrs. Knutson's defeat. While they would not oppose her publicly in the 1958 primary, it is no secret that they wouldn't support her again." Although she ran again in 1960, that, too, was unsuccessful. Byron Allen, Minnesota's commissioner of agriculture, recalled the "Coya Come Home" smear campaign: "That letter was one of the dirtiest tricks in politics I've ever seen. . . . She could have been in [Congress] for thirty years, but she was defeated by attacks on her morals." Coya paid all legal costs for her divorce from Andy in 1962. She went on to work as a congressional liaison for the Office of Civil Defense in the Pentagon, but never again had enough support, money, or initiative to get back into the national legislature.[26]

For Eugenie, as the dust began to settle after the Rochester convention in 1958, facts came to light about the tactics used to swing delegates and ensure her defeat. Seasoned DFL member George Jacobson (husband of Dorothy Jacobson) wrote a lengthy letter addressed to Humphrey, Freeman, and Rolvaag, soundly chastising them for their abstinence from duty and fair play:

> Because you men failed to take a stand, you left a vacuum, and whenever a vacuum is created, others move in. It is the law of nature and the law of human relations. . . . The person in particular, the agile, unscrupulous, and power-hungry [state chairman to the Democratic National Committee Gerald] Heaney, took over the political leadership as a result of the abdication by the elected officials. Jerry went after the job of naming his Catholic friend, Gene McCarthy, with the zeal of a convert. . . . They were going to put him over come what cost there may be. . . . Heaney as well as some of his other associates used tactics that would have been a credit to the boss manipulated Republican conventions. They bargained, threatened, cajoled, intimidated, spread false and true rumors, spread half-truths, and in cases they did what amounted to character assassination. They left a scar on this Party by their conduct . . . which will long be felt by the DFL Party.[27]

Many convention delegates wrote to Eugenie expressing outrage over the steamrolling. One of them declared, "Frankly, I shall find it nearly impossible to forgive our National Committeeman, Gerald Heaney, for his unscrupulous tactics during the campaign!" Mitch Perrizo, former campaign manager for both Humphrey and Adlai Stevenson, reported from Washington that "HHH closed the door for one of his private huddles when he returned from Rochester. It was apparent that a great deal of emotional energy had been expended." Perrizo went on to say: "My overall impression, Mrs. Anderson, is that each person found good and proper reason for what they felt they had to do but continued, nonetheless, somewhat uncomfortable. I suppose politics, like international relations, must ultimately revolve around self interest."[28]

The most important perspective on the fallout was, of course, Eugenie's. How much did she know, and had she been forewarned leading up to the convention, as the Coya Knutson scandal broke, and during the battle in Rochester? The best overview of her experience is in her own words, written to her close friend and DFLer Doris Tullar Heller. This letter, excerpted below, also reveals Eugenie's knowledge that not only were Eugene McCarthy's backers behind the Coya Knutson scandal, but that Coya herself used her influence to sway delegates away from supporting Eugenie.

> Red Wing, Minn
> June 29, 1958
> Dearest Doris,
> You know, I am sure, the basic fact that Gene got the endorsement, although I doubt if you know the real story behind it. None of the press here did a very good job of reporting it . . . the McCarthy backers *did* get dirty, as they got desperate, and indeed their tactics were such that I was glad not to have any part of it. The real reasons behind my defeat were that Humphrey & Freeman . . . remained neutral, which meant that the leadership of the Party was seized by [Gerald] Heaney, [John] Blatnik & Bob Hess who were backing McCarthy. . . . In retrospect, I can see that I should have decided against trying for the endorsement once Humphrey & Freeman had decided that they could no longer back me. It should have been obvious that their "neutrality" would give the advantage to McCarthy. . . . To finish things off at the Convention the Coya Knutson fracas was involved in it, since her backers in the 9th District refused to support me . . . (I learned incidentally that the whole sorry business of her husband's "Come home, Coya" letter was engineered by McCarthy's backers who were using this to try to create sentiments against me as another woman candidate. It did not have that effect, but it did get the 9th Dist. organization in a fresh state of uproar,

with Coya's backers completely irrational in their fanatical opposition to anyone who might in any way threaten her—apparently she had also made it clear that she did not want another woman from Minnesota in the Congress.) . . . Many people do not believe that Gene can win, but it appears to be such a strongly Democratic trend this year, that I think it is quite possible that he will. I feel sure that I could have won, and of course this was one of the reasons that it was disappointing to lose the endorsement.[29]

Eugenie Anderson admitted years later: "I don't regret that effort on my part, but I did decide that I wouldn't seek public office again. I felt that I had learned a great deal, maybe made some small contribution to our political process in the state, but I didn't wish to try again."[30]

It is possible that she may have healed faster, or found her way back to seeking office, if a deeper rift had not opened between herself and Hubert Humphrey after the convention. Humphrey, as he had done over the previous year's holidays, delayed speaking directly to Eugenie. It was a full six weeks before he wrote: "I have been wanting to write you ever since the convention, but I suppose I just didn't know what to say and, therefore, subconsciously found a reason not to write. . . . Just remember that despite all the heartache and other emotions that come from one of these convention experiences, my respect for you is all the greater and my affection for you all the more sincere. We need a good visit." He also noted: "You are a wonderful person and a true and loyal soldier in the ranks of liberal democracy." Bowing to the party's (and Humphrey's) expectations, Eugenie agreed to help launch McCarthy's candidacy. A week after receiving Humphrey's letter, Anderson wrote: "I attended a luncheon for McCarthy in Minneapolis at which I introduced him. It was not easy to do, and I am thankful that that is over. I now feel as if I have done enough to demonstrate my 'Party loyalty' and 'good sportsmanship,' and that from now on I can forget about the McCarthy campaign and concentrate on whatever I prefer to do."[31]

Unfortunately, the drama and betrayed feelings of the Rochester convention continued to revisit both Eugenie and Humphrey and complicate their already damaged friendship. In the upper DFL ranks, word started circulating that Hubert had "double-crossed" Eugenie. And, as rumors and gossip are bound to do, the story went from ear to ear, gaining new false layers with each interpretation. The "game of telephone" reached Eugenie in early August. The root of the matter was that Eugenie had allegedly confided to Geri Joseph that she never would have run for Senate in the first place if she'd known that she would not have the full support of Hubert Humphrey. By the time this tidbit reached Humphrey's ears, it had traveled through at least three other narrators, with a resulting insinuation that Humphrey had double-crossed Eugenie. Hubert exploded, infuriated that *he* should be so maligned. He sent a long, heated letter to one of the steps in the rumor mill (Alpha Smaby) and cc'd the rant to Eugenie: "I did not double cross Eugenie. For anyone to think so is to lose my friendship and my respect. Eugenie knows I did not and I would expect her to say so. I don't intend to be made the target of people's complaints and frustrations." Responding to an accusation that he had initially encouraged Eugenie's campaign, Humphrey outright declared: "It is not true that I asked her to run." How intensely painful it must have been for Eugenie to see those words in print, after all the years of partnership, trust, mutual respect, and shared goals. *Shall I drop Ed Thye a note and tell him to pack up and get ready to move, or would you rather do that yourself?* Hubert had joked, three years before. But that was before Humphrey lost so bitterly in his 1956 vice presidential bid. It was before the popularity began brewing for Senator John F. Kennedy, a rising storm that could eclipse Humphrey's hopes for 1960. Facing that reality in August of 1958, Humphrey had no choice but to focus on the bottom-line best strategy for his own presidential ambitions. And those ambitions needed the people behind Eugene McCarthy. Closing the angry letter above, Humphrey wrote: "I have no intention of spending any more of my time defending myself against allegations that are not true. If a person can't be trusted by his friends, then there is little to look forward to." One can imagine Eugenie felt the same way.[32]

Uncharacteristically, Eugenie did not instantly leap to a diplomatic reconciliation. She was honest with Hubert and called him out: "I must say that I feel badly that you accepted as fact a third-hand report . . . before you took the trouble to ask me what I had actually said, if anything. The fact is that I have never criticized you, (except to your face,) and indeed I have always defended and supported you. The only thing that I had said to Geri Joseph (about a month after the Rochester Convention) was that I felt badly because I had not heard from you since." Eugenie asked for the chance to get together in person soon, but again, Humphrey's schedule did not allow it. The situation dragged on unresolved for months. In spite of the devastating rift, Eugenie was not deterred from considering her future, even if it was significantly different from what she had hoped: "If the international situation were not so serious, I think I would feel as if I might forget about politics for awhile. But I don't think I can or should really do this—what I should do, and plan to do, is to use this time more for study and reflection, so that when there is some potential task in the future which seems really important again, I will be better able to work at it."[33]

Eugenie stayed home at Tower View. She and John spent pockets of time taking care of their one-year-old granddaughter. And she committed large amounts of time to reading, comparing the worlds of current governments and foreign policy, past political intrigue, and the literary art of fiction: books like Henry Kissinger's *Nuclear Weapons and Foreign Policy,* Sandburg's multivolume biography of Abraham Lincoln, and E. M. Forster's *Howards End.* Studying informed her. Reading soothed and inspired her. Everything lent itself to the restoration of her crusading spirit. By the end of October, Eugenie notified Max Kampelman that she and Humphrey were back on the road to reconciliation: "Hubert and I finally did have a talk. . . . While we did not have enough time after all that had happened, nevertheless, it was a beginning, and I think that we both understand each other." Kampelman's reply urged Eugenie to accept offers to reinforce bridges from everyone, especially Orville Freeman and those who would be instrumental in Humphrey's 1960 presidential campaign. The words Kampelman used were "destroy the divisiveness."[34]

Plans were already underway to begin a virtual campaign for Hubert H. Humphrey (of which Senator Humphrey was supposedly not a knowing participant), spearheaded by Governor Freeman. When Humphrey left on a monthlong tour of Europe, attending UNESCO meetings in Paris; a NATO conference in Geneva, Switzerland; nuclear test suspension talks; and other meetings in Berlin, Copenhagen, Stockholm, Helsinki, Leningrad, and finally Moscow, he and Eugenie reestablished a lively correspondence that helped bring them back together. Writing to each other in depth about democratic principles, national security, and foreign policy did more for their relationship than confessions or apologies. It reminded Eugenie, at least, of her most dearly held goals and brought her back to the belief that Hubert Humphrey remained one of the best conduits toward those goals: "As for 1960," Eugenie wrote to India Edwards, "I still feel that Humphrey would be the best President, and the best Candidate too." To her son Hans, Eugenie admitted that she was becoming "more aware of my own continuing desire to return to the possibility of *acting* instead of only studying and talking. I am afraid it is as [secretary of state] Dean Acheson said, not so long ago, that once one has been in a center of decision and responsibility—no matter how relatively small my corner was—one will always want to be there again. Not just to feel at the center of things, but also to know that you are using your potentialities as fully and as well as you can—because this is always one of the greatest happinesses that a human can have."[35]

No matter that one road of Eugenie's political career had just been irrevocably blocked—in great part because she was a woman— she still maintained that politics was, for her, a matter of human potential, and not designated male or female. Minnesota would not send a woman to Congress for another forty-two years, when Democrat Betty McCollum won a seat in the House of Representatives in the year 2000. In 2006, Minnesota sent Democrat Amy Klobuchar to the Senate, and the 6th district elected Republican Michele Bachmann to the House. It was not until the 2018 elections that Minnesota began to significantly increase its numbers of women in Washington. Three women won their districts to join Congress: Betty McCollum, who was reelected; Ilhan Omar, who became the first Muslim American woman in the House; and Angie Craig. Amy Klobuchar won her Senate seat to begin her third consecutive term, and Tina Smith won a special election to hold Minnesota's second Senate seat. The simple math that adds eight House and two Senate seats—filled by five women and five men—shows that after 160 years of statehood, Minnesota was at last represented, at least for two years, along fifty-fifty gender lines.

"There is something valuable in learning to distinguish which things in life *can* be changed, and which things have to be accepted," Eugenie wrote. She recognized and accepted that, in her life, situated as she was in 1958, positions and opportunities in politics for women might exist, but they were rare exceptions to the rule. Eugenie made the decision to persist, not on behalf of women, but for her belief in democracy.[36]

Five
BREACHING the IRON CURTAIN

During her years in Bulgaria Mrs. Anderson
had opened the door for improved relations between the two
countries—contacts were made and expanded, exchanges were
promoted, some cultural exchanges took place, and a reservoir
of good will for Americans was built. By combining charm
with firmness, enthusiasm with dignity, Eugenie Anderson
had made herself both liked and respected in a nation
with which we have had more than our share of difficulties
during the chillier phases of the Cold War. She demonstrated
that intelligence, firmness, political experience, and understanding
are the most potent weapons a free government
can use against dictatorship.

VIRGINIA LANEGRAN, 1977

A NEW DECADE WAS DAWNING. NOW FIFTY YEARS— half a century—old, Eugenie Anderson recognized that reflection and study were all well and good, but action suited her better.

She had never given up on her belief in the Truman Doctrine: that Americans must be "willing to help free peoples to maintain their free institutions and their national integrity against aggressive movements that seek to impose upon them totalitarian regimes." Knowing that one of the best ways to pursue these goals was having a deciding vote on internationalist Senate committees, Anderson had tried, in 1958, to join that club, but she was denied the chance to be admitted. She could have run again, but it would mean waiting a full six years (to overwhelmingly negative odds), or until Humphrey gained higher office. Whether or not she secretly considered another Senate run, Eugenie accepted that Hubert Humphrey remained one of her best contacts in Washington. So she went to work for him, yet again.[1]

It was no secret that Humphrey would run for president in 1960. The Democrats faced a tough offensive: Eisenhower had been very popular, and Republican vice president Richard M. Nixon was set to step smoothly into the Oval Office. On one of her speaking tours for Humphrey, in December 1959, Eugenie told her audience: "American people need to be aroused to realize how close we are to losing our supremacy and our freedom to Communist Russia," citing hollow efforts by the Eisenhower administration to give glitzy shows of world summit meetings that led nowhere. Anderson's credentials, beyond that of former ambassador, showed that she had a seat at many tables: she was a member of several committees that included the Democratic National Advisory Committee on Foreign Policy, the board of directors for the American Association for the United Nations, and the US Committee for the National Atlantic Treaty Organization Congress. She also remained chairman of the Minnesota State Fair Employment Practices Commission. Still, far more effective means existed that Eugenie felt she was more than capable of joining—as long as she could stay connected to the people in charge of appointments. Her path led back to diplomacy and opportunities to support NATO, the United Nations, and the United States in their international foreign services. If she wanted to step back into that arena, it would have to be under a Democratic administration; therefore, she stuck with Humphrey.[2]

As America welcomed the 1960s, the Democratic candidates faced off. Hubert Humphrey and John F. Kennedy were the front-runners, but as it turned out, Humphrey didn't stand a chance against the charisma of—and the power behind—JFK. Eugenie could not bring herself to volunteer for Kennedy's campaign: "I felt that this was a kind of very ruthless machine operation that was quite different than Minnesota politics and I wasn't sure if I really wanted to be involved in it," she said.[3]

Eugenie rejoiced when Ceylon (now Sri Lanka) elected the world's first woman prime minister, Sirimavo Bandaranaike, in July 1960. A month later, she celebrated in Red Wing at Hans's wedding to Margaret Kaehler. On Election Day, November 8, John and Eugenie Anderson left Minnesota, bound for India, where they would set up a short-term residence in New Delhi near Johanna and Som Ghei and their young daughter, Kiren. The Andersons sailed out of Los Angeles before hearing the confirmed results of the election; it was some time later when they learned that John Kennedy had definitively beaten Richard Nixon. Traveling on a Danish freighter with about twelve other passengers, the Andersons made stops in Yokohama and Tokyo, Manila, Hong Kong, Saigon, Djakarta, Bangkok, and Singapore over a six-week journey. "I was very disappointed not to have more time in Saigon," Eugenie said, "because we had been reading . . . about the infiltration from North Vietnam, and about the beginnings of the terrorist activity of the Viet Cong." Typically, regrouping—for Eugenie—meant combining the joy of family time with the pursuit of political knowledge and potential involvement. She never took her eye off the Communists.[4]

From Singapore, the Andersons flew to New Delhi, arriving in January of 1961. Eugenie embarked on a lecture tour of a dozen major Indian cities and visited Nepal and Kashmir. "I found myself as an unofficial interpreter or representative you might say, of the Kennedy administration," she reminisced, "even though I was not a member of it. I did receive a letter from Sargent Shriver during that time asking me if I were interested in a diplomatic post. . . . I wasn't sure what I wanted to do, really, so I didn't answer it." To her family, Eugenie expressed her contentment being abroad: "We are having such an amazing trip that none of us can honestly wish ourselves at home . . . I think you would be quite surprised to see your 'old folks' so active."[5]

Anderson was not politically optimistic, in spite of Shriver's inquiry, for herself or for women in general while Kennedy was in office. She wrote: "As Doris Fleeson pointed out, the women have not been important up to now in Kennedy's campaign nor choice of appointments, and it appears doubtful if they will suddenly become so. After reading *Time*'s Jan. 20th (Asia Edition) feature about Jacqueline Kennedy, one would gather that Kennedy has never shared political decisions with her, this would indicate a general approach of ignoring women at political levels."[6]

It didn't happen overnight, but eventually, Anderson came around to a more cooperative attitude concerning the Kennedy administration. "I began to see that a man does change with the office," she said. "I think Kennedy did." John and Eugenie returned from India in the spring of 1961, and Anderson and Washington began sizing each other up. The wars in Laos and threats inside Vietnam worsened. The Bay of Pigs invasion in Cuba caused enormous strife, internationally and within the United States. American schoolchildren continued to hide under their desks or march to basement gymnasiums while fire alarms signaled nuclear attack drills. Betty Friedan scribbled in relative obscurity, drafting her thoughts that would soon coalesce to rally the cry in *The Feminine Mystique*. Russian cosmonauts and American astronauts raced each other to plant the first flag on the moon.[7]

Eugenie Anderson focused on the role she could play in President Kennedy's goals to open up relations with Eastern Europe. By October 1961, she was ready to answer Washington's call. She wrote to former President Truman: "I have learned recently that I am being considered by the White House for a diplomatic appointment. Our mutual friend, Senator Hubert H. Humphrey, who is now in Europe, has suggested that it would be helpful if you would write a letter, or speak personally, on my behalf to President Kennedy and Secretary of State Rusk." One week later, Truman replied, enclosing a copy of his letter to Kennedy. Both were brief to the extreme, and casual enough to show that he understood that this was merely a formality. To Eugenie, he could use humor. To Kennedy, a simple thumbs-up:

Dear Mrs. Anderson:
I am enclosing you a copy of a letter which I have written to the President of the United States. I sincerely hope that it will do you no harm.

Nothing would please me more than to see you back in the Diplomatic Service. Sincerely yours, Harry Truman

Dear Mr. President: I understand that there is a possibility of the consideration of Mrs. Eugenie Anderson for a Diplomatic place in the Foreign Affairs of the Government.

She was one of the outstanding Ambassadors in the Administration of which I was the head. She is pleasant and knows the score. Any consideration you give her will be highly appreciated by me. Sincerely yours, Harry Truman[8]

"She is pleasant and knows the score." Interpretation: Eugenie Anderson is a professional, will never embarrass the administration, and will not rock any boats. She knows the right people, knows her place in the hierarchy, and does her homework. Give her a job.

Only one other woman currently held a top-level ambassadorship for the United States at this time. Since Eugenie's "first" for Denmark, Frances E. Willis had served as ambassador to Switzerland from 1953 to 1957 and to Norway from 1957 to 1961; she had just been stationed to Ceylon (which not so coincidentally had a woman prime minister). Clare Booth Luce, who had been ambassador to Italy from 1953 to 1957, completed the roster of all US women ambassadors ever appointed. Frances Willis was a diplomat equal to Eugenie in expertise and talent, and she also held similar philosophies. Willis once said: "It takes certain qualities to make a fair success in diplomacy. A diplomat's sex has nothing to do with it. Mostly, I think, it takes adjustability, intelligence, and stability." The most recognized woman diplomat in the world was, of course, Eleanor Roosevelt. At age seventy-seven, she was still active and outspoken. Historians James MacGregor Burns and Susan Dunn wrote: "[Roosevelt's] principal focus was policy. She wrote to JFK about Berlin, disarmament, Vietnam, migratory farmworkers. When she learned that only nine of his first 240 appointments were women, she sent him a list of competent women."[9]

The State Department considered Anderson for placement in either Romania or Bulgaria; both countries shared deep isolationist histories and challenging positions inside a thick fog of Soviet-controlled Communism. "Kennedy apparently thought [Anderson's] people's diplomacy worth a try behind the Iron Curtain, and her impeccable anti-Communist credentials certainly did not hurt her," wrote political historian Philip Nash. Kennedy's people, Eugenie recalled, "felt that our career diplomats had been maybe overly cautious and hadn't made enough efforts to improve relations with the people and with the governments of Eastern Europe." Was her appointment, perhaps, a situation like Eugenie's early forays to reach the Senate? *It's a lost cause, so let's let a woman try it.* Very likely. But Eugenie loved to prove doubters wrong, especially when she could prove that being a woman was irrelevant in terms of her usefulness, so she pursued the appointment wholeheartedly. On May 26, 1962 (Eugenie's fifty-third birthday), the Senate approved the nomination, and Anderson became the first American woman minister to head a legation behind the Iron Curtain. Eugenie and John Anderson were given six weeks to make arrangements and move to Sofia, Bulgaria.[10]

The first obligation was, of course, to meet with President Kennedy and the State Department and formalize relationships. Eugenie made journal notes at the time about her invitations to "Camelot": "I attended a White Tie Dinner at the White House (in honor of the President of the Ivory Coast). I was seated next to Attorney General Robert Kennedy, who greeted me by my name as if he knew me, but then asked me if I were the Ambassador to Ceylon, apparently confusing me with the Career Ambassador Miss Frances Willis." Upon introduction to President Kennedy at the

On May 28, 1962, President John F. Kennedy and Eugenie Anderson meet in the Oval Office to discuss her appointment as minister to Bulgaria. Anderson recalled that they went over Nikita Khrushchev's recent visit and insulting remarks to Bulgarians, and the severe breakdown in relations between the United States and all Eastern Bloc countries that desperately needed improvements to hold off Soviet encroachment and propaganda. Anderson also wrote: "While the photographers were 'shooting,' we talked about Red Wing and the Pres. said he liked the name of it and alluded to Stephen Vincent Benet's poem about liking American names." *Eugenie M. Anderson papers, box 27.*

same dinner, Eugenie later wrote: "He greeted me very cordially ... and said, 'It's a sin to send you to Bulgaria.' I suppressed my natural reaction which was to say, 'Well, you're the one that's doing it, Mr. President.'" A few days after the dinner, Anderson made her official visit to the White House Oval Office to authenticate the appointment and sit for a photographer. Afterward, she wrote:

> May 28, 1962
> I was ushered in to see [President Kennedy] at 10:10, and he greeted me cordially and asked me to sit down by his rocking chair in which he seated himself facing me. He began by thanking me for being willing to accept such a hard appt. and said he was afraid I was going to find Belgrade (sic!) rather a dour, dreary place to live—said that when he was there several years ago he thought it most depressing. I agreed it would be.[11]

JFK confused Sofia with Belgrade, the capital of Yugoslavia. RFK mistook Eugenie for Frances Willis. Perhaps the post in Bulgaria was not terribly important to the Kennedys, but Eugenie came away from meetings with secretary of state Dean Rusk with enough confidence to feel excited about her mission: "I really became very enthusiastic. . . . Although I also realized that it was going to be a very difficult assignment and one quite in contrast with the years that I had spent in Denmark. We were looking forward to it, however, partly just because we realized that it was a rare opportunity and a rare challenge."

The announcement of Anderson's Bulgarian post certainly didn't attract press features the way Denmark had for its historic appointment in 1949. Many of the newspaper pieces that did come out characterized Anderson as a quiet, soft-spoken grandmother. However, Stewart Hensley, veteran State Department reporter writing for the United Press International service, attempted to show that nine years had effected a more enlightened attitude toward women in government: his fifteen-paragraph July 5, 1962, article never once referred to Anderson as a female (or any equivalent feminine adjective) diplomat, never mentioned her appearance or made reference to female manners or qualities, and did not compare her to other female diplomats.

> In Bulgaria Mrs. Anderson faces the problem of dealing with one of the most rigidly doctrinaire of communist states.—The most isolated from western influence of any except Albania. . . . There is no American business community in Sofia and U.S. tourists are not very numerous. . . . She will find herself called to the foreign ministry to receive official protests whenever one of the North Atlantic treaty organization (NATO) countries in the neighborhood, Greece or Turkey, holds military exercises. . . . Mrs. Anderson will find that the Sofia atmosphere is not receptive to open American propaganda. . . . All in all, it is not too enviable an assignment, but Mrs. Anderson's Washington superiors are confident she can handle it with credit.[12]

Nationally, most publicity followed in this vein. But locally, Minnesotans could not (or were not allowed to) divorce themselves from Eugenie's overwhelmingly feminine press image. Margaret Crimmins, writing "One Woman's View" for the *St. Paul Pioneer Press*, wrote that "President Kennedy knew what he was doing when he appointed this attractive, intelligent and quietly confident grandmother. If anyone can present the American way of life with its love of the family, the arts and its belief in an independent spirit, Eugenie can." When Crimmins asked, "Does she consider her sex a handicap or asset?" Anderson was quoted as replying: "Anything a woman does is more complicated because of home and family responsibilities, but I've never considered it a handicap. . . . The most important thing for any woman in public life is to forget first that she *is* a woman and concentrate on her objectives."[13]

The *Minneapolis Tribune* could not resist giving Barbara Flanagan free rein in the Sunday women's section. A teaser the day before told readers to watch for "Flanagan's report about Mrs. Eugenie Anderson, U.S. Minister to Bulgaria. You'll learn about the fashionable wardrobe she is wearing for her diplomatic duties." A full page was devoted to Eugenie's wardrobe plans and collaboration with a Minneapolis fashion house owned by Angela Strem.

Eight tall sketches showed Eugenie, like a paper doll, in different day and evening wear, and a large color portrait highlighted a formal gown. While the first half of the article dwelt on Anderson's designer choices and charming past reputation in Denmark, it did find its way to current times. Flanagan stated that "Mrs. Anderson believes women haven't moved ahead in public life, although they have made progress in the business world." Then she quoted Eugenie: "'Women really aren't willing to choose between a career and a family,' Mrs. Anderson said. . . . 'You know, men have to be convinced that women can help a cause,' she said. 'Men, you see, are in the position of choosing.'" Ever determined that women must commit themselves to any work they wanted, regardless of sexism or historical patriarchy, Eugenie Anderson never backed down from her belief that participation was a matter of personal willpower, not gender. At her time and place in the early 1960s, she continued to eschew feminism and women's solidarity, still firmly convinced that each woman should fight her own battle to succeed for herself. To forget that she *is* a woman.[14]

John and Eugenie Anderson arrived in Sofia, Bulgaria, in mid-July, 1962, having traveled to a diplomatic mission that had been vacant for ten years, from 1950 to 1960. (Eugenie's predecessor, Edward Page Jr., a career foreign officer, manned the desk in Bulgaria from 1960 to 1962.) Although the Andersons knew ahead of time that their residence in the city would be comparatively smaller and less comfortable than embassy residences in most other countries, they

In a feature written by Barbara Flanagan, the August 12, 1962, *Minneapolis Sunday Tribune* published a photograph of Minister Anderson in a sophisticated evening gown, accompanied by "paper doll" sketches of her diplomatic wardrobe. The color scheme of all her clothing included a range of blues and greens, with some neutrals; Anderson would wear no red (the signature color of Communism) during her tenure behind the Iron Curtain. Flanagan recalled that the sketches were drawn by French-Algerian refugee Jean-Pierre Girard, hired as an artist by the paper. *Portrait by Gerald Brimacombe, newspaper in author's collection.*

Minneapolis Sunday Tribune

MINNEAPOLIS, MINN., SUNDAY, AUGUST 12, 1962

Women's SECTION
PART ONE

Nicollet Av. Dresses a U.S. Envoy

Navy silk suit by Italian designer, Roberto Capucci.

Navy suit with soft tie at neckline, buttoned pockets.

Jacket dress in printed blue and green batiste.

Emerald green silk jacket dress from Nina Ricci.

Gothe's blue lace and satin evening dress.

Marine blue wool suit from collection of Paul Parnos.

Blue and green flowers on white silk by Fontana of Italy.

Ricci's navy silk worn with Jensen silver brooch from Denmark.

Minneapolis Tribune Sketches by Jean-Pierre Girerd

Minnesota's Ambassador for the U.S.: Eugenie Anderson

By Barbara Flanagan
Minneapolis Tribune Staff Writer

If Mrs. Eugenie Anderson's first two weeks in Communist Bulgaria were as busy as the first two weeks in free and easy Denmark, the woman diplomat from Red Wing, Minn., will have scored again for the U.S.A.

The crowd gathered even before the ship Jutlandia was at the dock that December day in 1949 when the Andersons arrived in Copenhagen.

Some even questioned the idea that a woman should serve as ambassador to their country.

Others figured Mrs. Anderson was a social butterfly with a yen for politics. And they all wondered what her husband, John P. Anderson, was going to do.

The sticklers for protocol—and even a few of the fun-loving Danes are—worried about where he was going to sit at diplomatic dinner tables.

Mrs. Anderson charmed the press in one short interview on shipboard. The crowd warmed to her the minute she came down the gangplank; followed by her husband and two children, Johanna and Hans.

The city band, handled against the cold, enthusiastically blew a chorus of "Oh, What a Beautiful Morning."

WHEN THE SUN CAME OUT, even the meanest among the onlookers seemed impressed. The sun doesn't shine too often in Denmark in December.

Mrs. Anderson went Christmas shopping followed by crowds of smiling Danish well-wishers.

She smocked at a press conference and made headlines. One newspaper, an underground resistance organ during World War II, wrote Mrs. Anderson an open letter in English.

"Don't get kidnaped by party-givers," it warned. "Get acquainted with the Denmark that works."

A week later, Mrs. Anderson gave her first party—for the 80 workmen and their wives who had refurbished the 37-room embassy residence.

Mrs. Anderson coped immediately with the Danish language. She learned it and delighted Danes with her fluency.

Along with the children, Mrs. Anderson also mastered another Danish tradition—how to ride a bike.

MRS. ANDERSON MADE FRIENDS for the United States in Denmark. Even today, Danes speak fondly of Minnesota's Eugenie as their favorite diplomat.

It was this along with a solid record of diplomatic accomplishment that helped President Kennedy decide to appoint Mrs. Anderson as minister to Bulgaria.

She is the first woman to be appointed to a diplomatic post in an Iron Curtain country, and currently, only one of two women in the foreign service.

"It's unfortunate, I think," Mrs. Anderson said recently, "that more women are not used in diplomatic posts because I believe they are most effective in diplomacy for various reasons.

"A WOMAN'S SPECIAL SKILL is in human relations. She has an understanding of people. And if she has had political experience, she is even better equipped."

Mrs. Anderson believes women also haven't moved ahead in public life, although they have made progress in the business world.

"Women really aren't willing to choose between a career and a family," Mrs. Anderson said. "I was fortunate because my family was able to accompany me to Denmark. (This trip, only John Anderson will be at Eugenie's side. Their children are married.)

"You know, men have to be convinced that women can help a cause," she said. "Men, you see, are in the position of choosing."

IT IS TYPICAL of Eugenie Anderson that even before she left Washington after a U.S. State Department briefing, she was studying Bulgarian.

Although Danish is often thought an improbable tongue—even by the Danes—Bulgarian is almost impossible.

To begin, one needs to learn the Cyrillic alphabet. Mrs. Anderson, studying from records, mastered it before she left.

She also has learned to count to 10, say "thank you," "good morning," and "good evening."

At her new residence in Sofia—not as big as the 37-room Rydhave in Copenhagen, but comfortable and

Mrs. Anderson
Continued on Page Two

Mental Patient: Don't Forget Us

DEAR ANN: I am a patient in a mental hospital. I know I am ill, just as a person who has pneumonia is ill. I know, too, that my illness is temporary and that I am getting better. One day I will be a useful citizen and perhaps even contribute something to society.

I am writing this letter in the hope that people who have friends and relatives in mental institutions will have a better understanding of the mental patient and his needs. More than anything, we need to know we are not forgotten.

On the Fourth of July we were served a lovely chicken dinner and there was a movie afterwards. I would gladly have exchanged the dinner and the movie for just one visitor. I have a daughter, grandchildren, brothers, sisters and cousins, but no one dropped by to say hello.

I'm not the only person who walks week after week for a visitor. It's as if our people are ashamed of us and they don't wish to remember we are here. We patients discuss this often — never in a self-pitying way, only with a feeling of sadness because others do not understand.

The staff here at San Bernardino is wonderful. What grand people they are—but we are so many, and they are so few. They do what they can but nothing builds morale like a visit with family or friends. These links with the outside, more than anything else, speed a patient's recovery.

Please print this letter. It is too long, I know, but perhaps you can trim it so it will fit in the paper. You could help so many by printing this word. God bless you.

Ann Landers

ANN SAYS: Thank you for your beautiful letter. Yes, it's about twice as long as most letters which appear in this column, but I couldn't bear to cut a word of it. So here it is—as you wrote it.

DEAR ANN: One month ago I sent for your booklet "How To Be Well Liked." I put the advice into effect the very day it arrived. I have already had some wonderful results. It has brought me new friends and has changed my whole outlook on life.

Please print this letter. It is too long, I know, but it possible to become a different person. Thank you very much. Ann.

ANN SAYS: How nice of you to write! There's nothing really new in that booklet, but it's useful to be reminded of things we learned a long time ago—and forgot. If people only understood that ALL of us are hungry for kindness and acceptance, every one of us would be more likeable.

(Ann Landers will be glad to help you with your problems. Send them to her in care of the Minneapolis Tribune enclosing a stamped, self-addressed envelope.)

MRS. EUGENIE ANDERSON'S diplomatic wardrobes —worn as U.S. ambassador to Denmark, 1949-53, and now as U.S. minister to Bulgaria—have come from Angela Strem's fashion studio, 1038 Nicollet Av. The elegant moss green satin and beaded lace reception gown,

Minneapolis Tribune Photo by Gerald Brimacombe

a Dior, is a good example of how closely Mrs. Anderson and Miss Strem agree on fashion. The clothes selected by Mrs. Anderson include silhouettes from several European and American designers—but all keep to one color scheme.

conversation piece
They're Talking About . . .

Ned and Rita Mayo's new Greenhouse Gallery at Mayowood in Rochester, Minn., crammed with art and plants and antiques and pottery by Jim Gettner, assistant director of the Rochester Art Center. He bunks upstairs. (The greenhouse was built by Dr. Will Mayo from old X-ray plates.)

Bob Moulton, bouncing into a reception for young Swedish visitors and enchanting them with his get-up, the University of Minnesota professor and choreographer was decked out in a Billy the Kid in cowboy clothes and boots. The Swedish teen-agers, here as guests of Minnesota Lions, were entertained by Swedish Consul and Mrs. Gosta af Petersraine.

Another famous Minneapolis face stunning New

York — Danna Stewart, first Miss Downtown Minneapolis, now blowing smoke rings on TV.

The Minnesota Twins, the season's doughtiest darlings, and their newest Ladies Day favorite, shy and freckled Rich Rollins.

Tippi Hedren, director Alfred Hitchcock's "new English discovery," actually a pretty ex-Minneapolitan and a cousin of Mr. and Mrs. James Hedren, Osseo. Tippi, really named Natalie, but always Tippi to friends and relatives, moved to California with her parents, the Ben Hedrens, during her high school days. A modeling career in magazines and on TV helped Hitchcock discover her. Now she's the star of his newest film, "The Birds."

were unprepared for its dismal, neglected state. The dark rooms, in a house which had not been refurbished or updated since before World War II, mirrored Eugenie's instinctive feelings about the city's atmosphere as a whole: "It evidently was a place where the people were very oppressed and fearful and I was conscious of this almost immediately."[15]

One of Eugenie's first actions, when ordering grocery and household items to stock the residence, was to put, at the top of the list, 130 cartons of American cigarettes. John smoked, of course, and Eugenie did so occasionally, but ordering twenty-six thousand cigarettes indicated that these would be used as frequent gifts to staffers, guests, and anyone who could benefit from a little whiff of free capitalist America.

On August 3, 1962, Anderson officially presented her credentials to Bulgarian Chief of State Dimitar Ganev and commenced her Ministry of the American Legation. The press release afforded a brief notice in the *New York Times* ("Sofia Greets New U.S. Envoy"), but there was no fanfare as there was in Denmark, no cheering crowds, and no swarms of photographers. Eugenie reported to family at home in the same weekly newsletter format that she had used in Copenhagen. For the next two and a half years, Eugenie walked around with her handwritten letters in her purse, never letting the bag out of her sight. Only after the drafts had been typed and sealed in a diplomatic pouch to be safely mailed were the originals destroyed. The Andersons had been warned by the State Department, of course, that one of the main conditions that made Sofia a "hardship" post would be the Communist surveillance and censorship of all American communication, over all degrees of public and private material. But nothing could prepare them for the pervasiveness of the Big Ears and Eyes, or how quickly the lack of privacy would begin to challenge their fortitude. Outgoing and incoming mails in secure diplomatic pouches were safe. Everything else was vulnerable to scrutiny, censorship, and/or translation not only to Bulgarian officials but directly to Soviet secret police as well. More personally debilitating, however, was the relentless attention given to bugging the American legation, as well as Eugenie and John's private residence. Legation offices had one "safe" room inside a room, a cube made entirely of soundproof glass on four sides and the ceiling, with a raised concrete floor, swept daily for bugs and used for meetings and conferences, but the Andersons' residence had zero guarantee of privacy at any time. It was understood that everything said out loud within its walls would be overheard and recorded. Before they had been in Bulgaria even a month, Eugenie wrote home:

> The next time you want to settle an argument, just try doing it on paper. You will discover that no matter how furiously you scribble you cannot write as fast as you talk. Of course, you can't interrupt each other in writing either. Nor can you express your emotions with the intensity that two people who love each other deeply can often feel during the course of a day.
>
> I also have a strong need to be able to talk freely with John out in the open where there is, we hope, no trace of 1984 around us (naturally we will thoroughly examine ourselves, our clothes and our picnic baskets too, remembering that such innocent looking things as a bottle opener or a bread knife could in fact be the ever-present big ears around us.) . . . It *is* frustrating to go for ten days without being able to talk freely even with your nearest and dearest.[16]

Eugenie and John routinely communicated by writing notes, which were immediately torn up and flushed down the toilet. In the early days, for the most part, they tried to have a good sense of humor about it: "You should have seen the huge spider that was in our bathtub this morning. . . . I do not like to kill anything, but I insisted that this one had to go the way of all flesh, which in this case was down our trusty toilet, or should I say 'security file.'" When they entertained guests, it was common knowledge that somewhere nearby, the secret police were listening for inflammatory remarks in every toast, joke, and burst of laughter. One guest, Eugenie explained in a letter, "seemed to know about the dangers of talking in this house, however, and said that she had been told that when this house was remodeled for the Americans (several years ago) that wiring and microphones were built into the walls." Every ring of human connection around the Andersons was subject to constant scrutiny: themselves, their families, guests and acquaintances of all nationalities, but perhaps most intensely, the Bulgarian employees inside both the residence and offices. Every single one of them was required to report to the police once a week with a summary of activity, observation, experience, and impression within the American subcommunity. "I realized," Eugenie wrote, "what kind of demands must be made on even the most faithful of our household staff, and what a miserable situation they are in, especially if they want to be honest and loyal. Of course it is our responsibility simply to see to it that the items they have to report on us are of no significance." The vigilance necessary to keep any staff from seeing or hearing sensitive material was exhausting: "I will admit that I get tired of always having to be so careful about papers, letters, etc. around our rooms, although that is less annoying than not being able to talk freely. The latter is more than a mere annoyance—at times one feels it is a monstrous, unbearable invasion of one's privacy." Employees were even questioned about Eugenie's moods, what sort of personal conversation subjects she introduced or encouraged, or whether she tried to entice confidences. The wife of one trusted employee, Eugenie found out, "had been questioned specifically about my 'smiles'"—apparently, other Western diplomats kept themselves much more aloof and disinterested with staff.[17]

One of Eugenie's primary directives from the State Department was to attempt to bring a positive image of Western capitalism to the Bulgarian public. This public, served only by Stalinist-oriented propaganda under one news service, had severely narrow reference points on American life. And ordinarily, neither Minister Anderson nor anyone affiliated with the legation was allowed to distribute anything that smacked of American propaganda to the Bulgarian people: not advertisements, pamphlets, books, photographs—nothing material. An international trade fair (begun in 1892 and still in existence today) provided a legal exception to the tight censorship. Huge crowds attended the fair in Plovdiv, a city about ninety-three miles southeast of Sofia, walking through exhibits from many countries that displayed everything from the tiniest sewing needle to the largest factory machinery. Before 1962, the United States had been allowed a presence at the fair only once. This year, granted space to exhibit a modern American kitchen, the legation facilitated the display more as a starting point for building trade and public relations, since almost none previously existed. Anderson's staff negotiated a small pamphlet, rewritten several times over a period of months between the legation's cultural attaché and a representative in the Bulgarian Ministry of Commerce—a "very bland, innocuous little pamphlet," Eugenie called it—that included greetings and photos of both President Kennedy and Minister Anderson. The pamphlet was grudgingly approved by the Bulgarian government, and the legation was given clearance to have it printed and available at the Plovdiv trade fair.

Eugenie and John Anderson, accompanied by the legation's cultural attaché, Alexander Bloomfield (who acted as constant Bulgarian language interpreter and eventually became a close friend), traveled to Plovdiv the day before the fair opening. Eating dinner in their hotel, the Andersons, Bloomfield, and some staff members were accosted at their table by Alexander Popov, the representative of the Bulgarian Commerce Department and overseer of the Plovdiv fair, who claimed no prior knowledge of the legation's clearance to share their pamphlet with the public. Popov told Eugenie Anderson, rudely: "We are not at all pleased with your exhibition. Furthermore, this brochure which you are intending to distribute is completely unacceptable and we don't intend to permit you to distribute this." Eugenie explained that they already had government permission, but Popov continued to argue. Sensing immediately that a precedent needed to be set, Eugenie told Popov that business of this nature belonged in her office, and she stood up and left. It would be the first of many times she openly defied and walked out on the Communists.

Eugenie's strategy to overrule Popov and any authority he might have with the local customs officials was to target Bulgarian prime minister Todor Zhivkov and publicly hand him a pamphlet before they could be confiscated. When the opening ceremony of the fair concluded that first morning, Zhivkov and his entourage visited the Soviet pavilion first (of course). From there, they made their way to the American pavilion, as yet unaware that any controversy surrounded Anderson's "innocuous" little pamphlets. US Minister Anderson greeted Prime Minister Zhivkov personally, said a few welcoming words in Bulgarian, and "did immediately hand him one of the brochures, which he innocently accepted. It was very amusing that almost immediately one of his aides grabbed it from his hand from behind, not intending to let him be photographed with it, or caught with it, so to speak." The high contingent moved on, and Anderson and her staff continued to hand out the pamphlets. Word spread that customs officials did not approve of the literature and could be seizing it from the Americans at any minute, which only created more curiosity among the Bulgarians touring the fair. Foot traffic picked up through the American pavilion, not to see the matching modern stove and refrigerator, but to score a rare copy of President Kennedy's smiling face and see what the illicit, decadent hype was all about. "They were falling all over themselves to get these brochures," Eugenie remembered, "and it was almost dangerous for our officials to hand these out because they were just being mobbed by the people." The secret police began snatching away the brochures as soon as people exited the American pavilion, going so far as to recruit young Communist boys, called party youth "Pioneers," to confiscate, or pickpocket, the pamphlets. After three days of vigilance, the legation staff physically protecting their leaflets and locking them up at night, Alex Bloomfield instructed Anderson to meet with the customs officials to clear things up since they still had another week to get through. She did, informing them that she would instruct her staff to continue distribution "even if we had to use force," refusing to back down from thuggish secret police intimidation. Grudgingly, the officials complied and reduced the harassment. Bloomfield heard from his contacts that Bulgaria's minister of foreign trade admitted that they "underestimated the determination of your minister," adding, "We didn't know the Americans could be so tough." Neither did the Americans. Although the State Department reacted with a congratulatory telegram after receiving Minister Anderson's report on Plovdiv, they remained uneasy and cautious. In 1962, one of the highest objectives of the United States was to maintain any relations with the Soviet Union that forestalled nuclear conflict. "They [the US government] felt that to talk about opening things up with Eastern Europe would rock the

Minister Anderson greets Bulgarian citizens in Sofia, 1964. *Photo by John P. Anderson, Anderson family collection.*

boat," said Anderson in a 1973 interview. Her public presence was beneficial in Bulgaria to show American goodwill, but not necessarily entrepreneurship.[18]

Global nuclear threat came to the forefront just weeks after the Plovdiv trade fair closed. During the Cuban Missile Crisis of October 1962, it was transparently obvious that the Bulgarian government would uphold any and all directives from the Soviet Union. Eugenie recalled, "The Bulgarian press was carrying on a very shrill campaign of vilification against the Americans during all this. And there was indeed great tension." Anderson wrote to President Kennedy: "Your resolute actions of the past week have been exhilarating not only to all the Americans here, but also to our friends and Allies. . . . We have gained a new initiative, and Soviet weakness has been revealed." Bulgarian chief of state Dimitar Ganev, naturally, did not view the outcome of the Cuban Missile Crisis, nor Kennedy's actions, the same way at all. At a reception honoring Bolshevik Revolution Day, which included diplomatic guests from many countries, delegates to the congress of the Bulgarian Communist Party, and a variety of top officials, Ganev verbosely accused the United States of "bandit-like" acts and "piratical actions" against Cuba. Provocative remarks by the Soviet ambassador Georgiy A. Denisov also spurred Ganev to declare: "Anger and disgust filled our planet when the aggressive forces of the United States, violating all norms of international law, tried to put a blockade around small but heroic Cuba and began piratical actions in the region of the Caribbean Sea, openly preparing an armed attack on revolutionary Cuba in order to eliminate the Socialist order." Standing nearby with the visiting head of the Eastern European Division of the State Department, Harold Vedeler, and her attaché Alex Bloomfield, Eugenie Anderson understood that she was supposed to overhear these remarks. Furthermore, it was understood that beyond knowing Eugenie would recognize their grossly insulting tone of voice, Ganev and the Communists knew she would also get an instantaneous English translation from Bloomfield. She was supposed to be humiliated and ridiculed in her public vulnerability. But they didn't yet know Minister Anderson.[19]

Eugenie quickly and discreetly consulted with some of the other ambassadors from NATO countries at the reception, many of whom did not have interpreters and were in the dark as to what anyone said in Bulgarian. She also, as a formality, informed Harold Vedeler from the State Department that she intended to walk out in protest. Then she instructed a deputy from her staff to inform the NATO ambassadors, especially the British and the French, that she would be leaving, and recommended that they do so as well—many did indeed follow. As Western newspapers later reported: "Bulgarian officials rushed over in an attempt to smooth things over, diplomatic informants said, but Mrs. Anderson would have none of it." Her walkout caused something of a short sensation, but its real significance was that it added to her growing reputation as a tough cookie. Initially viewed by both Kennedy's advisers and strangers in Eastern Europe as a harmless, soft-spoken grandmother, Anderson was debunking that stereotype at every turn. Loyal Gould of the Associated Press took notice:

U.S. DIPLOMAT IS NO PATSY
Bulgarian Reds took on more than they bargained for when they tangled with a silver-haired American grandmother here. "They figured she'd be a pushover," a Western diplomat said, "but they didn't know Babitschka." Babitschka, the Bulgarian for grandmother as she is known affectionately among some of her friends here, is Mrs. Eugenie Anderson, American minister to Sofia and the first female U.S. diplomatic chief of mission in an Iron Curtain country.... Obstacles include secret police action, insults at diplomatic receptions, and so-called "spontaneous" anti-American demonstrations.[20]

Eugenie had a fine-tuned instinct for finding the proper line between protocol and protest. She knew how to keep her dignity in controversial situations, particularly while representing her country's best interests. One of her most trusted heroes and mentors, a person she strove to emulate, had always been Eleanor Roosevelt.

Eugenie took many of her cues from Mrs. Roosevelt's examples of tenacity on behalf of democracy. She owed a tremendous amount to Mrs. Roosevelt's good faith and sponsorship. The very morning of the Bolshevik Revolution Day reception (where Eugenie would end up staging her walkout), Anderson would have read in her daily diplomatic reports that Mrs. Eleanor Roosevelt had died the day before in her Manhattan home at the age of seventy-eight. Alongside that news, Eugenie would have received instructions from the White House to lower all American flags to half-staff to honor the great lady's passing. One could say that Eugenie Anderson was honoring Roosevelt in her own way, too, when that evening she rallied the democratic voices around her at the international gathering and refused to be intimidated, silver-haired grandmother or not.

As 1962 drew to a close and Eugenie made plans to fly back to the United States for meetings in Washington and holidays with family, many people were surprised to discover that John would not be accompanying her. Bulgaria—only five months into the post—was proving stressful and frustrating for Eugenie, but for John, it was close to unbearable. Eugenie, at least, had a purpose and a philosophy of her big-picture political contribution; whether or not her mission in Bulgaria came out successful in any way, her appointment gave her historic status and more credentials for future work. John, on the other hand, had no clear objective outside of photography and emotionally supporting Eugenie. His reversed role as the subordinate spouse to the chief of mission, even though press and publicity were not as much of an issue, was even more highly pronounced in company than it had been in Denmark. John also lacked the rewards of family management that had helped him in Copenhagen. There were no longer any children to look after. In addition, there was no one equivalent to a Niels Bohr with whom he could visit nearby, scheduled or spontaneously, for brandy or coffee and long discussions about science, art, or, God forbid, subversive Western topics of any nature. John became so depressed that, instead of traveling home with Eugenie in December, he isolated himself further and took a trip into Greece alone with his cameras. Hans wrote: "It seems no one here really knows where you are, or what you are doing! A day or so after Mother arrived here I sent a letter to Salonika, and right now I do not know where to send this." A week later, John surfaced in Athens, to which Hans sent his New Year's greetings for 1963: "I feel at times that we do seem to have roles, parts as it were, that we play out, and at these times I feel that yours, my father's, is a difficult one. You are a gifted and sensitive man, John, and it goes hard for you but perhaps in the next year there will be a few moments even longer times when you will be feeling good and life will seem real."[21]

John and Eugenie had been married for thirty-two years. On the whole, they had weathered the years surprisingly well, considering the fact that they wrestled with public stresses (image, role reversal, and career expectations) as well as private difficulties (John's struggle with alcoholism and unrealized hopes for his art, and Eugenie's ambitious, outgoing nature). But while each year bound them closer together and deepened their love and commitment, each week, each day, was a different story. The Andersons were not uniformly content and often spent time apart, sometimes amicably, but sometimes in utter frustration. Donald Tice, employed as an economic officer in the legation from 1964 to 1967, revealed one impression of the Andersons in an interview: "At one point there were several anti-American riots in Sofia, and [John] went out to take pictures of them. These took place near the Legation. Eugenie was absolutely furious with him for putting himself in what was potentially 'harm's way.' I felt very uncomfortable being present when at the residence she was really 'dressing him down' for having taken those pictures. This was the Ambassador talking to him."[22]

The above comment ended in laughter between Tice and his interviewer. And the very fact that any instance of the role reversal between Eugenie and John could be repeated or translated as a joke—to Americans or to Communists—was what made the dangers and oppressions of Sofia so very hard on the Andersons' marriage, and on Eugenie as a woman diplomat. Eugenie did not want to look like a virago; neither could she look away when something threatened her tenuous political authority in a hostile environment. Everything around Eugenie and John—Bulgarian and American staff, diplomatic corps, government officials, twenty-four-hour surveillance and bugging—all of it put enormous stress on their relationship, between themselves, and on their role-reversed image to the public.

Over the holidays in December 1962, while John was traveling in Greece, Eugenie returned to Washington, spending most of her time politicking. She managed a few days with Johanna and Hans and their families, but otherwise she worked her way down a substantial list of objectives for the time stateside. First, she had to insist (again, and this time in person) that the State Department approve the budget for refurbishing the horribly dilapidated offices and residence in Sofia. Second, she needed to get the State Department to confirm her authority to negotiate financial war claims settlements in Sofia. These settlements (money and property value owed to Bulgarians by the United States; and the same to Americans by Bulgaria) had been dragging out for seventeen years, since the end of World War II, and had become a messy legal tangle. Eugenie believed that "I would never be able to make any kind of diplomatic headway in Bulgaria unless we settled this question of the financial war claims settlement." Third, she attended meetings and debriefings concerned with foreign policies based on the aftermath of the Cuban Missile Crisis. Fourth, she appealed to the Kennedy administration to upgrade the Bulgarian status of trade to "most favored nation," a tariff perk enjoyed by Yugoslavia and Poland but denied to Bulgaria because it was Communist. (On this initiative, Anderson's attempts would fail to both President Kennedy and later President Johnson.)[23]

Of 1963, Eugenie recalled that it "was a very active year and I think without a doubt it was our best year in Bulgaria." Graham Hovey, European correspondent for the *Minneapolis Tribune*, agreed. On

July 7, his column listed multiple "firsts" and high achievements for Minister Anderson. She had painstakingly brought the financial war claims settlements to a close and signed off on the amounts due to each party. She had officiated at the opening of an American "Plastics USA" exhibit in Sofia and reinforced her tough reputation when she called out a Bulgarian commerce official for rude remarks about the dubious quality of unexceptional American goods. And she had addressed Bulgarians, over both radio and television, on July 4, Independence Day: "This was not only the first occasion on which Bulgarian television time had been granted to any Western minister," Eugenie recalled, "but also the first time any diplomat from any country had spoken to Bulgarians on TV in their own language. Beneath the scrupulous politeness and friendly warmth, it was a tough message to give on TV in a Communist-run country."[24]

In order to find access to real, everyday Bulgarian people (as opposed to stiff, vetted government officials and police), language proved to be an even higher commodity than it had been in Denmark: "I just wanted to [learn Bulgarian] so badly because I was convinced that it was the key to communication with the people. This was true in Denmark as well as in Bulgaria. If I hadn't done this, I think that the people in both countries would hardly have known that I existed. But because of this, the people knew in Bulgaria that not only was there an American Minister who cared enough about them to learn their language and to speak to them in it, but they suddenly became aware of me as an individual."[25]

Other diplomats, most of whom thought learning Bulgarian was a ridiculous whim, suggested that if Eugenie wanted to waste her time, she might as well study Russian. But Anderson's point of person-to-person mutual accessibility was lost on many of the career Foreign Service people, and she furthermore thought that trying to converse with Bulgarians in Russian would be insulting. Richard E. Johnson, deputy chief of the Bulgarian mission from 1963 to 1965, was interviewed in 1991; the following memory of Eugenie Anderson provided an example of her dynamic outreach:

Eugenie had a great public relations orientation; she liked to shake hands and to get out and around. Of course, Bulgaria is a very difficult place to do that, but Eugenie nonetheless tried. She dressed very beautifully, both in terms of her personality and intelligence but also her appearance; she spoke well for the USA as obviously a prosperous woman. She and her USIA guy, a guy named Alex Bloomfield, would pile into her Cadillac and just shoot off for a day visiting different people, not with prearranged appointments necessarily, but going into the marketplace, and the mobs would descend around this huge Cadillac and Eugenie would shake hands and, through Alex Bloomfield who spoke excellent Bulgarian, she would tell everybody how the U.S. only wanted friendship with Bulgaria and that we hoped there would be some exchanges eventually, but the Bulgarian government wasn't doing much on that.[26]

Over time, cultural attaché and interpreter Alex Bloomfield, and his wife, Ruth, had proved to be completely trustworthy, invaluable friends and advisers to the Andersons. Alex's multilingual communication skills and talent for pragmatism were supplemented by his good instincts in situations with the Communists that necessitated "fight or flight" diplomatic responses. Eugenie relied heavily on Bloomfield's assistance through many deep political waters. The brutality and insidious nature of the Bulgarian government's tactics to keep its people submissive and fearful erupted on Easter Sunday 1963. In a small group that included Alex Bloomfield and the Israeli minister Zvi Avnon and his wife, the Andersons went to the midnight Easter service at the Alexander Nevsky Cathedral, expecting a modest crowd, peaceful cultural observation, and beautiful music. Instead, they found the square outside the church packed solid with up to ten thousand young Communist party agitators, organized to bully and disrupt the religious proceedings. "Once inside, the crowd was even more dense," wrote Eugenie, and "we all had a feeling of danger because it was so clear that this was largely a mob of young Communists who had had orders to jam the church, disrupt the service, make a noisy demonstration and as much confusion as possible. They certainly succeeded." Eugenie

Eugenie converses with a Bulgarian woman in a Plovdiv street market in November 1963. *Photo by John P. Anderson, Anderson family collection.*

likened the uproar of noise to a sports event. Separated from their group by pushing and shoving, Eugenie's secretary, Vivian Meisen, witnessed a chair-throwing fight in the balcony. John and Eugenie, with Alex Bloomfield and Minister and Mrs. Avnon, were squeezed into a corner by the altar, where they watched a tight clutch of young men try to prevent the cathedral patriarch from ascending to the pulpit. "The youth looked very calloused, hard-boiled, and unintelligent," Eugenie remarked. "It was horrifying to think that this was a sample of the coming generation of Communists here. . . . Several older people to whom Alex spoke expressed their shock and shame, but could only say, 'This is the way the young people today are being trained.'" After an hour, during which it was clear that nothing would improve and that the police were aiding the disrupters by blocking doors and watching passively, the Andersons found a side door. John forced it open with his shoulder, unbalancing the policeman on the other side. Eugenie admitted: "The types of secret-policemen that one sees in such a situation as this are reminiscent of Hitler's storm troopers. It was hard to get to sleep that night, and I am still haunted by the brazen, wanton faces of the young destroyers, as well as their cruel masters."[27]

In October 1963, Anderson flew to Bonn, Germany, to attend a conference with the complete roster of American chiefs of mission to European countries, both Eastern and Western. "A number of other top State Department officials were there, in addition to Secretary [of State Dean] Rusk, so it was quite a large group, of which I was the only woman at the Conferences." For two days, the Western chiefs held meetings among themselves; Secretary Rusk then met with the entire group; and for an additional two days, the Eastern chiefs held their discussions. After Dean Rusk gave his central talk, the Eastern European mission chiefs had an opportunity for a roundtable of sorts with him. Eugenie sent the following account to her family, describing "an amusing bit of repartee took place between Rusk and myself": "Rusk was explaining to the group that he felt that the present dynamic situation in Eastern Europe offers the U.S. definite possibilities to help the individual countries towards more independence. 'If Eugenie will permit me to use the phrase, I might say that we should use the methods of seduction and not of rape in this process towards their freedom.' When I interjected, 'Perhaps a woman has a certain advantage in this situation'—everyone laughed, someone said 'Touché!' and Rusk joined in heartily."[28]

No hesitation, no flinch, no fumble. Secretary of State Rusk threw a rape metaphor at Eugenie, who, without blinking an eye, diminished its potency with skillful banter. And not only did she take ownership of the analogy, but she deflected any continuing emphasis on the fact that she was the only woman in the room. *Can't take a joke* is one of the oldest and most treacherous methods of segregating women from the men's club. It took quick reflexes, guts, and political expertise to grab that violent analogy, dilute it with her own sense of humor, and squash it before the metaphor got any more disgusting or confrontational. No doubt, Eugenie had parried dozens of times before with similar verbal challenges and probably preferred crossing swords with men she could call fellow patriots over Communist Party officials bent on their own agendas of intimidation.

When Eugenie returned to Sofia from the State Department conferences at Bonn, while she was certainly aware that East-West relations were strained, complex, and rapidly cooling, she could never have predicted how the next few months would play out. The Communists had internal political battles in multiple countries, the ideological split between the Soviet Union and China being the largest. Soviet interference in all of their satellite countries, as

November 1963. Minister Anderson stands in front of the American legation in central Sofia with a deputy minister, among the crowd that gathered daily to see photos and news of American life. Cultural attaché and interpreter Alexander Bloomfield is at far left. *Photo by John P. Anderson, Anderson family collection.*

well as the growing menace in Vietnam and the close proximity of Castro's Cuba, kept the United States on constant high alert. And then the unthinkable happened. On November 22, 1963, President John F. Kennedy was assassinated in Dallas, Texas.

Minister Anderson draped the picture windows at the American legation in black, gradually adding photographs and news of President Kennedy's life and tragic death. These windows were not inconsequential, nor were they unknown to the outside world. Free world newspapers called them "the most popular USIS [United States Information Service] photo display in the world. The three large store windows filled with news and feature photos attract a constant crowd of 50 to 100 people from dawn to nearly midnight, and in summer an average of 5000 Bulgarians stop by [daily] to get this glimpse of outside information." Like the pamphlets at the Plovdiv trade fair, the legation windows offered visual evidence of American life, something that was either contorted by Communist propaganda in their own newspapers and magazines or, more often, absent altogether. When President Kennedy was assassinated, thousands flocked to the window displays, a line of spectators in dark coats snaking around the block, waiting their turn to see for themselves what had happened on the other side of the world. Approximately eight hundred Bulgarians actually entered the legation, climbed the steps to the second-floor offices, signed the guest register as mourners, and shook the hand of Minister Eugenie Anderson, who welcomed them and thanked them, in Bulgarian, for their respects. Brave visitors even whispered words of their own.[29]

Minister Anderson was allowed to tape a televised address to the country, speaking in Bulgarian, following the days of mourning, when she thanked the country for its sympathy, especially the visitors who had come in person to the legation. Although the text of her message was constrained by a government censor, her voice—the accent, the timbre, the emotion, the very individuality—could not be altered. Eugenie's persona, christened "Babitschka" (an

endearment of *grandmother*), along with her perseverance to use
the Bulgarian language whenever she could, gave her allowances to
be seen and heard around the country that a male career diplomat
would have been denied.

The Bulgarian government was far from pleased by the out-
pouring of sympathetic sentiments from its people. Soviet directives commanded that the Bulgarian population should only see
and hear material that reinforced America's reputation as imperialist, decadent, aggressive, and selfish. Something had to be done
to counteract the widespread fascination with America and the
tragedy-diorama of the murdered president, his suffering widow,
and the dangerous personal associations that their fable could stir
in vulnerable hearts. Communist officials and journalists latched
on to the highest-profile story of the moment that could distract
the Bulgarian public and vilify the Americans: the spy trial of Ivan-
Asen Khristov Georgiev. Arrested in Moscow four months prior to
the start of the trial, fifty-six-year-old Georgiev had been part of
the Bulgarian mission to the United Nations in New York City from
1956 to 1961, headed by ambassador Peter Voutov. Georgiev was
accused of feeding Bulgarian secrets to the US Central Intelligence
Agency for the previous seven years. His picture, his history, and
his traitorous crime saturated the Bulgarian TV news, radio, and
papers. Prosecutors sent investigators to observe and document
any possible links between Georgiev and the American legation in
Sofia. Deputy chief of mission Robert B. (Bob) Houston recalled the
surveillance and the cloak-and-dagger atmosphere straight out of a
John le Carré novel:

> They captured [Georgiev's] radio transmitter and radio schedule.
> . . . The Bulgarians tried to use this radio communication link to
> set up a meeting with the spy on the main street in Sofia, to be
> attended by someone in the legation. Well as it came out later in
> some newspaper article, at the very hour of the assigned meeting
> and on the street corner where this fellow was waiting and was sup-
> posed to be picked up, I walked past him just as I did every evening

on my way home. Again their suspicions must have been aroused, "What was this guy Houston up to?" The worst thing was that in press articles later, they did not describe me by name. They just said that a short time after one legation officer went by, smartly dressed, another legation staff member "in a cap and a crumpled raincoat" came walking by, trying to disguise himself. Well, my raincoat was crumpled and I did wear a cap, so I was sure they were talking about me. Later, in talking about this with John Anderson, the husband of Minister Anderson, he said, "You think that was you, I'm sure it was me." So it is a matter of dispute who the guy in the cap and the crumpled raincoat was whom Bulgarians thought was trying to meet the alleged spy that evening.[30]

Georgiev was imprisoned and interrogated for four months. When his trial began on December 26, 1963, Eugenie Anderson was in the United States, visiting for the holidays, but John Anderson was in residence in Sofia (they were spending a second Christmas apart). The court proceedings were closed to the public, but news reports throughout Eastern Europe were detailed and inflammatory. It was during the first two days of testimony that Communist organizers rallied three thousand people to hold a demonstration in the streets of Sofia, supposedly expressing, independent of the government, the *people's* disapproval of America's seduction of Georgiev. "It was claimed that the reason for this demonstration was because of the Georgiev spy trial. The United States was portrayed as the enemy of Bulgaria and as a wicked imperialist power," Eugenie recalled.

I was in Burlington, Vermont, spending Christmas with my daughter and son, and I was informed by the Department of State . . . that a mob of Bulgarians had stormed the legation, the chancery, and had smashed all the big windows in the front of the legation and had overturned and smashed three or four, maybe five, cars belonging to legation personnel. . . . Of course, I knew immediately that this signaled more than simply a reaction to the Georgiev spy trial. It signaled also a reaction of the Bulgarian government to the fact that I think they felt that we were getting along too well, that we were making too much headway in Bulgaria.[31]

The mob of mostly young people gathered midmorning several blocks away from the legation. At the same time, John Anderson had driven his blue Mercedes to the office to pick up some mail that had come in while he was traveling the previous week. About 11:30 AM, he parked the car in front of the big picture windows. Shortly after, someone in the legation was tipped off that there could be trouble and that large numbers of demonstrators were moving along the street, yelling, waving placards, and chanting phrases that translated to things like "down with the imperial masters and their puppet spies." A few agitators arrived early. John got out his camera and light meter and started to take exposure readings. But a legation staff member warned him to get his car off the street before the mob arrived; John saw reason and got back in his car, but only after witnessing the first rock fly, crashing through the plate glass. As he drove away, he could hear the roar of the crowd advancing. Richard Johnson, left in charge during Eugenie's absence, described the situation as it felt from inside the building, under siege while angry protesters smashed windows for the third or fourth time since the start of Anderson's ministry two years prior:

> These were quite frightening occasions . . . I was worried that these mobs would set fire to the post. They always broke windows and started climbing into the windows. And we had the whole embassy staff to protect. We would be up on the top floor . . . most of the embassy staff was there, because many of us lived there, and they were sort of cowering in a corner while rocks rained through the windows into the offices of the embassy. And, as soon as I could, I would have to try to get out the front door of the embassy, pushing against this surging crowd, and make my way through the crowd, with all sorts of taunts and insults and being spat upon, to the Foreign Ministry.[32]

David Binder, special correspondent to the *New York Times*, sent an article over the wires that day. He reported that "two American Foreign Service officers, who asked not to be identified, were roughed up as they attempted to enter the legation . . . in downtown

Sofia. One of the young diplomats was slapped in the face by a demonstrator and the other was kicked in the groin and punched by several Bulgarian men. . . . At the height of the assault, phalanx after phalanx of young and middle-aged men swept into the boulevard. They were armed with such missiles as rocks, beer bottles, and chunks of ice as big as softballs." Binder also acknowledged that "United States diplomats voiced astonishment over the assault. . . . For the last year, under the bold leadership of Mrs. Anderson, the legation established ever warmer relations with Bulgarian officials and with ordinary Bulgarians." The attack became international news overnight. On December 28, the *Minneapolis Tribune* picked up the AP story that reported: "It was obvious that such an incident could not have occurred at all—much less lasted for an hour, as this one did—without the connivance of the Communist government. Police did not arrive to disperse the crowd until an hour after protection was sought by U.S. officers in the legation. Some members of the ruling Communist government have chafed at the recent Cold War 'thaw' engineered by Minnesota's Eugenie Anderson, U.S. minister in Bulgaria."[33]

In the hours before New Year's Eve, when the sun went down on 1963, Ivan Georgiev was found guilty of espionage for the United States and sentenced to execution by firing squad. Used as the justification for the attack riots on the Americans, the truth of Georgiev's guilt or the questionable level of his actual importance was never established. When Eugenie was interviewed in 1971, she still did not know at that time what Georgiev's fate turned out to be, or whether he was indeed executed. But in the first days of 1964, as Eugenie prepared to travel back to Bulgaria and workers measured the tall picture windows for new glass, few people doubted that Georgiev's show trial was just used as a distraction and that the Communist government sacrificed him as an expendable figure. A major feud between the Soviet Union and Red China was threatening the safety and balance of power on the planet—not to mention the Cold War between East and West. Any means were fair

John Anderson photographed the aftermath of the December 27, 1963, riot that smashed legation windows, injured guards, participants, and bystanders, and destroyed everything on the street in front of the American offices. *Photo by John P. Anderson, Anderson family collection.*

game for Communists to demonstrate that none of their people were soft on capitalists or sympathetic to Western overtures. David Binder looked back on the trial in his book *Fare Well, Illyria*. Binder attributed the entire orchestration of the trial to Bulgaria's highest officer, Prime Minister Todor Zhivkov, who was so threatened by softening relations with America and so desperate "to put forth Bulgaria as the most loyal and doctrinaire of the Soviet Union's satellites" that he was eager to resurrect the type of show trials more common under Stalin in the early 1950s—trials Zhivkov had also been involved with personally.[34]

Upon her return, Minister Anderson called on the Bulgarian foreign minister "with a very vigorous protest directly from the State Department" demanding the immediate replacement of all the broken windows. The glass and carpentry repair took several weeks. Damaged relations, however, never quite recovered. "The

Bulgarian [officials] also were very unfriendly, very severe, stopped coming to our residence, stopped accepting our invitations. There must have been several months there when U.S.-Bulgarian relations were practically what I would call in a deep freeze." The offices and chancery of the legation, at the outset of 1964, were somber and lifeless. If Eugenie had a weakness, it was her impatience with working at a dry, perfunctory level. Accomplishing nothing, she decided to take a leave: she and John traveled for three weeks in March, spending two weeks in Egypt (one in Cairo, a second in Luxor), then toured the United Arab Republic and Jerusalem, Israel. Only weeks after returning to Sofia, they packed their bags again and commenced a tour recommended by the State Department, visiting Bucharest in Romania, Warsaw and Krakow in Poland, and multiple cities in the Soviet Union. They arrived in Moscow just in time to attend the grand May Day parade in Red Square (John's movie footage attests to the striking reputation of Communist glorification). After a few days in Leningrad (St. Petersburg today), experiencing the northwestern culture of Russia, they turned south and explored a completely different culture through Tashkent, Samarkand, and Bukhara in present-day Uzbekistan and Tbilisi in Georgia, finishing in Kiev.[35]

Within days of returning to Sofia, another legation window was smashed. A staff member telephoned Eugenie early in the morning; she only temporarily kept her cool and informed the staff to make her an appointment with the foreign minister immediately so that she could deliver a formal protest. Hanging up, she "exploded," letting loose of her usual composure, knowing that every word would be overheard through the bugs in the house: "I was simply furious. . . . I expressed my feelings without any inhibitions about how I thought this was outrageous, that here we had just sort of begun to recover from one window smashing when it happened again . . . I felt quite sure that my voice was heard almost immediately at the foreign office because within fifteen minutes I had a call from the foreign minister expressing his personal apologies. . . . He told me that he was sure that this was an accident . . . and that it must have been the work of a deranged person."[36]

The international reactions to JFK's assassination had not, in any procedural manner, changed the Bulgarian post or created difficulties on top of those that already existed. But the overall sense of the mission—the feeling that Anderson was making no progress—continued to spiral downward. Eugenie despaired that no matter what she tried, nothing would change in the foreseeable future. As one deputy chief of mission put it: "Bulgaria was one of the most rigid of the Warsaw Pact states. If people caught a cold in Moscow, Bulgarians would sneeze in Sofia." Soviet control, secret police saturation, and the absence of Western press remained absolute.

Eugenie toed the line and duly presented her official protests to offenses large and small to the Bulgarian government whenever she could (knowing that the protests would be filed or simply ignored). For the most part, John was cautious and realistic about what he could and could not get away with out in the streets or while touring the countryside around Sofia. But sometimes the temptation for a photographic subject caused him to overstep his common sense. On one occasion, he had driven and then hiked up the side of a broad hillside overlooking Sofia. Charmed with the rooftops and vista laid out under good light (versus the brown smog that sometimes blanketed the city), John began shooting pictures with a telephoto lens. When a policeman arrived and began to question him (in Bulgarian), John realized that he had left his wallet at the house and had no way to communicate to the officer that he was the husband of the American minister. The police attempted to seize John's camera, but he refused to turn it over. He was escorted back to Sofia and detained until, after many hours, the police agreed to find an English interpreter.

> He was taking pictures which he had no idea were of any forbidden military installation. He thought he was taking a picture overlooking Sofia. And suddenly police popped up, as they were likely to do when you didn't have any idea they were around they would appear,

and they arrested him, actually held him for several hours. . . . They had a gun and so he had no choice except to stay where he was. . . . And when they found out that he was my husband, they were rather scared. I think they realized that they would get a strong protest from me, which they did.[37]

John was unraveling. "My husband was not well," Eugenie confessed, "and I felt that his health was being adversely affected by our staying in Bulgaria. He not only was very depressed but he had a rather severe stomach trouble. . . . The life there was simply too much tension, too much isolation, and really very, very depressing, more so for him than for me. . . . I always could manage this by simply the fact of working so hard to try to do something."[38]

What had started out amid the glamour of a new age under a Democratic administration—JFK and Jackie, American resolve through the Cuban Missile Crisis, space exploration, and the barest glimmers of cultural movement for women away from the 1950s "feminine mystique"—now ground to a standstill for Eugenie's objectives. She began counting the days until the November 1964 election. No matter who prevailed, President Lyndon B. Johnson or challenger Barry Goldwater, she planned to resign her post and— for lack of a better metaphor—get the hell out of Dodge.

Hubert Humphrey was "at the peak of his powers" in 1964. His intense efforts with President Johnson on the historic Civil Rights Bill confirmed his reputation as the hardest-working man in Washington and someone who actually had a shot at uniting people in a rapidly changing political decade. "To be floor manager of the civil rights bill is almost a superhuman task," he wrote to Eugenie in April. "I do not shun it, however. I want it and am pleased to be in charge. I hope I can do a good job." Eugenie sent encouragement and support in her replies, reminding Humphrey that this initiative was just the latest phase of his lifelong goals: "I often think of how fateful—and how right—were your decisions at the 1948 Philadelphia Convention. Once again, a most crucial point in your life— and in our country's history—is tied up with your leadership and of the Civil Rights struggle. Of course, I know that Presidential, and Vice-Presidential politics are the most hazardous in the world, but I have confidence that this time the right decisions will be made, and thus that you are now on the threshold of momentous times."[39]

A month later, Eugenie sent congratulations to Hubert on pushing the bill, after an agonizing seventy-five-day filibuster, through the Senate, creating into law the Civil Rights Act. Humphrey wrote to Eugenie: "This was a historic day for America. I was indeed honored to have had an opportunity to assist in securing passage of this measure which will help banish second-class citizenship from this land." Hubert was not the only Humphrey with whom Eugenie corresponded. She also exchanged letters with his wife, Muriel. After President Johnson extended the official invitation for Hubert to join him on the November ticket as the vice presidential candidate, a letter of Muriel's to Eugenie revealed some of the understanding between them: "You are so wonderful to write to me especially, Eugenie, and encourage me. What you have thought of me and what I do to help Hubert has meant a good deal. You know I don't have all the self-confidence in the world. I think there is one thing that you and I share—we look calm, at ease, and poised as though we could handle almost anything but underneath each of us has self-doubts. I look to you for strength many times and when you approve of what I am doing, I feel it is o.k."[40]

While Democrats blazed through the autumn of 1964 campaigning for Johnson and Humphrey, Anderson flew home for the month of October. Secretary of state Dean Rusk had informed Eugenie that ambassadors were discouraged from actively campaigning for any national candidates, so any work she did on behalf of Hubert Humphrey was put down to off-the-record socializing. Anderson's reputation in Washington was stellar. But even as more and more political insiders continued to take her seriously and on her own merits (rather than her being an exception as a woman), newspapers and writers persisted in focusing attention on the contradictions of her femininity. Neil Hurley, a business writer for

the magazine *International Commerce,* published an article titled
"Blue-Eyed and Faithful, the Minister's a Doll." In the piece, he
described his impressions of the legation in Sofia:

> There was hardly a picture to brighten a wall but a third-floor suite
> was as cheerful as a daiquiri, made so by its occupant, the Minister
> of the United States legation, Eugenie Anderson. . . . "Just do not
> mistake the natural warmth in her expression for tolerance," said
> an embassy official. "Those baby-blue eyes can turn icy as Siberian
> weather." . . . Mrs. Anderson is a lady in the fine sense . . . pretty as
> a magnolia in springtime Charleston. She serves at this austere out-
> post with faith as strong as the Marines. . . . Oftentimes femininity
> takes over. At a United States reception this week, she asked an aide
> to perform minor chores before guests arrived while she checked
> a main concern—the arrangement of canapes. Except for perhaps
> Mrs. Frances Willis, recently of Ceylon and Mrs. Kathryn White in
> Denmark, she is the only U.S. chief of mission in the world to put
> priority on the delicacies. . . . One evening the Minister, at a busi-
> ness reception, carefully coiffed and wearing a fashionable dress of
> green silk, stood before a standing, pushing crowd of 500, packed
> into a space small enough for a cloakroom. In Bulgarian first, then
> translating herself into English, she spoke of her hopes for friend-
> ship and trade. . . . An American stepped to the stand when the
> crowd dispersed. "Madame Minister," he said, "you are a doll." And
> she really is.

Still aware that she was best served by ignoring labels like *doll,*
dame, or *lady boss,* Eugenie felt the quips were getting old. In the
last month of her mission in Bulgaria, delivering yet another protest to the Bulgarian Foreign Ministry for some transgression or
another, Eugenie recalled—using that familiar code phrase for her
anger—"one rather amusing thing":

> Finally the deputy foreign minister, his name was Angelov, he was
> quite stern, he was an old Stalinist . . . he said in desperation, "Mrs.
> Anderson, I really don't like to be rough with you because you are a
> very charming lady. But after all, I cannot accept your protest." And
> I said, "Mr. Minister, I am not in your country because I am a lady.
> I am here making this protest as the American Minister and I insist

that you must accept it on behalf of my government." I was really furious to be told that he didn't like to do it because I was a charming lady! . . . When I said this, reminded him that I wasn't here as a lady, he was a little bit embarrassed. He didn't really quite know what to say, what to do. I think in the end I walked out and left the paper on the table.[41]

It would not be long before Eugenie could walk away for good. Johnson and Humphrey were indeed elected to the White House on November 3, 1964. While many diplomats carried over their missions since Johnson was continuing his own Democratic administration, several used the transition as an opportunity to resign. And while customarily chiefs of mission were expected to remain at their posts until after the inauguration and letters of resignation had been officially accepted and persons dismissed, Eugenie and John Anderson would not delay their departure any longer. Four hundred students gathered in front of the American legation on November 25, carrying signs protesting US aggression in the Congo; allegedly, the masses of students, who threw rocks and smashed the huge plate glass windows yet again, were mainly composed of African and Chinese Communist protesters. But it was clear that no matter who attacked the legation, or who was behind it, or how many times the Bulgarian government threw up its hands and offered meaningless superficial apologies, no channels of support existed (in Bulgaria or at the US State Department) that could improve the present situation even to the slightest degree. Minister Anderson submitted her letter of resignation to President Johnson and began packing. On December 8, 1964, the Andersons returned home.

After the ordeal in Bulgaria, Eugenie had barely caught up on her sleep before diving back into work. Within a few weeks, she was accepting speaking engagements. And before two months had passed, her name popped up frequently in both Minnesota and Washington rumors—everything from future runs for senator or governor to appointments as assistant to the secretary of state or other cabinet or diplomatic positions. The sixties were at the halfway point, but opportunities for women in politics were not yet improving. In fact, in each congressional session between 1965 and 1971, the House of Representatives lost a woman, lowering their number from thirteen to ten. Margaret Chase Smith of Maine remained the sole woman senator in the nation (she was first elected in 1949). There was, as yet, no discernible women's movement on the horizon. Betty Friedan's new, provocative book, *The Feminine Mystique*, was getting plenty of press and buzz, but most people still thought of it as the guilty secret that housewives in curlers were reading under the bedcovers while their husbands watched Gomer Pyle or *The Jack Benny Show* on the davenport with a scotch. A reviewer in *LIFE* magazine called the book "an angry, thoroughly documented book that in one way or another is going to provoke the daylights out of almost everyone who reads it."[42]

"Are women trapped?" asked Jean Libman Block, arguing with Friedan's premise. "Far from it. The chains are off and it's time to end this myth of misery." Block's dissent mirrored what one could imagine Eugenie Anderson thinking: "The great irony is that we gripe while women around the globe fight tooth and nail for the very freedoms of choice that are already ours. So let's put an end to lamentations, bury our self-pity and set about our task of each woman realizing her own potential as she sees best—in the office, the laboratory, the classroom, at the drawing board, at the controls of a jet or sitting serenely in her living room with dinner on the stove."[43]

Regardless of the success or derision of Friedan's book, it was capturing attention. And even though most American women were consuming it privately, turning the notions around in their own heads rather than discussing it over coffee in consciousness-raising groups (a movement that would not catch hold for another four or five years), at least the public was exposed to the possibility that maybe, just maybe, it was natural and acceptable for women to want, to need, and to pursue activity and employment outside the home. Plenty of women were already doing it; why not acknowledge that shedding the "mystique" and involving oneself in the workforce could provide—in addition to more financial benefit— just as much satisfactory intellectual, physical, and spiritual advantages as home and motherhood did?

Eugenie herself had always argued that women had special talents when it came to human relations (i.e., politics) because of their role throughout history as caretakers, facilitators, mediators, and keepers of social and cultural traditions. Did Eugenie read Friedan's controversial best seller when it first came out? *The Feminine Mystique*, though partially based on scientific study and inclusive of Freudian theories, was viewed by many as just another piece of popular culture, and hot topics were not generally given shelf or table space among the piles of government journals, newspaper clippings, serious biographies, fat histories, and dense philosophical tomes at Tower View. But the times, they were a-changing. Almost a decade before, college freshman Hans Anderson had asked his parents for classical Beethoven albums for Christmas. Now he admitted, "As you know, I like Beatles records and Bob Dylan songs."[44]

At the beginning of 1965, Eugenie was still committed to the Democratic Party. She had every intention of pursuing an influential position, relying on her basic tenet that participation in democracy should have nothing to do with gender. But she would cling to beliefs, methods, and words that were becoming outmoded—styles that had once set her apart as a young woman with fire and unique character, but now lumped her in with "the establishment" or the aging reputations of her champions, Hubert Humphrey and President Johnson. She worked in the decades between feminist movements—far too late for the suffragists; far ahead of the libbers and Friedan's NOW campaign.

Sit with the wives or the chiefs? No contest. Eugenie approached 1965 with a consistent agenda and a US vice president in her corner. She had paid her dues in Bulgaria: on to better things.

$\mathcal{S}ix$ HOLDING the LINE

*I wanted you to know that I have spoken to the President
and the Secretary of State about you . . . I have reason
to believe that you are going to be appointed as our
U.S. Ambassador to Canada if you want it.
We will keep at work on this.*

HUBERT H. HUMPHREY, DECEMBER 23, 1964

$\mathcal{U}$PON RETURN FROM BULGARIA, EVEN BEFORE CELE-brating the Christmas holidays, Eugenie had the communication of her ambitions well in hand. She wanted Canada, and many believed that she was the perfect diplomat to serve as liaison between the two North American countries. There were many possible hindrances to Anderson achieving the prestigious Canadian post, but in the end, her sterling reputation as a cool-headed chief of mission with great potential in the future of the State Department was undermined by the fickle temper of the president. "Lyndon Johnson had a low boiling point, particularly for leaks that accurately predicted what he was about to do," wrote Tom Wicker in a 1982 article for the *New York Times*. Johnson "was known to cancel . . . nominations to high office when word about them got out before he or his press secretary could make an official announcement."[1]

Democrats closest to Eugenie—Hubert Humphrey and India Edwards (who still kept her insider sources active)—tried to keep a tightly sealed lid on the impending announcement. "No leaks so far as I know about you," wrote India in mid-March. But two weeks later, *Newsweek* magazine published the following on its "Periscope" page of government news: "Capitol Hill: Eugenie Moore Anderson, who recently resigned as minister to Bulgaria, has her eye on the U.S Embassy in Canada. With strong backing from her fellow Minnesotan Hubert Humphrey, Mrs. Anderson will probably get her wish if a suitable slot can be found for career diplomat W. Walton Butterworth, now our man in Ottawa." Eugenie wrote to Max Kampelman: "I have the impression that quite a bit of intervention may be required . . . the insidious NEWSWEEK leak has disturbed me to no end. . . . I can only hope that it will not ruin everything."[2]

It did ruin everything. India Edwards discovered that Canadian Ambassador Butterworth's son, who worked for the Department of Commerce, had been circulating rumors for weeks around Washington that Eugenie was a certain interloper for his father's post. The whispers led to an anonymous leak, triggering Johnson to slam on the brakes and put an end to Eugenie's hopes for this promotion. While talk remained that Butterworth might still be transferred out of Ottawa, ultimately he remained chief of mission there until 1968.[3]

Meanwhile in that spring of 1965, Johnson, Humphrey, and the entire country were absorbed in wars on two fronts: the escalation of US and Soviet aggressions in Vietnam, and stateside chaos following the Civil Rights Act of 1964. On March 2, President Johnson approved and launched Operation Rolling Thunder, a bombing raid on North Vietnam that was meant to last eight weeks but essentially continued for the next three years. And on March 25, Rev. Martin Luther King Jr. completed a grueling march from Selma, Alabama, walking up the steps of the state capitol in Montgomery, achieving historic triumph for nonviolent protest following several months of criminal racist backlash to the Civil Rights Act in the South. A month later, on April 17, young people and civil rights activists took Rev. King's philosophy and message and applied them to global issues, marching on Washington to protest the Vietnam

War. Among the cosponsors of the march were members of Women Strike for Peace. Women did not yet have a nationally recognized movement of their own, but they were deeply involved in civil rights, pacifism, and other highly visible activities. A cofounder of Women Strike for Peace, Bella Abzug, would later join Betty Friedan, Shirley Chisholm, and Gloria Steinem to found the National Women's Political Caucus in 1971.

The Johnson-Humphrey administration appeared to be genuinely supportive of promoting women, their political involvement, and their interests. However, India Edwards heard through the grapevine that Johnson's true motives were suspect, and she relayed to Eugenie: "A friend of mine heard . . . at a recent dinner party that the appointment of so many women by LBJ was purely a political move, which saddened me for I really thought we had a President who believed in women; and their ability." Johnson received much praise for his appointment of the first African American woman to an embassy: on May 20, the White House announced the selection of Patricia Roberts Harris as ambassador to Luxembourg. In a congratulatory letter to Harris, Eugenie Anderson wrote: "I trust that you will find your new assignment as fascinating and satisfying as I felt that my two diplomatic posts were. While a woman ambassador does have a more complex life, I did not feel that it was a disadvantage to be a woman diplomat. I hope that you will have the same positive experience."[4]

The same day as Harris's appointment, Eugenie's daughter, Johanna, sat down to write her mother a letter. In it, she reported: "Currently reading The Feminine Mystique by Betty Friedan. Have you read it Mother? I think it is excellent & am really enjoying it—of course not everyone has fallen prey to these social pressures & influence but she has a lot of evidence & has woven it into quite a convincing thesis." Perhaps Eugenie did peruse the book upon the advice of her daughter, a person whose opinion she trusted much more than unknown book reviewers or critics with their own political agendas. In any case, Eugenie, in typical fashion, continued to look forward rather than back. She did not consider herself one of those postwar women duped into the feminine mystique (those who had "fallen prey" to the syndrome labeled by Friedan, nor those who were acolytes of the book by that name). She did consider herself a seasoned, valuable contributor to foreign affairs, particularly as the Vietnam arena was heating up so quickly, and American representatives were needed who had experience dealing with inscrutable Communists.[5]

An unexpected event changed the direction of Anderson's potential usefulness. Adlai Stevenson, cornerstone of the Democratic Party and current head of the US delegation to the United Nations, died of a heart attack in London on July 14, 1965. The vacancy left by Stevenson was of critical importance based primarily on the war in Vietnam and its complex international impact. Replacing Stevenson was an extremely important and delicate choice. Lyndon Johnson, looking for a ringer, shocked everyone by convincing a Supreme Court justice to fill the role, naming Arthur Goldberg to the job six days after Stevenson's sudden death. On August 26, the *New York Times* announced the Goldberg team in a list that "named a career diplomat [Charles W. Yost], a Negro educator [James Madison Nabrit Jr.], a former woman politician [Eugenie Anderson] and a Roosevelt [FDR and Eleanor's son James] to serve under Arthur J. Goldberg, United States Representative to the United Nations." Part of the new delegation's mission was to reinfuse Congress with a stronger opinion of the United Nations' effectiveness, in addition to bolstering the United States' reputation within the United Nations itself.

Doris Fleeson, nationally syndicated (and previously mentioned) political columnist, leapt to the defense of the displaced UN team headed by the late Adlai Stevenson and ousted by Goldberg and President Johnson, delegates whom she believed "deserved much more than the cold abruptness of the change." Eugenie was replacing Mrs. Marietta Tree, a very well-liked personality in the Democratic Party. Perhaps it was Fleeson's resentment on behalf of Mrs.

Tree, but the rather condescending summation of Eugenie's credentials went against the columnist's usual championing of women politicians: "Mrs. Eugenie Anderson of Minnesota is a veteran of its activist politics and a former ambassador. Her like is to be found, though perhaps she is more simply dressed, in the good works sector of every American town and city. She is an articulate and sensible expert in the soft sell." Likening Ambassador Anderson to a volunteer socialite was a low blow. The complexity and challenges of Eugenie's international work—both past and present—deserved much better consideration, especially by other women.[6]

Ann Geracimos of the *New York Herald Tribune* provided a much more affirmative portrayal: "If Eugenie Anderson didn't exist, a horde of feminists would have to invent her. If a musical were made out of her, she could probably play all the roles. The new U.S. Representative [to the United Nations] . . . is one of those women that men are never quite ready to believe in. She's got it all—the home, the hobbies, the family, the career, the charm, the brains—direct from the Minnesota heartland. Housewife From Red Wing Makes Good. And she says she couldn't have done it without her husband."[7]

The grueling two and a half years in Bulgaria—a political appointment that Eugenie had deemed necessary and part of a larger chain of work—had taken a harsh toll on John's overall health. The Andersons had been together for so long that even if certain periods of time or geography were particularly hard on them, they had come to expect, as a team, that challenge and compromise and occasional "agreeing-to-disagree" were always going to be part of their marriage. John had settled back into Tower View, not magically nor quickly recovered from the ordeal of Eastern Europe, but no doubt relieved and comforted to be home. Family letters indicated that he was contemplating new avenues for his painting and drawing. John and Charles Biederman even buried the hatchet long enough for John to assist with the arrangements for Charles's exhibit, titled "The Structurist Relief, 1935-1964," at the Walker

Ambassador Anderson on a New York street between her apartment at 25 Sutton Place and the United Nations Plaza near the East River in Manhattan, 1966. *Photo by John P. Anderson, Anderson family collection.*

Art Center in Minneapolis in March 1965. The brief detente fizzled soon after, but Eugenie and Mary were always grateful when the two men managed to communicate, much less collaborate, to any degree. When Eugenie accepted the appointment to the United Nations delegation in August 1965, the job required her to keep a residence in New York City. She sublet a small apartment in Manhattan on Sutton Place near the UN building, but it was several months before John came to visit her, and even then, he continued to live primarily in Minnesota. John and Eugenie kept their domestic decisions and itineraries quite private; even their children were not always sure whether John was in New York or Red Wing from month to month.

There was also a widening chasm of opinion between Eugenie and Hans and Johanna and their spouses concerning the Vietnam War. "The Viet Nam situation seems to be growing . . . into a horrible malignant cancer," wrote Hans to his parents in the summer

of '65. The differences of attitude between younger and older generations of the Anderson family typified what was rippling across
America and creating serious rifts, socially and politically. At the
time when the first draft card was burned in protest on October
15, 1965, Hans was in the middle of his residency in psychiatry in
Rochester, New York. He had already deferred one draft notice in
1964; it was only a matter of time before the draft board called him
up again for his value as a medical doctor, whether or not he was a
sole breadwinner or father of two (soon to be three) young children.
"We came to completely an anti-war stance," Margaret Anderson
recalled, "but the only options for our family were to flee to Canada or for Hans to go to prison, neither of which we could do or
would do. So it was very conflicting." Hans agreed: "It was awful. . . .
We used to argue with my parents, who at that time were still very
much in line with the administration . . . and the people who were
running the war. And they thought it was a necessary evil, to fight
the Communists."[8]

Eugenie Anderson was very much in line with the Johnson
administration's position on Vietnam. While there were endless
discussions with friends and colleagues over the ethics and repercussions, intricacies and results of every government decision and
every day of fighting that went by, ultimately Eugenie stood by her
support of the president and her belief in the aggressive program
that the United States continued in Southeast Asia. Both Eugenie
and her friend Vice President Humphrey each had their own work,
political maneuvering, and internal grapplings to do—over myriad issues in the rapidly changing world of the 1960s, conflict over
Vietnam being the most prominent and symbolic of those changes.
Humphrey would come to a "softening" on Vietnam policy sooner
than Anderson. In the meantime, even while Eugenie held onto her
hard-line stance supporting efforts against any global expansion of
Communism, it was not long before she was disillusioned with the
means by which she, individually, could help those efforts. In other
words, she realized that the United Nations—so glorious in theory

as an observer—was far more complicated from the inside: "My post at the United Nations, of course, was very different than any that I had had before and in many ways it was very fascinating, very educational. . . . It was during the period of the Vietnam War, the escalation of the war, and I must say that in spite of the efforts of Ambassador Goldberg to get this in the United Nations and to deal with it there, he was never able to do this."[9]

On January 16, 1966, the *New York Times* featured Eugenie in an article about her work with the United Nations: "U.S. 'Woman's Voice' at the U.N. Has Faintly Midwestern Accent." The piece outlined Eugenie's strides in her career, as well as progress for all women over the last few years. "Her rank is that of Ambassador, which was not accorded to most of her predecessors. Her main area of concentration is in colonialism and trusteeship matters. Women members of the United States delegation have been largely restricted to the field of human rights and social welfare." After a brief overview of current work and past assignments in Denmark and Bulgaria, the article presented Eugenie's objection to her earlier press image: "Although amused, she is still troubled by the Anderson 'image' that was created of an aproned Minnesota housewife going off to do battle with hostile Bulgarian officials. She feels the image was distorted, and came from a widely publicized photograph showing her answering a rural, old-fashioned telephone in her Minnesota kitchen. 'It is true I love to cook,' she commented. 'I like my home and enjoy entertaining—though not all the housekeeping details.' But she objected to the implication in the image that she was a political innocent."[10]

Eugenie—together with the world's most prestigious newspaper—was acknowledging the same distorted image that Friedan and other up-and-coming feminist activists were discussing. Not all women were happy housewives. Not all women needed the same social constructs for security or inspiration. Not all women were naïve, politically or fundamentally, regardless of how they dressed or how the media portrayed them.

US Delegate Anderson sits at the UN General Assembly in alphabetical order next to Upper Volta, 1966. *Anderson family collection.*

Assigned to the ambassadorship in charge of the Trusteeship Council and issues of colonialism, Eugenie took up the tasks of studying the current state of US trust territories, reporting her findings to both the United Nations and the US Department of the Interior, and making recommendations for ongoing relationships and maintenance of the areas under trusteeship. It proved to be a frustrating, and ultimately fruitless, task: "It was even more difficult to affect U.S. policy in relation to the trust territory because this was considered a very low priority in terms of U.S. policy and interest. I found this rather incomprehensible in view of the rather rapidly escalating war in Vietnam."[11]

The only possible way to gather real facts and present practical means for assisting the trust territories was to visit them. In November 1965, Eugenie was invited by the Congressional Committee on Interior and Insular Affairs to join their tour of Micronesia and other Pacific islands. Accompanied by John, Eugenie, with several members of Congress and directors and commissioners of various territories, spent three weeks touring islands on boats and planes of all sorts and sizes. Eugenie recalled: "The tragedy was, we felt, that [the islands] had not developed much since the Second World War. . . . I had learned a great deal about the neglect of those islands, what their essential needs were, what the dangers for the future would be if the United States did not listen to the people, did not really help them to develop. But I also felt it was going to be very difficult to get anyone's attention. However I was determined to try."[12]

After the holidays, Eugenie submitted her report to the White House. Its response came from Hubert Humphrey: "I brought to the attention of the President your report. He is impressed and grateful. Right now I simply can't get you in to see him. He is just too deeply involved in decisions relating to Vietnam. He has asked, therefore, that I work closely with you and with Secretary Rusk and Ambassador Goldberg. I have a feeling that he will accept the recommendations that the four of us make."[13]

"I tried to see the Secretary of State," Eugenie recalled. "I tried to see the President. I was unable to see either of them, presumably they were at that time already so involved with Vietnam that almost nothing else could get their attention." One of Eugenie's top recommendations, based on her observance of widespread hazardous sanitary conditions throughout the islands, was to appeal to the Peace Corps for assistance. This initiative made its way through Washington channels. "In less than a year after I had gone there," Eugenie recalled, "there was a group of 500 Peace Corps volunteers in Micronesia and within the next six months, I believe, about 300 more were sent. This was the largest single group of Peace Corps volunteers in any place in the world excepting India."[14]

In addition to representing the United States on the Trusteeship Council, Eugenie also served on a subgroup called the Fourth Committee for Colonial Issues, which dealt with countries and territories that extended beyond those with trusteeship status, still fell under a colonial status, or were not yet independent. Most of these small countries were in Africa or the Caribbean and had political ties to Great Britain, France, Australia, the Soviet Union, or the United States. "We [the US] didn't win many issues," Eugenie stated. "We were not only always on the defensive but always in the minority. . . . This was a propaganda committee for the most radical African groups, states, and for the Soviet Union and some of its satellites. I found these meetings just intolerably frustrating because we really had to listen to a great deal of attack on us."[15]

In the spring of 1966, Eugenie and John packed their bags and joined a large UN junket to Africa. International members of the Committee of 24—including staff and secretaries, composing a group of almost ninety people—toured Tanzania, Somalia, Ethiopia, Egypt (Cairo/UAR), and Algiers. "[We] were in sessions most of the time; it was no sightseeing trip," Eugenie said.

> We had meetings, somewhat more stormy meetings than in [New York]. I suppose for propaganda purposes the African countries, especially the very militant ones, stepped up their attacks on the

United States in most of the countries which we visited, and also the Soviet Union and other countries did. Once again, I felt that our position was much too conservative and too backward, and I felt that we were mostly in a defensive position, which is always a weak position.

I might say I was losing most of my illusions about the United Nations by this time. . . . One couldn't be there very long without understanding what an intensely political organization it is and without realizing how limited its real powers are. . . . I really didn't expect very much good to come of this trip to Africa.[16]

The African tour was intensive and exhausting, intellectually and physically. But immediately upon return, after a quick respite in Minnesota, Eugenie hurried back to New York for the opening of the Trusteeship Council sessions. She was also given the temporary promotion, during the vacation absence of all four of the other US delegates (including Arthur Goldberg), of heading the entire US permanent delegation and serving on the Security Council. On July 14, UN secretary-general U Thant was notified that Ambassador Anderson was appointed as an alternate to the Security Council, the first American woman to be so named.[17]

When President Johnson announced the new appointments for the twenty-first session of the UN General Assembly in September 1966, Arthur Goldberg's team increased to a total of ten members. Eugenie remained the only woman on the delegation. Only four women in the United States held chief of mission posts for the State Department in 1966, but President Johnson seemed to view this minuscule number as a triumph: "The Administration," he said, "is not running a stag party."[18]

Johnson's administration may have started to open a door or two for women, but that didn't mean the climate inside the clubhouse was any more favorable. In his memoir *The Good Fight*, Walter Mondale reminisced about his time as a freshman senator during the early days of Johnson's presidency. He made note of Hubert Humphrey, his mentor, advising him to seek out as much connection as he could to senate seniority, on the floor and off: "One of the best places to build these relationships was a little office just off the Senate floor known at that time as 'Mansfield's hideaway.' . . . The office was popular as a place where senators could relax between floor votes, make phone calls, or rest up if we were headed for a midnight session. . . . Sometimes, after hours, you would just have a drink and swap jokes. [It] always seemed to have a supply of excellent bourbon. . . . Whatever the tone, you could get to know other senators personally and build friendships that transcended politics."[19]

When I met with Mr. Mondale in September 2017, I asked him about Mansfield's hideaway, curious to know if he remembered any women who might have been admitted. After he qualified that "there weren't even restrooms for women in those days," I asked, based on a hypothetical situation, if Eugenie had been in the Senate at the time, whether she might have gotten inside. "The hideaway?" he pondered, "I would bet *yes*. But I don't know. If they liked her." Then he smiled and asked, "Would *she* like to go to the hideaway?" I didn't have to think about it. "Oh yes," I answered. "She would have." Mr. Mondale chuckled and said, "It was a highly distinguished group."[20]

While Mondale learned the ropes in Congress, Humphrey was quickly disabused of any hopes he might have had for a positive, collaborative partnership with President Johnson. Women were not the only creatures LBJ chewed up and spit out. Less than a year after pushing the Civil Rights Bill into law, Humphrey was kicked off the implementation of its programs: Johnson gave the whole thing to Senator Robert Kennedy. White House aide Joseph Califano recalled the meeting when the president stripped Humphrey of the program leadership for which Humphrey had fought his entire career. "Like all of us in the Oval Office at that moment," Califano wrote, "[Humphrey] knew he'd just been castrated."[21]

Humphrey also had a long and well-documented battle of conscience over his position on Vietnam policies, both as vice president (and obligatory adherent to President Johnson's stance) and on his own as a presidential candidate later in 1968. In the fall of 1966, Eugenie remained an outspoken advocate of following Johnson's directives, but she also had her ear to the ground and recognized that many of her old Democratic friends and colleagues, Hubert Humphrey included, were diverging greatly in their trust and philosophies. Humphrey's letters to Eugenie were short, terse, and filled with frustration. "My life gets so complicated that I seldom know just what's happening," Humphrey wrote. "We have had some busy days which only a private conversation can explain. . . . I am very anxious to see you and deeply regret that our appointments have not worked out. Frankly, I'm mad as hell." Hubert and Eugenie continued to look to each other as friends and allies as they became older and more buffeted by the same winds of change.[22]

Time surged forward into 1967. "We are going back to the President on Canada," wrote Humphrey to Eugenie, after he had appealed for assistance from under secretary of state Nicholas Katzenbach, attempting to move Eugenie into that ambassadorship. In the end, Johnson's attention could not be obtained, nor could Butterworth be pried away from Ottawa. Eugenie herself was absorbed in work for the United Nations on multiple fronts. And throughout it all, she persevered with her perennial credo on gender: "The most important consideration in my work has been to approach it not as a woman, but as a human being," read the caption by her photo in the news on February 15, 1967.[23]

Besides devoting the majority of her time to committee work at the United Nations, Eugenie also accepted speaking engagements around the country, at which she was often required, beyond explaining current world affairs and conflicts, to justify the role of the United Nations and its reputation, which flickered between negative and, worse, invisible. Eugenie's high-profile status was a good media draw for lectures and keynote speeches, but she continued to see a split in her publicity between the hard news pages and the lightweight "women's" sections. One article about Eugenie's appearance at an Akron, Ohio, Jewish Center for its Women's Day event labeled the room a "hen party," and in spite of some good commentary and substantial overview of Anderson's information regarding the United Nations, headlined the piece with a misleading quote: "People Just Expect Too Much." Adjacent on the page ran the prominent headline: "In Doubt About Makeup? Ask Your Husband, Expert Advises."[24]

Some women were beginning to organize—against the dualities, against the contradictions, against the glass ceilings, against the inequalities. They had a long road ahead of them. "The shrill voice of the feminist movement is being heard across the land," reported the *St. Louis Post-Dispatch* on March 2, 1967: "The voluble Mrs. Betty Friedan, author of 'The Feminine Mystique' and mother of three, has organized something called NOW, which stands for National Organization for Women." Arvonne Fraser, veteran DFL organizer and wife of congressman Don Fraser, had started the low-profile Democratic Women's Forum (DWF) in Washington a full decade before the national establishment of NOW. Only in the late 1960s were the long years of quiet meetings coming to fruition toward mass movement and nationwide involvement. Arvonne, determined to work and be heard in Washington beyond the role of behind-the-scenes hostess for her husband, looked into the Washington, DC, chapter of Friedan's brainchild NOW and discovered, to her dismay, more talk than action. She also knew that "while the civil rights movement was treated with respect, at least by the liberals, the new women's movement was the butt of jokes."[25]

While organizers like Friedan and Fraser were attempting to spark the second mass women's movement of the twentieth century (fifty years after the first), marches and protests against the Vietnam War were growing larger and more compelling, and Humphrey's difficulties more confounding. The cover of *TIME* magazine on May 5, 1967, depicted General William Westmoreland saluting a joint session of Congress with Hubert Humphrey applauding behind him. Two weeks later, the US Navy drafted Dr. Hans Anderson into service. Under the Berry Plan for medical doctors, which had allowed him to defer his enlistment for three years while he completed an internship and partial residency training, Hans did manage to avoid being sent in-country to Vietnam. He reported instead, with Margaret and their three children (including a four-week-old newborn), to the Great Lakes naval base in Illinois, where he would serve in its hospital for the next two years as a psychiatrist. "I saw so much damage that was done in Vietnam," Hans recalled. "And also, damage that was done to kids in boot camp, who had no idea what they were getting into. . . . And they were psychologically so damaged that they couldn't even talk about it." Margaret Anderson, herself submerged in the night-and-day care of a newborn and two little ones, recalled the stress between generations when John and Eugenie would come to visit: "They were visiting Great Lakes when Hans was in the Navy. And we were voicing our opposition to the war. . . . And Eugenie said to me, 'Margaret, would you want Hans on the front lines with*out* the protection of the bombing?' It was really difficult; I had to leave the table and go to the kitchen. And Hans came after me and tried to calm me down."[26]

Like so many others around the nation during the Vietnam War, the Andersons could not keep fundamental moral beliefs out of their politics, and it brought the conflicts to the family table. In Washington, Hubert Humphrey persisted in consulting friends with controversial views at his table, too. Solberg described the vice president's situation in the spring of 1967:

> The old liberal who loved late-night bull sessions was even getting harder to talk to. . . . He turned the evening into one long monologue on the Johnson line. . . . In a wrangle about the Vietnam bombing, he said, you had to listen to the generals. . . . Late at night, after the tension had subsided somewhat, Humphrey dropped the only remark that even faintly suggested he might not go all the way with LBJ. Several times he referred to Vietnam as a "morass." Later he asked

those at the table whether the United States should stop bombing, and when all said yes, he said very quietly, "On balance, I think you are right. But the President's advisers don't agree."[27]

Hubert had begun to admit privately that he was torn. Eugenie remained firm. Determined to hold the line in principle against the Soviet infiltration of North Vietnam, as she did with all Communist aggression, Eugenie found herself in meetings over another globally threatening crisis when the Soviet-influenced Arab Republic and US-backed Israel went to war on June 5, 1967. Returning from a visit to the Midwest, she missed the first meeting at the UN Security Council: "I was later sorry that I had taken my vacation at all that year because soon after I left the issue of the beginning intensification of the conflict between Syria and Israel came before the Security Council and I missed that." The Six-Day War, as it came to be known, began when Israel launched a preemptive strike against its Arab neighbors. After the United States readied a deployment of naval carrier battleships, Soviet prime minister Alexei Kosygin, having received the intelligence that the US action was offensive in nature, activated the hotline to the president in Washington for the first time since the Cuban Missile Crisis of 1962. Nuclear war was avoided when both the Soviets and the Americans ultimately abstained from sending in ships. But the violence in the Middle East had far-reaching consequences, which, in effect, are still with us today. At the time, Eugenie strongly supported the defense of Israel. But she also recognized the crucial need for immediate peacekeeping. "There was still some hope that the United Nations might be able to do something," she stated four years later in 1971: "I was there all during that summer and again in the fall when the United States was trying to get a resolution in the Security Council that all sides would agree to as a fundamental framework for a peaceful settlement of the Arab-Israeli conflict. . . . They were finally able to hammer out an agreement on a statement of principles . . . to serve as a settlement of the conflict. But of course, now it's four years later and there still is no real progress toward an implementation of those principles."[28]

Eugenie also revealed years later that before the crisis of the Six-Day War, she had been in consideration to be appointed the ambassador to Israel. Admitting to frustration with the essential inability of the United Nations to *act*—in any practical sense—on its resolutions, Anderson let it be known that she was interested in a more influential assignment. Ambassador Butterworth still had an ambiguous reputation but could not be budged from Canada. Similarly, Ambassador Walworth Barbour in Israel, a career Foreign Service officer entrenched in Tel Aviv, was not universally liked. On Eugenie's behalf, Arthur Goldberg and Hubert Humphrey spoke to President Johnson and secretaries Dean Rusk and Nicholas Katzenbach. "It was apparently decided that the most likely and best assignment for me would be Israel. . . . It was, I would say, close to the final stages of being approved when the crisis, the Arab-Israeli crisis really heated up. Then, of course, it was quite clear that it would be a mistake to change ambassadors." The matter was shelved and not revisited again.[29]

During the summer, while Eugenie attended UN sessions in New York, Hubert Humphrey sat in on all the meetings at the White House to cope with the Israeli crisis. At the end of June, Humphrey stood in for President Johnson and flew to Korea with a US delegation to attend the inauguration of the new president, Park Chung-hee. This last-minute assignment meant that he had to back out of several engagements, including a Fourth of July speech in Philadelphia. Hubert asked Eugenie to substitute for him there.

Eugenie Anderson gave the address for the city's Freedom Day ceremonies in front of the old Liberty Bell statehouse in Philadelphia. The Associated Press reported that Anderson "told a crowd of 5,000 at historic Independence Hall that every country in the world is 'entitled to the same rights as we claim for ourselves. . . . In both the middle east and in southeast Asia, we seek an end to the fighting and a peaceful solution.'" As she spoke, police kept three hundred anti-war demonstrators separate from the rest of the crowd. They held up "Vietnam Veterans Against the War" placards and chanted slogans like "Futile Death." One small group, pushed farther behind a barricade, waved a Viet Cong banner.[30]

Political protests, racial unrest, and chaos only increased over the summer. Urban riots in Newark, New Jersey, and Detroit, Michigan, kept Humphrey on the move as Johnson's liaison to the cities' mayors. As Carl Solberg noted: "The president never made the recommended appeal for racial reconciliation. Faced with the immense cost of the war and stiff resistance in Congress, he hunkered down in the White House through that 1967 summer of America's most violent urban storms." The rioting eventually quieted down, but student protests of the Vietnam War continued. President Johnson's approval ratings, already shaky, plummeted as voters watched coverage of the bloody war on their television sets every night. "As one who lived by the polls, Johnson grew obsessed with the problem of how to 'get it across to the people we're making progress.'"[31]

One of Johnson's tactics was to employ voices of nonmilitary public figures, sending proponents to Vietnam in order for them to return with glowing testimonials to the press of the good work being done. These voices could help assure the confused public that, yes, the Americans were needed, they were making a difference to the innocents abroad, and they would prevail against the evil Communists. Eugenie Anderson agreed to be one of those voices.

Intending to resign from the UN delegation, in November 1967 Eugenie met with President Johnson in the Oval Office. As the meeting concluded, the possibility of a study tour to Vietnam was introduced. Johnson called a special assistant on the spot and gave orders that Eugenie's name should be put on a list with Secretary of Defense Robert McNamara, and that the next time a group was organized, she would be on the plane. Eugenie left the meeting with the assumption that a trip might materialize in four or five months—if at all. By that same evening, the White House called to confirm that she was invited to join a tour headed by Ellsworth Bunker, ambassador to South Vietnam, and they would be leaving in a week's time. Eugenie prudently said no, she couldn't possibly be ready, and hung up the phone. But it was less than an hour before she reevaluated the window of opportunity, called back to accept, and booked a flight home to Minnesota, where she could pick up summer clothes, get a broad spectrum of shots, and celebrate a hasty Thanksgiving with her family.

"I'll have to say my husband was not very happy about it," Eugenie recalled. "He didn't think . . . my going to a war zone was a very good idea." When the interviewer asked, "Were you nervous about it?" Eugenie didn't miss a beat before replying, "No, not a bit." If the president and the secretary of defense thought it was safe, that was good enough for her.[32]

Two other women joined Eugenie on the trip. Anna Lord Strauss, age sixty-eight and a suffrage-era feminist, was a former president of the League of Women Voters and former US delegate to the United Nations. Dorothy Buffum Chandler was an executive of the *Los Angeles Times*; her husband, Norman, was its publisher. Both women, like Eugenie, had key ties to the media and would receive extra inches in reporters' columns when they returned from the war zone, based on their feminine bravery and initiative. Bunker's party made it as far as Yokota air base in Japan on a US Air Force Boeing 707. After fueling up, and ten minutes after taking off on the last leg of the journey, one of the starboard engines burst into flames, and they were forced to turn around for an emergency landing. A C-141 cargo jet was fitted out with seats, into which the passengers were loaded for the final flight to Saigon. They arrived only four hours late.

The guests were hosted by the embassy in Saigon and escorted to various diplomatic functions by Ambassador Bunker, deputy ambassador Eugene Murphy Locke, and Civil Operations and Revolutionary Development Support director Robert W. Komer. (Other descriptions refer to Komer as the special assistant to the president in charge of pacification in Vietnam.) They were also scheduled to fly to a number of locations by helicopter, accompanied on some of the trips by General William Westmoreland, to inspect the great progress that the South Vietnamese were accomplishing with the political and military support of the United States. A correspondent for the *New York Times* interviewed the group when they first landed in Saigon. Ambassador Bunker said: "'I hope when [the ladies] return they will report what they have seen here and will have a greater understanding what our objectives are. . . . I promise not to brainwash them,' Mr. Bunker added with a smile."

The *Minneapolis Tribune* reported that "Mrs. Anderson and her companions have covered the country from one end to the other—concentrating on visits to hospitals, schools, refugee centers, and especially to some of the 'revolutionary development' projects in Vietnamese villages. Such aspects of the Vietnam situation, [Anderson] said, 'have not been as well reported or as fully understood as the military side' because of a natural focus on the American combat troops here." Eugenie mentioned nothing of danger, risk, or negative impressions. Her primary comment was, "If people at home could know how other Americans are involved and committed here it would give them a greater feeling of involvement. We should be so proud of our people here."[33]

After eight days in Vietnam, Eugenie traveled back to Washington and drafted a succinct report for President Johnson on the "evidence of progress and new hope among the people" of South Vietnam. She stressed particular emphasis that the government should give "a much greater sense of urgency and priority" to the growing refugee population. Anderson was able to submit her report to President Johnson personally, meeting with him on December 8. "It was the day before his daughter Linda's wedding," she recalled, "so there was more excitement around the White House. . . . But he was very interested in my observations. . . . As I left that day he told me that he hoped I would reconsider my resignation and that he would be in touch with me later."[34]

UN Ambassador Anderson presents the report of her Vietnam study tour to President Lyndon B. Johnson in the Oval Office. Eugenie had returned home from Vietnam on December 6, 1967; her sister Ruth Stanley died unexpectedly on December 7; Anderson kept her appointment with the president on December 8 as he finished official business before his daughter's White House wedding on December 9. *Anderson family collection.*

Eugenie did not follow up on the conversation immediately, because her oldest sister, Ruth Moore Stanley, had died only the day before, on December 7. Much of December was occupied with family visits, arrangements, reconnecting, and deep mourning. At the same time, Eugenie was planning to move out of the New York apartment on Sutton Place and ship of all her belongings and files back to Tower View in Red Wing. She was not aware that her resignation letter had never gone through the official channels for acceptance—and that, in effect, she had not been formally dismissed from the UN delegation.

*   *   *

*In the years since 1968 I've spent a lot of time thinking
about the legacy of Vietnam. From time to time this country
goes through a period when, as a people, it changes its
mind about something big. I believe that's what we were watching
in 1968. The country went into that year supporting the war
and came out opposing it. Yet, as a party, we just
couldn't manage the break with our past.*

WALTER MONDALE, 2010

For Eugenie, 1968 would prove to be as pivotal as 1948 and 1958 had been. Each decade marker had brought her political career full circle. In 1948, she backed President Truman and helped attach his name to Hubert Humphrey's historic civil rights speech at the Democratic convention. In 1958, she put her own name in for Senate consideration and lost to Eugene McCarthy. At the beginning of 1968, she fully supported President Johnson; by year's end, she would witness the presidential loss of Hubert Humphrey to Richard M. Nixon, a loss hinging in part on Eugene McCarthy's failure to support Humphrey. The dizzying unspooling of many tragic events throughout 1968 changed all Americans' lives. And they substantively changed—and contributed in ending—Eugenie Anderson's career. Dan Cohen wrote in *Undefeated: The Life of Hubert H. Humphrey*: "The presidential year of 1968 began on an ominous note, setting the tone for a period that would bring the nation closer to anarchy than at any time since the Civil War. Assassinations, resignations, campus revolts at Berkeley and Columbia, rioting in the ghettos, rioting in the streets of Chicago, all would follow the first grim surprise—the Tet Offensive."[35]

As the year began, Eugenie could never have known, of course, what lay ahead. In January, she gave interviews to the press about her recent tour in Vietnam, in part to strengthen Johnson's public image as a reformer of civil rights and building efforts there. "We Just Have to Persist," Eugenie was quoted in a headline. She told one reporter: "As far as Vietnam is concerned, we should be there. We have to be there, the issues are quite clear. . . . The United States is the only country in the world capable of resisting Communist expansion and aggression." In March, Eugenie accepted a position as special assistant to secretary of state Dean Rusk, and she also continued accepting speaking engagements. After the Viet Cong Tet Offensive began, and four thousand American soldiers were killed between February and March 1968, Anderson's public comments began to change subtly. She gave a talk to college students in Winona, Minnesota, on March 25, 1968, and while the press titled it "Eugenie Anderson Defends Nation's Role in Vietnam," the content revealed both cracks in Anderson's arguments and resolve and rising hostility in her audience's reaction: "Mrs. Anderson had criticized the terrorism of the Viet Cong, including assassination and kidnapping of village leaders. A student asked if our use of napalm and destruction of villages did not also constitute terrorism. She replied that the American press—she singled out television for special attention—shows only what American forces do, not what the Viet Cong do. 'People have gotten a distorted picture . . . I don't think any war is humane. Every war is a failure of human relations, diplomatic relations.' She concluded, 'What alternatives do you have?'"[36]

Opinions differed widely in the Democratic Party, from hardline stances on continuing the war (Johnson hawks) to waging peace (McCarthy doves). Speculation over the Democratic ticket for the presidential election of 1968 hinged, of course, on whether or not Lyndon Johnson would seek another term. "You never knew when

LBJ had made a decision or what it was until he revealed it," wrote Joseph Califano. "The address on March 31 stunned the nation. Its ending caught most of the White House staff and cabinet by surprise." Only Johnson's family, Hubert Humphrey, and "a handful of others" knew what the president would announce: "I shall not seek—and will not accept—the nomination of my party for another term as your President." Johnson's unexpected withdrawal from the race sent Eugene McCarthy and Robert Kennedy, who had already launched their own campaigns, into frenzied reformulations of their support, delegates, and poll numbers. Hubert Humphrey faced the biggest challenge of all of them: approaching a campaign in which he *must* be seen as a powerful individual worthy of the presidency, while still fulfilling his duties as a vice president entirely in line with the current administration. Solberg wrote that initially, "for all his loyal service, Humphrey got no invitation to run in Johnson's place, and certainly no pledge of support." Just as Humphrey had felt compelled to claim neutrality (and refrained from choosing a favorite) when Eugenie Anderson and Eugene McCarthy had vied for a Senate seat in 1958, now Hubert was the victim of *his* superior's rationalized withholding. LBJ had told the nation that the presidency needed to rise above the partisan fighting that was dragging the country down and threatening its very existence, that the presidency must rise above divisiveness within his own party, acting and speaking only for unity. On such grounds, Johnson felt he could not instantly favor any candidate over another. His endorsement would have to be earned.[37]

Eugenie's career prospects in 1968 would be strongly affected by Hubert Humphrey's success or failure come November. Philip Nash wrote: "As a domestic liberal but international hawk, Anderson had much in common with the original [Democratic] neoconservatives. . . . But unlike many of them, her foreign policy views did not change much between the early and late Cold War." In 1968, Peggy Lamson published her book *Few Are Chosen*, outlining the careers of ten prominent political women. In Lamson's chapter about Anderson, she, like Nash, reveals Eugenie as a politician caught in uniquely challenging times: "Mrs. Anderson's position is a lonely one for a liberal of such long standing. The woman who helped push President Truman toward a more progressive civil rights plank in the 1948 platform now finds herself alienated, on the issue of Vietnam, from most of her old liberal friends. Not, however, from all of them; her closest political ties have always been to Hubert Humphrey and they remain so today. . . . [But] Eugenie Anderson's convictions appear to stem more from her deeply ingrained hatred of Communism than from her unwavering admiration of Hubert Humphrey."[38]

In hindsight, it's easy to accuse Anderson of being "old school" in 1968—clinging to post-World War II Truman Doctrine ideas that just didn't conform to the complexity of new conflicts and global change. But at the time, Eugenie did not see herself as outdated. She constantly read newspapers and magazines and political commentary on current national and world affairs. She studied the journals and reports from the State Department and the United Nations. And her own children were against the Vietnam War. None of her opinions went unchallenged or unexamined by herself or by those nearest to her heart. As she followed her conscience and maintained her unswerving belief in democracy for *all*, Eugenie also continued—based more on realism than on principle—to stand apart from the burgeoning women's movement. She was not marching, organizing, or linking her efforts with up-and-coming feminists; affiliation would not have served her own political objectives. Eugenie had strong, lasting friendships with women from different spheres of her life; she was close to her daughter, her sisters, and John's sisters, and she had five beloved granddaughters. But she viewed these as personal relationships and separate from her work and political abstracts of the future. As a woman politician reliant on the sponsorship of Hubert Humphrey and other Democrats (predominantly men), Eugenie projected her energy toward maintaining those ties. Jo Freeman wrote: "Men did not sponsor just any woman. They sponsored women who were loyal and accommodating. While party men might tell women that to get ahead they had to act like men, by and large male politicians did not feel comfortable with women who acted as they did; they preferred women who brought traditional feminine qualities to the political sphere."[39]

In order to stay close to her sponsors and their intricate networks of influence, Anderson never advocated loudly for women's rights. Instead, she subtly asserted them under the radar in the guise of appearing like a culturally conservative grandmother, using the language of a traditional, loyal wife. A hefty feature of Eugenie in the *St. Paul Pioneer Press*, in February 1968, reiterated what Anderson had been advising all of her adult life:

> Since she feels the key to any married woman's success outside the home is the husband, Mrs. Anderson wouldn't advise any woman to work if her husband disapproved. . . . Many women are now going through a "transitional phase," she said—trying to find a new niche outside the home. And there are revolutionary strains. "Women are going to have to accept more conflicts if they're going to follow through on this," Mrs. Anderson said. . . . "I don't think there's ever been a time of greater challenge." Contrary to popular opinion, this grandmother of six doesn't think there's any special "trick" to handling men in her work. "I believe that if you women approach your work—diplomatic or otherwise—with an attitude of getting the job done, you will be accepted by men and by other women on the same serious basis. If you approach your work on a more personal basis—thinking of yourself as a woman—then people become aware of you as a woman." And their prejudices, either way, affect their treatment of you, she said.[40]

Eugenie had been patient and enduring for years while politicians with greater power decided how, where, and when to utilize her talents and expertise. She had been reasonable, even after deep disappointments when discriminatory history worked against her. She identified herself, above and beyond everything else (including female), as American: duty-bound to the Constitution and honor-bound to the Declaration of Independence. In addition,

On January 28, 1968, *Parade* magazine announced: "Where Women Are Equal." Original caption: "Women at the United Nations are a powerful as well as attractive addition to the diplomatic scene. Shown here in U.N. Plaza are (left to right) Eugenie Anderson, of the U.S.; Angie Brooks, of Liberia; Anak Agung Muter, of Indonesia; Inez Lopez de Garcia, of Colombia, and Halima Warzazi, of Morocco." *Eugenie M. Anderson papers, box 17.*

she identified with the Democratic Party, and in that capacity, she turned her attention to Hubert Humphrey's presidential campaign. But based on the fact that she was still advising other women to advocate simply for themselves—individually, in politics, in diplomacy, and in the workplace as a whole—it was clear that Eugenie might identify herself as a role model, though certainly not as a ringleader. As she stated in the *Pioneer Press*, she believed, even in 1968, that *women*—not men—were going to have to "accept more conflicts" if they wanted equal consideration in a man's world. The language and tools that Eugenie had employed to stay at the table through the previous two decades were not nearly adequate for the upcoming wave of women entering male-dominated arenas.

Humphrey, too, struggled with maintaining his strength and was under attack as never before. His complicated relationship with President Johnson, his conflicting loyalties, his conscience, his ambition, and his future historical influence and reputation were on the line. One of his main personal challenges was keeping the trust and support of his oldest DFL and Democratic friends. Many of them, including Evron and Jeane Kirkpatrick, were also censured by the New Left as imperialists and warmongers. Other longtime friends, such as Arthur Schlesinger Jr., had serious reservations about Humphrey's mind-set and his political future:

> The tragedy of the [Vietnam] war is precisely this: that it represents such a catastrophic misapplication of honorable ideas—the idea of the containment of aggression and the idea of a global New Deal—the ideas which dominated the decade of the forties and which shaped, I fear forever, the mind of HHH. When I see Hubert talking about a Marshall Plan for the cities to audiences composed of people who were five years old in 1948 and have never heard of the Marshall Plan, I weep over his own failure of imagination and sympathy, and I grieve that this great and vivid time should have produced a condition of arrested intellectual growth for so many bright people. We went wrong on Vietnam because we imposed the truths of the forties—containment of a unitary communism; of social reform—on a world which has radically and fundamentally changed.[41]

Humphrey did not take the criticism well. "You write history, and I make it," he blasted Schlesinger. "My biggest problem in public life has been that I have been too far ahead of the times. I have never been a tag-along. I have been a leader, and you know it. So, in the parlance of the street, knock it off." Schlesinger countered: "If you do not understand and will not recognize that some of your old friends might oppose your candidacy on grounds of principle . . . then you have lost your own sense of reality and are in deep trouble."[42]

While Humphrey still had enough of the powerful Democratic Party structure behind him to drive his campaign, his battle with challengers Eugene McCarthy, Robert Kennedy, and later George McGovern and third-party candidate George Wallace, would weaken his image and eventually lead to defeat. The temptation here is to launch into a detailed analysis of the spring and summer of 1968, during which civil rights leader Rev. Martin Luther King Jr. was shot and killed; presidential hopeful Robert F. Kennedy was shot and killed; cities burned while African Americans rioted to express the two-hundred-year violent agony of their experience; crowds of passionate college students protested and marched and traded blame with the police for inevitable casualties; and far away in Europe, the Soviets invaded Czechoslovakia, signaling (to those few Americans listening) that totalitarian expansionism was not a past myth but a present threat. Eugenie Anderson, who had been convinced to stay on with the United Nations and had been elected president of the UN Trusteeship Council on May 28, 1968, recognized the ongoing Communist threat and believed that it warranted continuing vigilance—a philosophy that also encompassed the war in Vietnam. Unfortunately, there is a gap in the Anderson family letters, so any contemporary thoughts from Eugenie to her immediate family between 1967 and 1970 are either inaccessible or lost altogether. It is a disappointing omission in the story, because her own words, at the time of the upheavals in 1968, could have revealed ambiguities, shadows, and emotions that she would not have included in speeches, press interviews, or official diplomatic statements or records. In any case, it is safe to say that she fully supported Hubert Humphrey for president, and after fulfilling her UN duties at session meetings, she went to work on his campaign.

Eugenie flew into Chicago on Sunday, August 25, 1968, to join the rest of the Humphrey entourage preparing for the opening of the Democratic National Convention the next day. No one was expecting the convention to run smoothly. A municipal transit workers strike coincided with an electricians union strike, both situations severely limiting the physical freedoms and communications channels for all convention participants. Thousands of protesters, many peaceful and yet highly impressionable, were expected to gather around the city, but more worrisome were the political incendiaries and agitators who would be joining the crowds. Chicago mayor Richard Daley and his aggressive police force, against the protesters' involvement, proved to be much more provocative and dangerous than anyone had imagined.

Humphrey's team was not a team at all. As Lewis Chester wrote in the book *An American Melodrama,* "The Humphrey organization, in fact, was permeated, circumvented, and confused by a horde of old pals, old pols, eager beavers, and office seekers. . . . Countless other figures crowded the overcrowded campaign hierarchy. . . . So it was hard to be sure just who really had the candidate's ear, and harder still to know who spoke with his voice."[43]

Each day of the convention brought increasing tension, panic, violence, and the total absence of opportunity for healthy communication between opposing voices, either inside the convention hall or outside on the streets of Chicago. Weeks before, Eugenie had procured tickets for Hans and Margaret to attend parts of the convention, including an address that she would be giving to the delegates. On the first day of convening, Eugenie called Margaret at the Great Lakes naval base: "Don't come," she said. "It's far too dangerous." Eugenie herself had a room in the block reserved for Humphrey people in the Conrad Hilton Hotel, and she felt as confident as she could in her safety being escorted to and from the convention center. But the streets were completely unpredictable: one minute a flowing band of youngsters with peaceful banners, the next minute a war zone filled with clouds of tear gas and the threat of gunfire. Hubert H. Humphrey persevered, beating out Eugene McCarthy. He came through with the nomination, but even fifty years later, his efforts as the Democratic candidate for the presidency are studied, regretted, pitied, mourned, and held up as *the* perfect storm of politics.

Louis Menand, *The New Yorker*, 2018:
What everyone remembers are the attacks by police and National Guardsmen on demonstrators in the streets outside. . . . But the scene inside the hall—the Chicago Amphitheatre, on the South Side, near the stockyards—was tumultuous enough. The CBS reporters Dan Rather and Mike Wallace were roughed up by security personnel. After a vote on an antiwar platform plank failed, members of the New York delegation joined arms and sang "We Shall Overcome."[44]

Hillary Clinton, *What Happened*, 2017:
That summer, I was in Chicago's Grant Park when antiwar protests outside the Democratic National Convention turned into a melee that shocked the nation. . . . It was a terrifying, exhilarating, and confusing time to be a young activist in America.[45]

Norman Mailer, *Miami and the Siege of Chicago*, 1968:
These Humphrey politicians and delegates, two-thirds of all this convention, had lived their lives in the shadow of Washington's Establishment, that eminence of Perle Mesta parties and Democratic high science, they had lived with nibbles of society, and gossip about it, clumps of grass from Hubert's own grounds; but it was their life, or a big part of it, and it was leaving now—they all sensed that. The grand Establishment of the Democratic Party and its society life in Washington would soon be shattered—the world was shattering with it. So they rose to cheer Humphrey. He was the end of their line. . . . Everybody knew he would lose. The poor abstract bugger.[46]

In spite of the tangled organization, immense hardship, and myriad challenges that Humphrey and his candidacy endured, Eugenie Anderson did not waver. During the third day of the convention, she gave an address at the Food for Thought Luncheon in the Mayfair Room of the Blackstone Hotel. She titled it "Focus on the Future" and kicked it off with a quote from the early Greek philosopher Heraclitus: "Everything changes! Nothing remains the same!" Anderson touched on the Soviet invasion of Czechoslovakia: "The swift Soviet regression to the Stalinist mode of totalitarianism and aggression has revealed once again to those who had forgotten, and to those too young to remember, the nature of the world in our times." She also congratulated President Johnson for his March 31 declaration of "a drastic unilateral de-escalation of the bombing and [call for] peace talks which are now in progress in Paris." She insisted that the Paris talks reinforced "a policy which deserves our support, not attack or sabotage." Eugenie closed the speech by declaring: "It is our determination and our passionate desire for peace, freedom, equality, and human welfare which must unite us and sustain us now and in the fateful years ahead."[47]

Anderson left the historic convention and the battleground of Chicago, visited her grandchildren for a few days, and then returned to New York City. Within three weeks, she had resigned from the United Nations (permanently this time) and committed herself to a speaking tour schedule for Humphrey's campaign. She spent hours every day in meetings, organizing with the top campaign managers. With Orville Freeman, she drafted hundreds of pages of policy overviews, current issues, campaign strategies, reactions to public events and appearances, advice and recommendations for Hubert. In one set of handwritten notes, which Eugenie titled "The High Road," she made notes on foreign policy, and then wrote, and underlined: *"A new Humphrey position on Vietnam to which he would cling as to Gibraltar. Most Important of all—Firmness—no more changing."* She recommended that a mediator, either Senator Edward Kennedy or Orville Freeman, should present Humphrey's Vietnam language to President Johnson for its best hope of endorsement; furthermore, in order to defeat Nixon, it was "absolutely essential" to unify the Democratic Party by keeping Humphrey and Johnson aligned—but under Humphrey's initiative.[48]

In a memo to Freeman, Eugenie urged him to pass on language to Hubert that would label Nixon a "Cold Warrior" and a "Hard Liner," since, "Given the present extremely precarious situation in Europe, in the Middle East and in Vietnam, the American people are apt to fear a man as President whose instincts and record show a reflex action towards the military response to any dangerous situation." Perhaps it was the work Eugenie was involved in that fall of 1968, all the writing and research and time spent spinning comparisons and contrasts between Humphrey and Nixon, that influenced her own gradual move away from *absolute* pressure— including military—on Vietnam. She had always advocated the mission for peace in Southeast Asia with political, economic, and social development as most key, with the military and bombing efforts necessary to ensure their progress. But since the top priority in 1968 was to get Hubert elected, *Humphrey's* message must now take precedence. Through September and October, Humphrey flew around the country, appearing in a different city almost every single day (his itinerary revealed only two days without an event). "I want it said," Humphrey called out at a rally, "regardless of the outcome of the election, that Hubert H. Humphrey, in an important and tough moment of his life, stood by what he believed and was not shouted down." Legal historian Roberta Walburn wrote: "Everywhere Hubert went, it was the same. He was booed, heckled, jeered. Protesters threw urine on him, spit on his wife, and screamed obscenities. A 'public humiliation that no major candidate had ever known.'" Yale Archives director Michael Brenes agreed: "The protests agonized Humphrey. 'All I had ever been as a liberal spokesman seemed lost, all that I had accomplished in significant programs was ignored. I felt robbed of my personal history,' he recalled."[49]

When only five weeks remained before Election Day, Humphrey declared, in a televised address from Salt Lake City, "As President, I would be willing to stop the bombing of the North [Vietnam] as an acceptable risk for peace because I believe it could lead to success in the negotiations and a shorter war." He also stated that "I would move toward de-Americanization of the war . . . that the South Vietnamese take over more and more of the defense of their own country." The split was confirmed. HHH was no longer LBJ's man—and he was no longer adhering to the suggestions that Eugenie had outlined two months earlier when she had advised him to cling, "as to Gibraltar," to President Johnson's policies. But in truth, Eugenie was diverging from that road as well, maybe not as definitively as Humphrey when he announced his Vietnam turnaround, but toward that inevitable progression. Joining Hubert in a campaign sweep through Kansas City on October 15, Eugenie gave an interview to the press. The *Kansas City Times* reported: "Turning her guns on the Republican presidential candidate, Mrs. Anderson said she agreed with Humphrey's advocacy of a bombing halt and a de-Americanization of the war, but that Richard Nixon had not stated his views on Vietnam for voter appraisal."[50]

On October 26, Eugenie gave an address on the role of American women in US foreign policy. On October 28, she served as Humphrey's spokesman against a representative for Nixon at a World Affairs Council debate in Detroit. Throughout all of her speeches, travels, notes, meetings, and various topics of discussion that fall—especially those of women in politics—perhaps everything is most clearly defined by one handwritten, underlined reminder: "*In Conclusion,*" she scribbled to herself, "*Significance of November elections.*" Focused and realistic, Eugenie understood that all of her core beliefs and dearest-held ambitions relied on this presidential election. Any high-level position or influence that she might have going into the 1970s would become brilliantly possible, or come to a halt, after November 5. Moreover, better conditions and opportunities for all women in politics were also at stake. At the edge of the growing women's movement, finally there were voices changing and expanding the definitions of feminism. Eugenie believed that only under a Humphrey Democratic administration would the movement (like other civil rights and human rights efforts) find support and fertile ground to take hold; under Nixon Republicans, Vietnam would continue to supersede other agendas. She was right.

Senator Eugene McCarthy, waiting until October 29, six days before the election, at long last publicly professed his endorsement of Hubert Humphrey for president. It was too little, too late "when he finally provided . . . a 'mushy endorsement' of Humphrey's presidential candidacy. 'It was sad that the man who had provided a necessary voice for those who were vehemently against the war . . . couldn't get over his ego games.'" In my interview with Walter Mondale in 2017, the former vice president said: "[Eugene McCarthy] never felt a part of the Democratic structure. He was his own guy . . . a 'lone wolf.' And I think that it was a tough thing for Humphrey to deal with. Humphrey always liked McCarthy. But McCarthy never reciprocated." Mondale also wrote about the 1968 experience in his book, *The Good Fight*: "I've spent hours with old Minnesota friends wondering how that year might have played out differently if McCarthy had reconciled with Hubert before the convention ended. . . . He might have made a difference. We were praying for it."[51]

The perfect storm ended. Humphrey lost, by a hair. Roberta Walburn described it thus: "The margin of defeat was less than one tiny percentage point. . . . Many blamed Gene [McCarthy], saying that just the barest effort by him—an earlier and more robust endorsement . . . would have made all the difference. Hubert also thought that Gene could have 'turned it.' But he put much of the blame on himself. After four years as vice president, 'I had lost some of my personal identity and personal forcefulness,' he would say. 'It would have been better that I stood my ground and remembered that I was fighting for the highest office in the land.'"[52]

It has now been fifty years since that election. Multitudes of historians and political scientists have examined the devastation of Humphrey's bitter loss, bestowing upon him a tragic mantle he would wear ever after. Eugenie disagreed from the outset. She sent a long, detailed letter to Hubert one week after the election, on November 13, 1968, itemizing his challenges and the pride he should take away from the fight:

> All of these many forces were working powerfully against you, and any single one of them would have demoralized and defeated a lesser man. But you overcame all these cruel and undeserved obstacles, and by your own sheer courage, character, brilliance, humanity and will, came within a hair's breadth of winning! Just to have cut down Wallace's vote and Nixon's margin is a great thing for the future of our country.
>
> This was in truth a famous victory, Hubert, and I congratulate you and admire you with all my heart.[53]

Hubert replied a few weeks later, and the utter exhaustion from his ordeal was still raw: "I have read and reread your wonderful letter of November 13. It is an outline of our troubles, impediments and tribulations. . . . I guess we had to face almost every known obstacle but with all of that I can't help but feel a keen sense of loss and sorrow over our defeat." He closed with: "Let us hope and pray that the New Year will bring us some relief from the many aggravations of our time."[54]

While historians continue to ask "what if" about the 1968 presidential election, their hypothetical arguments are all (naturally) built around the same cast of characters: LBJ, HHH, RFK, MLK; McCarthy, McGovern, Nixon, and Wallace. At the end of 1968, during the fresh pain of Humphrey's recent defeat, some Minnesota Democrats were asking themselves: What if the playing field had developed differently over the previous decade? What if we had recognized sooner that Eugene McCarthy's stubborn individualism would backfire on Humphrey rather than help him toward the White House? *What if we had backed Eugenie Anderson in '58?*

Well, of course, that "what if" is a huge stretch. The equation could never be so simple: substituting one senator for another over a ten-year period—especially through the tumultuous 1960s. And perhaps more importantly, even though a Humphrey-Anderson senatorial team in Washington could have done great things for the Democratic Party for many years (even taking Humphrey to the presidency), the defining factor of Anderson's gender makes the whole "what if" scenario impossible to construct, even in hindsight. Jeane Kirkpatrick asked, in 1974: "Must it ever be thus? Is male dominance of power processes written in the stars and underwritten by human biology? I doubt it."[55]

At the outset of the 1970s, as the women's movement surged into new territory led by new voices, feminist leaders built on assertions like Kirkpatrick's doubt and boldly challenged the foundations of sexism, envisioning the possibilities for a different future. Jo Freeman, author of *We Will Be Heard*, wrote: "At the 1968 Democratic convention . . . I was a budding feminist and no longer oblivious, but I neither met nor saw anyone I recognized as a political woman. . . . No one—not political scientists, students, delegates, the press, or protesters—had one word to say about women; nor did I see any programs, posters, or panels on women's rights or women in politics." Understandably, the issues of civil rights, the Vietnam War, and other viciously divisive and violent problems among the American people took up most of the time, space, and energy of politics, media, and communication in the late 1960s. Women's rights—and the necessity to see them advance—existed, but they were constantly overshadowed by other agendas.[56]

Eugenie Anderson never served in politics on a national scale after Humphrey's 1968 loss. She did contribute her advice and time to Hubert's successful 1970 Senate campaign and his unsuccessful 1972 and 1976 presidential hopes. But she did not seek positions through the State Department or the United Nations, choosing instead to retire to Tower View in Minnesota. It would have been from her own living room and home office in Minnesota—and not from national committee meetings or Foreign Service

Members of the enduring Minnesota DFL attend an appreciation dinner for four-term Minneapolis mayor Arthur Naftalin on February 28, 1969: (L to R) Representative Don Fraser, Muriel Humphrey, Hubert Humphrey, St. Paul mayor Tom Byrne, Anderson, Senator Walter Mondale, Fran Naftalin, Arthur Naftalin. *Russell Bull, © 1969, Star Tribune.*

briefings—that she followed politics on all levels. International policy. Nuclear weapons. Environmental concerns. Political coups. Watergate. Women's lib and the ERA.

When Eugenie scored another first for women in 1971, the *Minneapolis Tribune* announced on its front page: "Minnesotan Again Leads Attack on Sex Barrier." Elected to the board of directors of the First National Bank in the Twin Cities, Anderson became the first woman named to the board of a business operation of that scale. The article noted that Eugenie "brings with her a deep interest in 'two special areas'—ecology and minority hiring. 'I have always been especially interested in equality of the races,' she said, then paused: 'And of the sexes.'" It is that *pause*—both the fact that Eugenie made one and the fact that the paper made a point of mentioning it—that insinuated a great importance on recognizing gender equality. It was as if Eugenie had been wanting to include women's rights in her comments all along, but only now was free enough from political criticism (and danger to her career) to include the issue in discussion in its own right, not just as a subset of human rights. Freeman wrote: "Knowing history shapes our sense of the possible. Leaving women out of political science and political history let students falsely believe that political woman did not exist, that politics was something properly reserved to men, and that women who tried to participate were 'idiosyncratic individuals' rather than engaged and effective political actors who faced a lot of resistance."[57]

From 1946 to the end of the 1960s, Eugenie Anderson kept herself in Democratic Party politics, at the national level, by deliberately attending to human rights; in other words, she relegated her discussion of women's rights to an intellectual subset of human or civil rights, because she fully understood the self-destructive career consequences of "shouting loudly" like a feminist. *She* knew what she believed inside, and she made a commitment to herself to fight the battles she thought she could win. But in order to fight, she had to show up. And no one—not Orville Freeman, not Hubert Humphrey, not even Eleanor Roosevelt—would keep inviting her to the table if she "acted too much like a woman—or, just as bad, like a man," and spoke too often or too aggressively about women's issues. As Jo Freeman encapsulated in *A Room at a Time*:

> Finally, the women who went into the parties did in the twentieth century what organized women—especially the WCTU and the women's clubs—did in the nineteenth century: they laid the foundation. They prepared women for political work and enlarged their sphere of activity. They did this through education, legitimation, and infiltration. When the political opportunity structure opened up, women in both parties were ready to take advantage of it. . . . Party women did what was possible to do in the conservative period between social movement clusters. And by doing what was possible, women went into politics the same way they got suffrage: slowly and persistently, with great effort, against much resistance, a room at a time.[58]

Seven
PASSING the STANDARD

She was a progressive . . . no question about it,
and she knew what discrimination meant for women,
'cause she was fighting it every day.

WALTER MONDALE, 2017

I F SOMEONE HAD WRITTEN A BIOGRAPHY OF EUGENIE Anderson in the 1970s or '80s, she might have been portrayed as a twentieth-century political woman abandoned too early by the system. But viewed in the context of our recent and explosive twenty-first-century women's movement— since another generation has passed, and Americans are recognizing (again) the longer history of feminism and its progress—Eugenie's life and efforts take on more dimensions. She was there, moving through one room at a time. If Hubert Humphrey had been elected in 1968, would she have been appointed to his cabinet? Is there any chance she might even have reached the level of secretary of state? Who can say? Humphrey lived and worked another ten years after his great loss. Eric Sevareid wrote: "The 'Happy Warrior' . . . never made it to the Presidency himself; he did not become the leader of the government; he became something rarer than that; he became the conscience of the government." Hubert, Muriel, and Eugenie nurtured their deep friendship and corresponded regularly on personal matters and political exchange. Through the 1970s, Hubert and Eugenie wrote frank letters to each other regarding the horrors of Watergate, President Nixon's demise, and, in most detail, their perspectives on foreign policy and the dangers of Soviet influence in the Middle East and its far-reaching threat to the future. Eugenie traveled to the Middle East three times: in 1969, in 1971 (when she met with Israeli prime minister Golda Meir), and in 1974.[1]

Life in Red Wing had found a rhythm, and Eugenie settled into a greater appreciation for not just the natural beauty of Tower View but also the peaceful existence of living permanently in the Midwest. Eugenie wrote to her daughter-in-law:

> I guess that we are at that time in life when more and more of our contemporaries are having serious health problems or are dying. It is easy to see how older people often succumb to gloom. We are so lucky—so far—to both be in good health and full of interests. Sometimes we realize that the things that we do now have little meaning for others, but as I often remind John, at least our lives are of

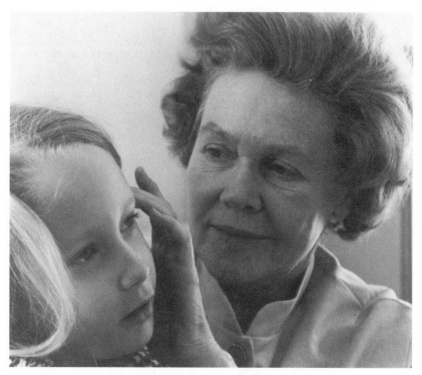

Eugenie and grandchild Jennifer Anderson, Christmas 1967, Great Lakes Naval Base housing, Illinois. *Photo by Hans P. Anderson, author's collection.*

significance to each other and to our children and grandchildren. I rather like Erik Erikson's description of life's stages, and try to remember that our stage of life—which we are hopefully just beginning—*should* be a development of wisdom.[2]

John Anderson had a productive life of his own with maintenance of the buildings and grounds on their ten-acre property, carpentry and machine shop work, daily attention to the fluctuations of the stock market and study of his long-term investments, and a vast amount of time devoted to photography: black-and-white prints, color slides, and movie film. In the mid-1960s, when Eugenie had been living in New York City, John had installed a large darkroom in the basement of the farmhouse. It proved essential to his happiness and creativity as he moved toward old age, when he felt unsuited to travel and adventure.

Charles and Mary Biederman lived just a mile away from Tower View, in a little house tucked behind the Cannon River from which Charles continued to design, construct, and exhibit his work. Mary Biederman taught kindergarten in the Red Wing school district to support them for many years, and while she and Eugenie remained close and dependent on each other for the irreplaceable buttresses of sisterhood, John and Charles never recovered their partnership or the mutual admiration of their younger years. In fact, it was a wry joke in the family that here were these two old men, living within spitting distance of each other, who had so much in common (historically and artistically) and so much to gain from letting bygones go—and yet they both stubbornly clung to their pride and unwillingness to reconcile.

Mary Moore Biederman died of a stroke in August 1975, at age sixty-four. While her death was not entirely surprising (she had undergone heart surgery two years before and suffered other serious illnesses as well), it was nevertheless sudden, and Eugenie was devastated. To date, it was the harshest and most personally difficult bereavement she had ever faced. A family member remembers Eugenie in a chair in her living room, sobbing inconsolably, bereft

Sisters Genie and Mary on Grandad's Bluff, La Crosse, Wisconsin, May 1975. Mary Biederman died three months later. *Photo by Hans P. Anderson, author's collection.*

of any of her usual control over emotions and propriety, crying, "I don't know how I am going to live without her." Charles was equally overcome, and besides that, he had never learned how to drive a car, had had struggles with his health, and was facing eye surgery that necessitated a huge amount of help for himself and his house. For many months, Eugenie took care of Charles and tried to accommodate both their households. Even immediately after Mary's death, Eugenie found it overwhelming:

> Now I am here attending a meeting of the Commission on Minnesota's Future. This is the first meeting I have attended since Mary

died, and while I did not really feel like coming, I decided that I should be trying to pick up the threads of my life again. . . . However, I am sure that this is one of the ways in which we absorb and eventually must accept the reality of death: we re-live so many times the exact ways in which it all came about, perhaps feeling that if we understand better *how* it happened, that then we will understand *why*—and thus in the end come to accept the inevitability of the final event.

I am far from reaching that stage yet, but I know that sometime I surely will have to. Meanwhile I know that it is a good thing that I have been so busy at home, although there are times every day when I wonder how long I can continue to carry on the kind of routine that I have been trying to do since Mary died. It probably will change, and I will eventually start changing it.[3]

The situation with Charles put a strain on John and Eugenie's equilibrium, of course, but, as with so many other rocky periods of their life together, eventually things settled down. Hans wrote to Eugenie: "We know that the pain of Mary's death and her absence continues to be just terrible for you, Mother, and as much as I admire and respect your caring for Charles as an expression of your devotion to Mary; I hope you will decrease your involvement as soon as his eyes are repaired. He will never assume responsibility for himself as long as someone else is taking care of him." Some months later, Eugenie put her foot down and forced Charles to find housekeeping help. For a man who smoked dense cigars and drank hard liquor practically every day of his entire adult life, Biederman lived exceedingly long and productively, remaining active, focused, and controversially opinionated well into old age. (Charles died in 2004 at the age of ninety-eight.)[4]

When Hubert Humphrey died of cancer in January 1978, more response and action was required than simply mourning an old friend. Eugenie wrote to Muriel, expressing her condolences in simple but honest words: "I hope that you are finding some comfort in knowing that we—and thousands of others—share your sorrow, and that we are deeply grateful for all that you and Hubert have done for us all." Next, in the days before and after attendance of the funeral, Eugenie accepted several interview requests from journalists who wished to write about Humphrey's early days, long career, and enduring legacy. During this same time, Governor Rudy Perpich was required to set the conditions for Hubert's replacement in the Senate and send someone from Minnesota to Washington to finish out the last year of his term. Six days after Humphrey's death, the *Minneapolis Star* reported on the possible replacement names floating around the DFL: Muriel Humphrey at the top of the list, followed by US representative Don Fraser. And somewhere in the pool of eight to ten other recommendations were old-timers Art Naftalin and Eugenie Anderson. Eugenie was never seriously considered (nor asked; nor would she have accepted), but she still represented a standard of political experience honored by the DFL. Muriel Humphrey was appointed, in the capacity of a "caretaker," to fill Hubert's seat. Serving from January 25 to November 7, 1978, she was the first woman to represent Minnesota in the US Senate. She chose not to run as a candidate in a special election later that year.[5]

As Muriel went to work at the Capitol, the DFL was contemplating its turning point as a party. "Founders of DFL Are Gone," announced the *Minneapolis Tribune.* "Is Armageddon Near for Party of HHH?" asked the *Minneapolis Star:* "The rift in the DFL party runs deep and serious. . . . It might have begun, some feel, with the death of party founder and patriarch Hubert Humphrey. When Humphrey was alive, he often was credited with bridging the gap between conservative and liberal camps that often were at odds within the DFL. No one has taken his place."[6]

Humphrey's passing marked the end of an era for DFLers, the *Minneapolis Star* reported Eugenie Anderson saying sadly. "I think that without his leadership and his marvelous quality of uniting people with different views, we are going to go through a very difficult period. I don't think it will ever be the same again."[7]

*   *   *

The 1970s. *Roe v. Wade.* Consciousness-raising groups. Betty Friedan's NOW. *The Mary Tyler Moore Show.* Gloria Steinem and *Ms.* magazine. Billie Jean King and the "Battle of the Sexes." Prime minister of India, Indira Gandhi; prime minister of Israel, Golda Meir; and finally, in 1979, prime minister of the United Kingdom, Margaret Thatcher. While Thatcher moved her staff into 10 Downing Street, President Jimmy Carter prepared for his reelection campaign against his challenger, Republican Ronald Reagan. The world faced the new decade of the 1980s and strengthening conservatism in the United States and Western Europe. Even so, many American women persevered in their climb toward what would soon be called the glass ceiling.

On February 4, 1981, the Reagan administration approved the appointment of Jeane Kirkpatrick as the US ambassador to the United Nations—she was the first woman to hold the highest command post of the delegation. Kirkpatrick's biography quoted her as saying: "A woman in high office is intrinsically controversial. . . . Many people think a woman shouldn't be in high office. Kissinger is described as a 'professor.' I am described as 'schoolmarmish.' Brzezinski is called 'Doctor.' I am called 'Mrs.' I am depicted as a witch or scold in editorial cartoons and the speed with which these stereotypes are used shows how close those feelings are to the surface. It's much worse than I ever dreamed it would be."[8]

Justice Sandra Day O'Connor, the first woman to be appointed to the US Supreme Court, took the bench on September 25, 1981. (She served as the sole female for twelve years, until Justice Ruth Bader Ginsburg joined the court on August 10, 1993.)

Eugenie Anderson's overall health weakened in the early 1980s. For stretches, she would be energetic and able to study and travel and attend political meetings, even give an occasional speech or commencement address at a university. But at other times, she suffered from the inevitable afflictions of age, slowing down, and a depression of spirits that she called "apathy"—dismay and sadness over global, domestic, and personal affairs. In retirement, Eugenie spent a great amount of time assisting and socializing (often doing both simultaneously) with all numbers of family, friends, former colleagues, and acquaintances. She took her grandchildren to lunch at Becky's Cafe on Hennepin Avenue in Minneapolis, then up the street to the Guthrie Theater to see *A Christmas Carol*. She visited frequently with her sisters-in-law in Red Wing, Elizabeth Hedin and Jean Chesley, as well as their children and grandchildren. She loaned Biederman constructions and paintings to gallery shows and museums, helping Charles with the arrangements. She made trips to see her older sister Julie in Oklahoma, and her younger brother Bill in Oregon. She still wrote dozens of letters every week. And every now and then, she would drive into Red Wing, pick up A. P. Anderson's widow Vinnie at the nursing home, and bring her to Tower View, where they would bake cinnamon rolls together, just as Vinnie used to do for Hans and Johanna in that same kitchen almost fifty years before. Vinnie lived to the great age of ninety-three; she died on April 29, 1981. Her hand-knitted afghans can still be found in the homes of her step-great-great-grandchildren.

A milestone celebration was coordinated for Eugenie's seventy-fifth birthday in Red Wing, at the end of May in 1984. Two months later, Democratic presidential candidate Walter Mondale chose a woman, Geraldine Ferraro, to run on his ticket for vice president. Ferraro was a US representative at the end of her third congressional term for the State of New York. The Mondale-Ferraro struggle for an optimistic campaign, and their landslide loss that November, created an enormous amount of debate over the health of the Democratic Party, both nationally and in Minnesota. From the *Minneapolis Star Tribune*:

> The party has lost some of the fire of those early days, say some who were there. "We say we are a Democrat," said Naftalin, 66, former Humphrey associate . . . "What do we mean by that?"
>
> "I don't know what it means to be a Democrat in 1984. I thought I knew 20 years ago. I would be a New Deal, Fair Deal, Great Society, New Frontier man—it all meant something. Government

John and Eugenie Anderson celebrating their fiftieth wedding anniversary at their home in the farmhouse at Tower View, Red Wing, Minnesota, September 1980. *Photo by Hans P. Anderson, author's collection.*

intervention to set things right, social programs, tax the rich to help the poor. . . . Nobody knows anymore what the Democrats mean."

Walter Mondale's massive loss in last week's presidential election did more than end the electoral career of another politician. It also marked the passing of a remarkable generation that emerged from one middle-sized state and that provided a succession of leaders who have been active at the national level in every presidential election since 1960.[9]

Even though Eugenie was solidly behind Mondale, and a woman was paired on a presidential ticket for the first time in American history, she committed herself to another first in her own lifetime: she publicly endorsed a Minnesota Republican for Senate. During that same election cycle of 1984, Republican incumbent senator Rudy Boschwitz requested a meeting with Mrs. Anderson in August; Eugenie invited him to Tower View, where they discussed Boschwitz's campaign and disagreements on foreign policy with DFL challenger Joan Growe. Specifically, they reviewed the ramifications of the proposed freeze on nuclear weapons production, testing, and deployment between the United States and the Soviet Union. Two months after the meeting, Boschwitz solicited Anderson's endorsement for his candidacy, and she gave it. Eugenie's public letter stated, in keeping with her lifelong hard-line stance against Communism: "We must never yield to the temptation of an unverifiable agreement with the Soviet Union . . . simply for the sake of yielding to popular pressures." Growe's campaign manager was quoted as suggesting that Eugenie was "out of touch" and "a wayward soul, who's lost her way." Out of touch? Certainly, due to extended and recurring periods of time in ill health. Neither Boschwitz's request for Anderson's public statement nor Eugenie's agreement should have taken place at all. At this point in her life, Eugenie was at the edge of inevitable separation from anything requiring rigorous activity or study.[10]

Eugenie succumbed to poor health and advancing dementia after 1985, declining slowly for many years. Her memory faded and her body weakened. By 1990, the "old DFL" had become legend. "DFL Convention Glory Days Lost in Past," lamented Robert Spaeth of the *St. Cloud Times*: "In those days the DFL was overflowing with political ideals and political pragmatism—and from the two the party built winning slates of statewide candidates who, once in office, made Minnesota great." As with all history, who tells the story makes a big difference in the overall effect—and the truth. Three, four, and five decades of storytelling, news making, and reputation building can bend all manner of truth, from the biggest picture to the smallest details. In this case, Spaeth deployed a scenario from the DFL Senate race in 1958 to substantiate his point about past glory: "In 1958 the Humphrey-Freeman group wanted Eugenie Anderson as the DFL candidate for the Senate seat held by Ed Thye. But Congressman Eugene McCarthy got the party's endorsement— and immediately the Humphrey-Freeman group united behind McCarthy in the election campaign. The result: another DFLer in national office." Well, Spaeth was right on one point: McCarthy won. But all of the players, Eugenie, Hubert, Orville, and Eugene, are lumped into a victory undeserving of its oversimplified glorification. Hubert withheld his support from Eugenie, who could not rely on Orville, who personally did not support Eugene, who used dirty tactics to usurp Eugenie (see chapter 4). Fast-forward thirty years to 1990, and the modern internal battles of the DFL looked pretty much the same—as do politics in our present world, an additional thirty years down the road.[11]

Helen Eugenie Moore Anderson—Genie—died on March 31, 1997. Only two weeks before her death, President William J. Clinton had announced the appointment of the first woman secretary of state, Madeleine K. Albright. In the limelight of her new position as the highest-ranking woman in the history of the United States, Albright said: "It is sad but still true that there are not enough women holding jobs in foreign affairs. . . . Correcting this is not simply about fairness. Today's world needs the unique set of skills and experience that women bring to diplomacy."[12]

Eugenie Anderson's obituaries cataloged her early groundbreaking roles in diplomacy. The *St. Paul Pioneer Press* observed:

> Before Madeleine Albright could have aspired to become a secretary of state, Eugenie Anderson had to break a glass ceiling in the diplomatic establishment.... When Albright was an immigrant girl, Anderson was serving as the first woman to fill an ambassadorship for the United States....
>
> Anderson's death after a long life rich in public service and politics reminds us that extraordinary women helped shape this half of a century that raced into the future. It was men and women of foresight and skill who were "present at the creation," as Dean Acheson put it, of a new world that saved itself and built prosperous democracies from the ruins of war.
>
> In many other ways—including party building, civic and business—Anderson also contributed generously to the common work of citizenship. Her many accomplishments came during an era when popular history mythologizes the American woman as a homebody. Not her.[13]

The "popular history mythologiz[ing] the American woman as a homebody" referred to the contradictions and restrictions on women described in *The Feminine Mystique*. Betty Friedan's sociological study was now history of its own, serving as a foundation element for those evaluating the roles of women between post–World War II and the early 1960s. And anyone looking back on Eugenie Anderson's life and choices immediately saw the refutation, if not the antithesis, of "feminine mystique." Mondale was quoted in the *Red Wing Republican Eagle*: "The sheer force of her mind and personality made her a power long before the women's movement arrived." And the *Minneapolis Star Tribune* added: "Former Vice President Walter Mondale said of Anderson this week: 'She was an extraordinary public figure, a pioneer in the women's movement. She hit that glass ceiling every day. But she was not just a flower pot in the corner. She thought well, spoke well and was genuinely confident in her own views.'" In that same article, Geri Joseph remembered, "When Eugenie walked into a room, you knew she was *somebody*. She had a regal bearing. She was generous with her political knowledge and encouraged us . . . to never sit back."[14]

Over the three decades in which Eugenie was most politically active, she rarely sat back. And if she did, it was often with a book about world history, or philosophy, or political theory. In quiet old age, she was devoted to and read, over and over, the works of Samuel Johnson. An eighteenth-century English poet and prolific writer of essays, biography, criticism, and lexicography, Johnson was the author of the famous statement: "A woman's preaching is like a dog walking on his hind legs. It is not done well, and you are surprised to find it done at all." Once, in a 1968 interview, Eugenie reflected on her early years of political exploration: "I wanted to have as much influence as I could on the course of events then happening in the world. And, frankly and unashamedly, I enjoyed the activity. It offered me a new potential I didn't know I had." In a way, Eugenie's soft-pitched but firm, resolute voice, speaking, advising, conferring, rallying, mediating, educating, and counseling, was akin to secular preaching. She preached for democracy and for human rights. She preached for moderation and for tolerance. She preached for compassion and civil rights. Combining her father's oratory skills and internationalist politics and her mother's quiet steadfastness and artistic appreciation, Eugenie spent her life pursuing and communicating the meanings and requirements of democracy. And she did not allow her gender to alter her message, change the course of her ambition, or narrow the global scope of her vision.[15]

AFTERWORD

GROWING UP, I WAS FORTUNATE TO KNOW ALL FOUR of my grandparents. Unlike so many born in the first decade of the twentieth century, they had all survived the dangers of infancy. Arnold Kaehler was the third of ten children and was raised on a farm in St. Charles, Minnesota. Edna Haverland had polio at age one and a half but recovered by age three. She would have been the middle child of five in Grand Forks, North Dakota, but two brothers died, very young, before she was born. John Anderson also lost an older brother before he was born, a little boy named Leonard, who died of meningitis. And Eugenie Moore lay in bed for months with scarlet fever, gradually fighting it off and living to witness almost the entire century until she died in 1997. All four grandparents had strong opinions, strong feelings, and strong agendas. Arnold was Grandpa: no smoking or drinking or pretension, quietly confident in his mischievous sincerity, always seeking something down the road. Founder and inventor of Sturdiwheat in Red Wing, Minnesota (the company originally called V-10), he saw to it that all of his six children got a college degree despite the fact that Arnold was often out of work during their childhoods in the Great Depression. Edna was Grandma. She was no nonsense, unfussy, hands rarely idle, and usually found in the kitchen, a coffee-and-knitting Methodist with a tremendous ability to focus on necessity. You knew she loved you if she gave you a quick swat on the bum when you walked by.

Many families have to differentiate between grandparents with nicknames or extras: Grandpa Joe versus Grandpa Jim; Bubbe versus Nanna, and so on. For my sisters and me, Edna and Arnold had a lock on Grandma and Grandpa—because my father's parents were simply Genie and John from the start. At some point, I must have questioned why, but I've forgotten the answer. They chose to be Eugenie (Genie) and John, without titles or suffixes or qualifiers to anyone or any generation in their families. As a grandfather (still an awkward reference in my ears), John was a fascinating combination of light and dark. When he was in a humorous mood, he had lightning-quick wit, jokes that seemed short and sharp on the surface but often had a professorial meaning behind them. Once I called something "very unique," and he spent twenty minutes explaining why the phrase was redundant and inapplicable. I've never used it since. Every summer, his skin above the waist turned dark cinnamon brown because he refused to wear a shirt when he mowed the grass in swatches around his ten-acre portion of Tower View. That was the light above ground. The light below flicked on when I followed him into the darkroom, where beautiful black and silver instruments made photographs appear, and shelves and boxes and cubbies contained the mysteries and treasures of not just the past—but *my* past. If you've ever smelled print developer or fixer, you know what the air contained. A picture of his mother hung next to a picture of an unknown small child and a goat in a country I'd never heard of. Drawers held hundreds of little tools and nails and pieces of wood fitted with brass and the promise of invention. If I stayed long enough for John to get used to me and realize that I wasn't leaving, he would get out boxes of prints and we would look at black-and-white images of faces and figures and patterns and buildings. I liked the family pictures best: both the laughing expressions and the captured innocence or maturity clothed in high collars, buttoned shoes, and the contrast that results from antiquated negatives under modern exposure. In the evenings, John would set up the slide projector, or the huge 16mm movie projector.

I would squirm in a scratchy wool chair (mid-century modern Danish of course) while everyone got up and down correcting the window shades and the screen that pulled down from the ceiling, then waited for Genie to bring in the coffee. No matter who turned off the lights first, they always came on again when John argued that he needed to rethread the film or adjust something important. Finally, as the coffee grew cold and the room went dark, the screen glowed with brilliant color and real, moving people. And history. Ourselves, when we were babies. Crowds of Soviets in Red Square at the Kremlin. Mom perched on Dad's old motorcycle. Toothless farmers leading a white cow down a red road in India. Eugenie beaming in full diplomatic armor. My dad, twelve years old, wheeling his bike in front of an embassy. My mom, impossibly beautiful, red hair under a bridal crown of white roses.

This biography of Eugenie Anderson's life and politics—the need that I felt to explore her work in government, diplomacy, and democracy—came about in part because I only knew Genie as my grandmother. Even though I was thirty years old when she died, and already had the first of my three children at that point, the opportunity I might have had to sit down with her at length to discuss her career ended, essentially, before I was even into my teens. It never happened. For me, Genie was a deep well of stories and connections and artistry and tangible beauty that I instinctually recognized as the outer body inside which a discerning mind and a beating heart held infinite knowledge. Truth and experience accrued from her past. Dazzling potential for those of us in her future. I wanted to know *her*. Mrs. Ambassador. Writing this book has allowed me to try.

The first memory I have of American politics was Richard Nixon's face, tinted green and wavering with the static of a bad signal, resigning from the presidency on television. It was August 1974, and I was seven years old. We were on vacation at Clearwater Lake on the Gunflint Trail in northern Minnesota, two miles from the Canadian border, without TV or telephone, and I remember standing at the door of the lodge owner's cabin, my parents apologizing: "We hate to intrude" (I didn't know what *intrude* meant, and it impressed me as deeply vulnerable), "but may we come in to watch Nixon's resignation?" My parents must have explained to me what the president had done that resulted in everyone's depressed and sickened faces, after the quiet trek back to our own cabin among rustling birch trees and skittering red squirrels. Ever after, the highest ranks of our government were discussed with doubt, suspicion, and anxiety. Truthfully—with cynicism. I have never known an America that regarded or cheered its top elected officials with more hope than worry.

Eugenie's first political memory was the end of World War I; the Great War, they called it. Instead of watching a president abandon office in shame for criminal behavior, witnessing from a private, isolated room, she was marching down the street on a bright autumn morning, waving an American flag behind her father, who led the parade past cheering crowds. The United States had joined their allies in Europe and led the world back from the brink of tyranny and oppression and evil. The future for democracy—all over the globe—was filled with hope and public unification and victory. No one country could have done it alone; only cooperation and fortitude and friendship between nations could have led to hope for the future. And that is what Eugenie grew up believing.

Many of my birthday and Christmas gifts from Genie and John were, of course, books. They were primarily little stories and short novels about characters striving for a better life or reflecting real-world struggles from a child's point of view: Lois Lenski's sharecropping families, Rudyard Kipling's *Riki Tiki Tavi*, Willa Cather, Helen Keller, *The Diary of Anne Frank*. But a certain book I picture in my head, the title and the cover, was *When Hitler Stole Pink Rabbit*. Honestly, it's possible I never actually read it, partly because I was sneaking into my sister's room and stealing Judy Blume books about preteen romance, but mostly because I equated Hitler, naturally, with unspeakable Evil. It was characteristic of Genie to share, and talk, and invite people of all ages to look evil in the face and examine it. But like many kids, I avoided confrontational literature. At twelve and thirteen, I wrote long, horrible, inane romance novels in spiral notebooks, and I even sent one proudly to Genie and John. How she must have smiled and cringed (and skipped whole pages) as she perused the childish story. But she wrote to me: "I think you have a truly remarkable gift for invention and for expressing your real feelings about people and situations. I hope that you will continue to write and will send us more of your stories."

I did continue to write, and gradually, in college and graduate school, I read and worked through many of the literary movements and authors that Genie had always recommended: Jane Austen, George Eliot (Mary Ann Evans), Charles Dickens, E. M. Forster, more Willa Cather, and Shakespeare and Shakespeare and more Shakespeare. I gravitated toward women's studies and discovered, as if they had never been discovered before, new approaches to Austen and the Brontës and Edith Wharton. *The Madwoman in the Attic.* Brilliant contemporary writers such as Toni Morrison and Louise Erdrich. I read Betty Friedan's *The Feminine Mystique* and my mouth dropped open with horror that women of my mother's and grandmother's generations had been brainwashed into slavish housewifery and sexual objectification. Wait . . . they were? Really? My mother, who wore leather miniskirts and fringed boots in the late sixties, painted nudes, defied sexism and racism and all "isms" that restricted humanity? My *grand*mother, who worked for the Democratic Party since my father was a baby, traveled the world, and spoke for civil rights? Suddenly the whole ball of female wax got stuck in my throat, and I am still not done digesting it, nor am I ever likely to swallow it completely.

American feminist movements. The first wave: suffrage and Votes for Women, recognized as beginning in 1848, but most aggressively fought between the 1890s and 1920. The second wave: mass movement resulting in the wider social and cultural acceptance of women outside the home, achieved between 1968 and the late 1970s. And third: the current wave, including the #MeToo and Time's Up initiatives, to balance human rights between women and men in all arenas of American life. It is no accident that I began writing my grandmother's biography in the years 2017-18: I turned fifty (and coincidentally, it has been fifty years since the beginning of the second feminist wave); an American population has risen up in protest, starting a third feminist wave; and it has been exactly one hundred years since Genie marched down a street in a small town in Iowa, a little Victory Girl waving her banner for freedom and democracy, just two years before her own mother could go to the polls and vote.

Eugenie studied the cyclical nature of politics across eons of history. She knew far more than I do about interdisciplinary philosophies that make history speak to politics, which speak to rhetoric, which speaks to language, which speaks to symbolic systems, which speak to music, which speaks to mathematics, which speak to the visual arts, which speak to psychology, which speaks to human nature—and all the intersecting threads between them. Somehow, among all of her reading and contemplation, she always maintained the ability to take her knowledge and apply it, to make it practical, to communicate it to others, and to *act*. Above all, she wished to be active.

Because of Eugenie's need to act, she insisted on that codicil to Humphrey's famous civil rights speech in 1948. That speech, and its reference to Truman, has been credited with helping to elect Truman to the presidency, while pushing the twentieth-century agenda for civil rights. Because of Eugenie's need to act, she proved, for the first time in American history, that a married woman with young children could occupy, and succeed at, the highest chief-of-mission diplomatic rank. Because of Eugenie's need to act, she accepted, for the first time in American history, a top post for a woman behind the Iron Curtain. Because of Eugenie's need to act, she became the first American woman to represent the United States (in the absence of the chief delegate) on the UN Security

Council. And because of her compulsory need to act, rather than simply study or witness, Eugenie showed that women in a democratic America could fight totalitarianism on a global scale, tackling the real systems and confronting the actual individuals who represented their threat to freedom. After Eleanor Roosevelt, Eugenie Anderson was the first woman diplomat to be taken seriously and receive national attention as a political force—not just a feminine presence or influence. Her legacy has risen above the publicity of her time, which emphasized her soft-spoken, fashionable, yet motherly persona, to reinforce, instead, what Eugenie had wanted known all along: that the message of one's politics should supersede one's gender.

India Edwards once said about politics: "If I didn't have the crusading spirit, I'd get the hell out and go home." Eugenie had that spirit. Part of it came from her Methodist upbringing and her preacher father's beliefs in promoting internationalist cooperation toward peace and tolerance. Part of it came from watching her mother's dedication to doing her part behind the scenes as foundational support. And a great part of Eugenie's crusading spirit came from the fact that, even though she questioned the traditions of all organized religions and their effects on the human condition, she always kept herself open to the possibilities of a greater meaning. In 1982, Eugenie wrote in a letter: "I still think—yes of course there must be a God—I know there is a force divine in all of us and in all of nature—there must be, no matter what we choose to call this immensely mysterious creative divinity. I often times feel when I am listening to Beethoven and Bach and Mozart that this could not just have *happened* and that those great men were communicating with that God, just as we long to do, and try in our way to do."[1]

Eugenie's spirit, her love of nature and science and beauty, is also reflected in this letter from July 18, 1958:

> Tuesday night we saw the orbiting Rocket of the Soviet Sputnik III. It was quite an experience to see it, and something I will always remember, I think, even if satellites get to be common occurrences.

... I stopped the car a little west of Cannon Falls where I had a clear view of the sky, and indeed had an amazing chance to watch it all the way across the heavens. It was even brighter than a planet, a clear, pulsating star-like light traversing the skies.... Even though I could not forget that it had been put there by Soviet scientists, I will have to admit that it was an awesome spectacle and a majestic one.[2]

Hold strong against totalitarianism. Speak for democracy. Uphold the basic rights that protect Americans. Fight for human rights—everywhere in the world. That is what my grandmother Eugenie Moore Anderson believed, and her words remain true, and hopeful, today: "There are voices today calling for withdrawal, for disengagement, for a retreat to the old 'America first' pattern. But we cannot turn back to the isolationism of the pre-nuclear era. Today there is no security in a fortress America faced by powerful nuclear adversaries. Instead we must now address ourselves to reality and to the future. For it is to peaceful change, and to a peaceful future, that we are all committed."[3]

ACKNOWLEDGMENTS

I SAT DOWN WITH MY FATHER, HANS ANDERSON, IN 2013, and pushed the red button on a small digital voice recorder, and then we proceeded to talk for (it felt like) a day and a half. The point of the conversation was to preserve Hans's own life memories, about his childhood, career, feelings, and choices—it had very little to do with his mother's career or my own writing. But the source material turned out to be invaluable, and I am ever grateful for Dad's openness, honesty, humor, and discerning compassion regarding his family and himself.

Shannon Pennefeather, editor at the Minnesota Historical Society Press, gave me far more than the "time of day" when I asked her for informational meetings several years ago and then fired ideas and questions about all kinds of odd history and potential publishing opportunities. She has always made it clear that the MNHS Press values *all* Minnesota history, from its celebrities to its least historically documented residents. She has made the whole process of building this book far less complicated than I thought it might be.

No book about Eugenie Anderson would be possible without the source materials—the archive of her papers that was organized and donated to the Minnesota Historical Society by my aunt, Johanna Anderson Ghei. Her great efforts have accomplished what Eugenie hoped: that everything would remain accessible to researchers, historians, and interested individuals. I also thank Johanna for answering my many emails and letters, not just for this project but for many family history quests over the years. Gratitude also extends to Gita Ghei, who followed up on photo searches both for the biography and for me, personally, and to Raman and Kiren Ghei for their sincere encouragement.

I spent over a year going back and forth to the Gale Family Library at the Minnesota Historical Society in St. Paul, methodically requesting each of the twenty-seven archived Anderson boxes. I stored my water and purse in the same locker every time (#9), sat at the same table, and smiled at the familiar, friendly librarians. I thank all of them for their work, expertise, and assistance.

Many people agreed to meet me for interviews, and all of them shared marvelously different perspectives and inspired new avenues of thought. I thank family members Barbara Hedin Bayley, Anna Biederman Brown, and Gretchen Chesley Lang. I thank three very warm, sharp, generous nonagenarians who knew Eugenie personally: former vice president Walter Mondale, the late Arvonne Fraser, and the late Barbara Flanagan Sanford. I also thank Lori Sturdevant for advice and shared knowledge of the wider political community in Minnesota.

I am grateful to the people and places that make up the Dakota County Public Library (especially the Wentworth location) and the Hennepin County Public Library (particularly Special Collections); also to John Wareham, librarian at the Minneapolis Star Tribune; and to Dr. Philip Nash of the history department at Penn State Shenango. It makes me very happy that an old high school friend, author Lyda Morehouse, helped me find the services of Aimée Bissonette, literary attorney. I also had a secret weapon in my nephew Henry Meger, who is fluent in many languages and helped me with obscure online research bits about Cold War Communists and identifications that could only be conducted in the Cyrillic alphabet.

Thank you to my friends who read, write, and cheer me on: Susan Jerabek, Lisa Marier, Katy Winker, Kari Arfstrom, Rebekah Dupont. Thank you to my wonderful sisters, Jennifer Anderson-Meger and Lydia Anderson. Thank you to my mother, Margaret Kaehler Anderson, who champions anything and everything I write. Thank you to my kids, Anthony, Juliet, and Clara, for being individually and collectively wonderful and brilliant and so conscientious and loving, to our family and to others. And after all, but at the root of everything, thank you, Patrick.

NOTES

Notes to Preface

1. Walter F. Mondale, interview with the author, 8 Sept. 2017, Minneapolis, MN.

2. Freeman, *A Room at a Time*, 7; "Pride of Red Wing, Attractive Eugenie Anderson, Will 'Just Be Herself' in Communist Bulgaria," *St. Paul Pioneer Press*, 8 July 1962.

3. "DFL Committeewoman Has No Time for Bach Now," *Minneapolis Star*, 17 Mar. 1949; Freeman, *A Room at a Time*, 9.

4. Some women had been appointed; Chase would remain the only woman until 1972. Sheed, *Clare Booth Luce*, 3-4.

5. "*The Feminine Mystique* was like an earthquake compared to the tremors about unhappy housewives that had registered before. Friedan described the problem in scorching prose that made it seem much worse than anyone had previously suggested. . . . The power of Friedan's writing, the wealth of statistics and anecdotes . . . made *The Feminine Mystique* a sensation when it was published in 1963." Collins, *When Everything Changed*, 59.

6. Eugenie to Hubert H. Humphrey, 23 Nov. 1958, Eugenie M. Anderson papers, box 6.

7. Family newsletter from Sofia, 15 Aug. 1963, 8, Anderson family papers; Clinton, *What Happened*, 326.

8. Clinton, *What Happened*, 129.

Notes to Chapter One: Leaving the Tower

1. Epigraph: Albright, *Fascism*, xiv. Eugenie Anderson, oral history interview, 7 May 1971, 31, 32, 33, Oral History Interviews of the Public Affairs Center Collection Oral History Project, Minnesota Historical Society (hereafter Anderson oral history interview).

2. Anderson oral history interview, 7 May 1971, 30.

3. Anderson oral history interview, 7 May 1971, 8.

4. Anderson oral history interview, 7 May 1971, 6.

5. Millett, *Minnesota's Own*, 254.

6. Hans P. Anderson, interview with the author, 20–21 Sept. 2013, La Crosse, WI.

7. Alexander P. Anderson to John, 19 Apr. 1929, Anderson family collection.

8. Anderson oral history interview, 7 May 1971, 16–18.

9. Eugenie to John, 25 Aug. 1930, Anderson family collection.

10. Eugenie to John, 30 Aug. 1930, Anderson family collection.

11. Eugenie to John, 29 Aug. 1930, Anderson family collection.

12. Jean Anderson Chesley to John, 12 Jan. 1931, Anderson family collection.

13. Hans P. Anderson, personal recollection.

14. Lydia in Red Wing to John in Chicago, 13 Jan. 1931, Anderson family collection.

15. Eugenie to John, 21 Jan. 1931, Anderson family collection.

16. Alexander P. Anderson to John, 29 July 1931, Anderson family collection.

17. A. P. in Honolulu to John in New York City, 23 Oct. 1931, Anderson family collection.

18. Anderson oral history interview, 7 May 1971, 27.

19. Anderson oral history interview, 7 May 1971, 23.

20. Anderson oral history interview, 7 May 1971, 29.

21. Anderson oral history interview, 7 May 1971, 30.

22. Barbara Hedin Bayley, interview with the author, 18 Apr. 2017, Eau Claire, WI; Margaret K. Anderson, interview with the author, 8 Apr. 2017, La Crosse, WI.

23. Larsen and Larsen, *Charles Biederman*, 106.

24. Anderson oral history interview, 7 May 1971, 31.

25. Hans P. Anderson 2013 interview.

26. Anderson oral history interview, 7 May 1971, 33; Lamson, *Few Are Chosen*, 165.

27. Lamson, *Few Are Chosen*, xxiv.

28. Friedan, *The Feminine Mystique*, 57.

29. Larsen and Larsen, *Charles Biederman*, 109.

30. Elizabeth Anderson Hedin to Eugenie, 14 Feb. 1939, Anderson family collection.

31. Mary to Eugenie, 20 May 1939, Anderson family collection.

32. Mary to Eugenie, 26 and 28 July 1939, Anderson family collection.

33. Eugenie to Mary, undated (presumed July) 1939, Anderson family collection; Larsen and Larsen, *Charles Biederman*, 133.

34. Anderson oral history interview, 7 May 1971, 39.

35. Larsen and Larsen, *Charles Biederman*, 159–60.

36. Anderson oral history interview, 7 May 1971, 40–41.

37. Larsen and Larsen, *Charles Biederman*, 166.

38. Hans P. Anderson 2013 interview.

Notes to Chapter Two: Joining the Party

1. Epigraph: Lamson, *Few Are Chosen*, 167. Anderson oral history interview, 7 May 1971, 42–44.

2. Anderson oral history interview, 7 May 1971, 43.

3. Anderson oral history interview, 7 May 1971, 45, 49.

4. Arvonne Fraser, interview with the author, 8 Jan. 2018, Minneapolis, MN.

5. Kampelman, *Entering New Worlds*, 67.

6. Friedan, *The Feminine Mystique*, 269.

7. Friedan, *The Feminine Mystique*, 273, 274.

8. Solberg, *Hubert Humphrey*, 113.

9. Delton, *Making Minnesota Liberal*, 97; Anderson oral history interview, 14 May 1971, 6.

10. Humphrey, *Education of a Public Man*, 72.

11. Solberg, *Hubert Humphrey*, 114, 115.

12. Constitution, Minnesota chapter, Americans for Democratic Action, Eugenie M. Anderson papers, box 18.

13. Solberg, *Hubert Humphrey*, 119; "DFLers Think Back on Birth, Uneasy Early Days of Party," *Minneapolis Tribune*, 15 June 1984; Anderson oral history interview, 14 May 1971, 10–11.

14. Solberg, *Hubert Humphrey*, 122; Fraser interview; author's knowledge from shared family history.

15. Hans P. Anderson 2013 interview.

16. Hans P. Anderson 2013 interview.

17. Friedan, *The Feminine Mystique*, 484.

18. Epigraph: Freeman, *We Will Be Heard*, 15. *ADA World*, April 1948.

19. Delton, *Making Minnesota Liberal*, 136, 139.

20. Humphrey, *Education of a Public Man*, 74; Solberg, *Hubert Humphrey*, 122.

21. Solberg, *Hubert Humphrey*, 125.

22. Anderson oral history interview, 14 May 1971, 14.

23. McCullough, *Truman*, 636.

24. Lamson, *Few Are Chosen*, 171–72.

25. Schumacher, *The Contest*, 45; Hubert H. Humphrey, 1948 Democratic National Convention Address, American Rhetoric: Top 100 Speeches, http://www.americanrhetoric.com/speeches/hubert humphey1948dnc.html.

26. Lamson, *Few Are Chosen*, 171; McCullough, *Truman*, 640.

27. Collins, *When Everything Changed*, 96.

Notes to Chapter Three: Representing America

1. Epigraphs: Hubert H. Humphrey to Eugenie, 2 Nov. 1949, Eugenie M. Anderson papers, box 2; Lamson, *Few Are Chosen*, 175. Mondale interview.

2. Anderson oral history interview, 14 May 1971, 22, 23.

3. Edwards, *Pulling No Punches*, 8.

4. Anderson oral history interview, 14 May 1971, 24.

5. "DFL Committeewoman Has No Time for Bach Now," *Minneapolis Star*, 17 Mar. 1949.

6. Hubert H. Humphrey to Dean Acheson, 23 Feb. 1949, Eugenie M. Anderson papers, box 2.

7. Anderson oral history interview, 14 May 1971, 28; Hubert H. Humphrey to Eugenie, 6 Aug. 1949, Eugenie M. Anderson papers, box 2.

8. "Ardent Truman Supporter," *New York Times*, 13 Oct. 1949.

9. Anderson oral history interview, 14 May 1971, 33.

10. "John Is 'Nice Guy, But Not Talkative', Reporters Agree at Eugenie's Swearing-In," *Red Wing Republican Eagle*, 29 Oct. 1949.

11. "U.S. Ambassador Arrives in Denmark," *New York Times*, 21 Dec. 1949.

12. John to Frank Chesley, 19 Dec. 1949, Anderson family collection; family newsletter, 25 Dec. 1949; "Lady Ambassador Poised—No Jitters for Eugenie," *St. Paul Pioneer Press*, 14 Dec. 1949.

13. Frank Chesley to John, 27 Dec. 1949, Anderson family collection.

14. Sheed, *Clare Booth Luce*, 120, 159.

15. "Mrs. Ambassador" draft, ch. 4, Eugenie M. Anderson papers; Nash, "A Woman's Place Is in the Embassy," 224, 229.

16. Family newsletter, 31 Dec. 1949.

17. Anderson oral history interview, 21 May 1971, 7.

18. Anderson oral history interview, 21 May 1971, 11.

19. Family newsletters, 22 Jan. and 26 Feb. 1950.

20. Family newsletter, 30 Apr. 1950.

21. Family newsletter, 22 Apr. 1950.

22. John to Frank Chesley, 3 Feb. 1950.

23. John to Frank Chesley, 3 Feb. 1950.

24. "Mrs. Ambassador" outline, part I, ch. 4, 15–18.

25. "Mrs. Ambassador" draft, ch. 4, 30.

26. Arthur Schlesinger Jr. to Eugenie, 21 May 1950, Eugenie M. Anderson papers, box 4.

27. Friedan, *The Feminine Mystique*, 101.

28. Anderson oral history interview, 21 May 1971, 20–21; Nash, "A Woman's Place Is in the Embassy," 229.

29. Family newsletter, 7 May 1950.

30. Eugenie to Eleanor Roosevelt, 30 June 1950, Eugenie M. Anderson papers, box 4.

31. Family newsletter, 8 July 1950.

32. Anderson oral history interview, 21 May 1971, 22.

33. "Mrs. Ambassador" draft, ch. 4.

34. Family newsletter, 15 Oct. 1950.

35. Family newsletter, 22 Oct. 1950.

36. Family newsletter, 22 Oct. 1950.

37. Nash, "A Woman's Place Is in the Embassy," 235.

38. Anderson oral history interview, 21 May 1971, 29.

39. Family newsletter, 25 Aug. 1950.

40. Hans P. Anderson, interview with the author, 8 Apr. 2017.

41. Hans P. Anderson 2017 interview.

42. Anderson oral history interview, 21 May 1971, 47.

43. Family newsletter, 3 Dec. 1950.

44. "Mrs. Ambassador" outline, part I, 40; draft, ch. 2, 1.

45. Family newsletter, 18 Feb. 1951.

46. Family newsletter, 25 Feb. 1951.

47. "U.S., Denmark Sign Pact on Greenland," *New York Times*, 1 Apr. 1951.

48. Eugenie to John, 13 Oct. 1951, Anderson family collection.

49. Eugenie to John, 17 Oct. 1951, Anderson family collection.

50. John to Eugenie, 9 Oct. 1951, Anderson family collection.

51. John to Eugenie, 19 Oct. 1951, Anderson family collection.

52. Eugenie to John, 29 Oct. 1951, Anderson family collection.

53. Hubert H. Humphrey to Eugenie, 24 Jan. 1952, Eugenie M. Anderson papers, box 2.

54. "Mrs. Anderson Slams Reds on Negro Issue," *St. Paul Pioneer Press*, 12 Jan. 1952.

55. Friedan, *The Feminine Mystique*, 47.

56. Eugenie to Arthur Schlesinger Jr., 30 Apr. 1952, Eugenie M. Anderson papers, box 2.

57. India Edwards to Eugenie, 29 July 1952, Eugenie M. Anderson papers, box 2; Edwards, *Pulling No Punches*, 159.

58. India Edwards to Eugenie, 10 Dec. 1952, Eugenie M. Anderson papers, box 2.

59. William Roll to Eugenie, 18 Jan. 1953, Eugenie M. Anderson papers, box 4.

60. Harold Strauss to Eugenie, 15 Dec. 1949, Eugenie M. Anderson papers, box 5.

61. "Mrs. Ambassador" outline, part I, ch. 4, 15–18; Lynn Carrick to Eugenie, 10 Mar. 1953, Eugenie M. Anderson papers, box 5.

Notes to Chapter Four: Reaching for Washington

1. Epigraph: Fraser, *She's No Lady*, 113, 282. Hubert H. Humphrey to Eugenie, 9 July and 17 Nov. 1953, and with attachment, 9 Nov. 1955, Eugenie M. Anderson papers, box 5; Eugenie to Hans, 16 Nov. 1955, Hans P. Anderson collection.

2. Beito, *Coya Come Home*, 109, 110.

3. Beito, *Coya Come Home*, 196.

4. Solberg, *Hubert Humphrey*, 175, 176.

5. Solberg, *Hubert Humphrey*, 176; Beito, *Coya Come Home*, 210.

6. Beito, *Coya Come Home*, 211, 212.

7. Mondale and Hage, *The Good Fight*, 37.

8. Katie Louchheim to Eugenie, 16 May 1957, Eugenie M. Anderson papers, box 7; "How About Eugenie?" *Minneapolis Tribune*, 23 June 1957; Hubert H. Humphrey to Eugenie, 29 July 1957, Eugenie M. Anderson papers, box 6.

9. Anderson oral history interview, 28 May 1971, 19; Lamson, *Few Are Chosen*, xxiii.

10. "Minnesota Legislators Analyze Wisconsin Upset," *Minneapolis Tribune*, 1 Sept. 1957; "Eugenie Anderson a Senate Candidate?" *Winona Daily News*, 18 Sept. 1957.

11. Anderson oral history interview, 28 May 1971, 15; Harold Zellerbach to Eugenie, 6 Nov. 1957, Eugenie M. Anderson papers, box 27.

12. Eugenie to Hubert H. Humphrey, 18 Dec. 1957, Eugenie M. Anderson papers, box 6; Max Kampelman to Eugenie, 27 Dec. 1957, Eugenie M. Anderson papers, box 7; Eugenie to Doris Heller, 5 Jan. 1958, Eugenie M. Anderson papers, box 6.

13. Sandbrook, *Eugene McCarthy*, 84; Eugenie to Hans, 15 Jan. 1958, Hans P. Anderson collection.

14. "Eyes Turn to First District for National Vote Hint," *Minneapolis Tribune*, 19 Jan. 1958.

15. Eugenie to Max Kampelman, 9 Feb. 1958, Eugenie M. Anderson papers, box 7.

16. Eugenie to Hans, 12 Apr. 1958, Hans P. Anderson collection.

17. Beito, *Coya Come Home*, 226–27.

18. "'Politics' Suspected in Knutson Flare-up," *Minneapolis Star*, 9 May 1958; *Austin Daily Herald*, 13 May 1958.

19. Beito, *Coya Come Home*, 233, 243, quoting *Washington Evening Star*, 13 May 1958.

20. Beito, *Coya Come Home*, 239, 279.

21. "Bjornson Says He's Weighing Governor Race," *St. Cloud Times*, 19 May 1958.

22. Beito, *Coya Come Home*, 263.

23. "DFL Endorses McCarthy," *Minneapolis Tribune*, 26 May 1958; Anderson oral history interview, 28 May 1971, 21–24.

24. Mondale interview.

25. Anderson oral history interview, 28 May 1971, 24.

26. Beito, *Coya Come Home*, 298–99.

27. George Jacobson to Hubert H. Humphrey, et al., 10 June 1958, Eugenie M. Anderson papers, box 7.

28. Mitch Perrizo to Eugenie, 29 June 1958, Eugenie M. Anderson papers, box 8.

29. Eugenie to Doris Tullar Heller, 29 June 1958, Eugenie M. Anderson papers, box 6.

30. Anderson oral history interview, 28 May 1971, 24–25.

31. Hubert H. Humphrey to Eugenie, 3 July 1958, Eugenie M. Anderson papers, box 6; Eugenie to Hans, 14 July 1958, Hans P. Anderson collection.

32. Hubert H. Humphrey to Alpha Smaby, copy to Eugenie, 15 Aug. 1958, Eugenie M. Anderson papers, box 6.

33. Eugenie to Hubert H. Humphrey, 28 Aug. 1958, Eugenie M. Anderson papers, box 6; Eugenie to Hans, 14 July 1958, Hans P. Anderson collection.

34. Eugenie to Max Kampelman, 25 Oct. 1958, and Max Kampelman to Eugenie, 30 Oct. 1958, both Eugenie M. Anderson papers, box 7.

35. Eugenie to India Edwards, 17 Nov. 1958, Eugenie M. Anderson papers, box 6; Eugenie to Hans, 22 Nov. 1958, Hans P. Anderson collection.

36. Eugenie to Hans, 12 Apr. 1958, Hans P. Anderson collection.

Notes to Chapter Five: Breaching the Iron Curtain

1. Epigraph: Virginia Lanegran, unpublished chapter on Eugenie Anderson, Barbara Stuhler papers, Minnesota Historical Society. Harry S. Truman, speech, 1947, quoted in Applebaum, *Iron Curtain*, xxii.

2. "Demo Feels Presidential Year Victory Chance Not Half as Good as Year Ago," *Salem (OR) Statesman*, 13 Dec. 1959.

3. Anderson oral history interview, 28 May 1971, 27.

4. Anderson oral history interview, 28 May 1971, 30.

5. Anderson oral history interview, 28 May 1971, 33; Eugenie to Hans, 18 Dec. 1960, Hans P. Anderson collection.

6. Eugenie to Hans, 19 Jan. 1960, Hans P. Anderson collection.

7. Anderson oral history interview, 28 May 1971, 36.

8. Eugenie to Harry S. Truman, 3 Oct. 1961, Harry S. Truman to Eugenie, 10 Oct. 1961, and Harry S. Truman to John F. Kennedy, 10 Oct. 1961, all Eugenie M. Anderson papers, box 27.

9. "Frances Elizabeth Willis: Diplomat," US Department of State, Diplomacy 101, https://diplomacy.state.gov/discoverdiplomacy /explorer/peoplehistorical/170214.htm; Burns and Dunn, *The Three Roosevelts*, 562.

10. Nash, "A Woman's Place Is in the Embassy," 230; Anderson oral history interview, 28 May 1971, 34.

11. Eugenie M. Anderson papers, box 25; Anderson oral history interview, 28 May 1971, 37.

12. "Minnesota's Lady Diplomat to Try Her Hand in Bulgaria," *Mason City (IA) Globe Gazette*, 5 July 1962.

13. "Pride of Red Wing, Attractive Eugenie Anderson, Will 'Just Be Herself' in Communist Bulgaria," *St. Paul Pioneer Press*, 8 July 1962.

14. "Minnesota's Ambassador for the U.S.: Eugenie Anderson," *Minneapolis Tribune*, 12 Aug. 1962.

15. Anderson oral history interview, 18 June 1971, 2.

16. Anderson oral history interview, 25 June 1971, 31; family newsletter, 29 July 1962, 12; family newsletter, 5 Aug. 1962.

17. Family newsletters, 13 Oct. (17) and 11 Nov. (11) 1962 and 27 Jan. (8) and 16 Feb. (1) 1963.

18. Anderson oral history interview, 28 June 1971, 18, 19.

19. Anderson oral history interview, 28 June 1971, 24; Eugenie to John F. Kennedy, 30 Oct. 1962, Eugenie M. Anderson papers, box 7; "Peking Aide at Bulgarian Meeting Said to Condemn Missile Withdrawal," *New York Times*, 9 Nov. 1962.

20. "Eugenie 'Takes Walk' in Bulgaria," *Minneapolis Star*, 8 Oct. 1962; "U.S. Diplomat Is No Patsy," *Chillicothe (OH) Gazette*, 26 Dec. 1962.

21. Hans to John, 18 and 23 Dec. 1962, Hans P. Anderson collection.

22. Donald C. Tice interview, Foreign Affairs Oral History.

23. Anderson oral history interview, 28 June 1971, 28.

24. Anderson oral history interview, 28 June 1971, 46; "Eugenie 'Firsts' Surprise Bulgaria," *Minneapolis Tribune*, 7 July 1963.

25. Anderson oral history interview, 28 June 1971, 51–52.

26. Richard E. Johnson interview, Foreign Affairs Oral History.

27. Family newsletter, 13 Apr. 1963, 6–8.

28. Family newsletter, 29 Oct. 1963, 1.

29. *Daily News*, 14 Dec. 1963, clipping in Eugenie M. Anderson papers, box 17.

30. Robert B. Houston interview, Foreign Affairs Oral History.

31. Anderson oral history interview, 25 June 1971, 12.

32. Richard E. Johnson interview, 23.

33. "Sofia Mob Stones the U.S. Legation Over Spy Charges," *New York Times*, 28 Dec. 1963; *Minneapolis Tribune*, 28 Dec. 1963.

34. The Bulgarian news agency released on January 6, 1964, that Georgiev had been executed, but no details were given. Binder, *Fare Well, Illyria*, 89.

35. Anderson oral history interview, 25 June 1971, 19.

36. Anderson oral history interview, 25 June 1971, 24–25.

37. Anderson oral history interview, 25 June 1971, 42.

38. Anderson oral history interview, 25 June 1971, 30.

39. Solberg, *Hubert Humphrey*, 242; Eugenie to Hubert H. Humphrey, 18 May 1964, Eugenie M. Anderson papers, box 6.

40. Hubert H. Humphrey to Eugenie, 24 June 1964, and Muriel Humphrey to Eugenie, 17 Sept. 1964, both Eugenie M. Anderson papers, box 6.

41. Anderson oral history interview, 25 June 1971, 43–44.

42. Quote used in book ad, *LIFE* magazine, 10 Mar. 1963.

43. "Who Says U.S. Women are Trapped?" *Cincinnati Enquirer*, 6 Oct. 1963.

44. Hans P. Anderson to Eugenie and John, 7 Nov. 1965, Hans P. Anderson collection.

Notes to Chapter Six: Holding the Line

1. Epigraph: Hubert H. Humphrey to Eugenie, 23 Dec. 1964, Eugenie M. Anderson papers, box 6. Tom Wicker, "Leak on, O Ship of State," *New York Times*, 26 Jan. 1982.

2. India Edwards to Eugenie, 14 Mar. 1964, Eugenie M. Anderson papers, box 6; "Periscope," *Newsweek*, 5 Apr. 1965, 17; Eugenie to Max Kampelman, 3 Apr. 1965, Eugenie M. Anderson papers, box 7.

3. India Edwards to Eugenie, 11 Apr. 1965, Eugenie M. Anderson papers, box 6: "Yes, I was appalled at the Newsweek item but hope and pray it has no ill effects. Marian Dennehy, who works for young Butterworth at the Department of Commerce, told me today that he had told her you were going to be appointed Ambassador to Canada weeks ago so it must have been general knowledge with Ambassador Butterworth in on 'the secret.' I imagine you are right in thinking someone in [the Department of] State was the source of the item in Newsweek. With HHH backing you, I do not think the item will stop your appointment."

4. India Edwards to Eugenie, 11 Apr. 1965, and Eugenie to P. R. Harris, 2 June 1965, both Eugenie M. Anderson papers, box 6.

5. Johanna to Eugenie, 20 May 1965, Eugenie M. Anderson papers, box 15.

6. "Johnson's Team Goes to the U.N.," *Washington Star*, 28 Aug. 1965.

7. "What a Way to Pick an Ambassador," *New York Herald Tribune*, Oct. 1965.

8. Margaret K. Anderson interview; Hans P. Anderson 2013 interview.

9. Anderson oral history interview, 25 June 1971, 48.

10. "U.S. Woman's Voice at U.N. Has Faintly Midwestern Accent," *New York Times*, 16 Jan. 1966.

11. Anderson oral history interview, 25 June 1971, 50.

12. Anderson oral history interview, 8 July 1971, 4–5.

13. Hubert H. Humphrey to Eugenie, 29 Jan. 1966, Eugenie M. Anderson papers, box 6.

14. Anderson oral history interview, 8 July 1971, 6, 8–9.

15. Anderson oral history interview, 8 July 1971, 21.

16. Anderson oral history interview, 8 July 1971, 29, 31.

17. U Thant of Burma, secretary-general of the United Nations from 1961 to 1971.

18. "It's Not All 'Man's World,'" *Orlando (FL) Sentinel*, 25 Sept. 1966.

19. Mondale had taken over Humphrey's Senate seat in 1965 when Humphrey shifted over to the White House as vice president. Mondale and Hage, *The Good Fight*, 38.

20. Mondale interview.

21. Califano, *Triumph and Tragedy of Lyndon Johnson*, 56–57.

22. Hubert H. Humphrey to Eugenie, 27 July 1966, Eugenie M. Anderson papers, box 6.

23. Hubert H. Humphrey letters, 21 Apr. and 31 July 1967, Eugenie M. Anderson papers, box 6; "Ambassador Sees U.N. Gain Strength at Age 21," *The Independent (Long Beach, CA)*, 15 Feb. 1967.

24. "'People Just Expect Too Much'—Anderson," *Akron (OH) Beacon Journal*, 7 Mar. 1967.

25. Fraser, *She's No Lady*, 148.

26. Hans P. Anderson 2013 interview; Margaret K. Anderson interview.

27. Solberg, *Hubert Humphrey*, 306–7.

28. Anderson oral history interview, 8 July 1971, 40, 42–43.

29. Anderson oral history interview, 8 July 1971, 44.

30. "Demonstrators Chant Peace Slogans at Independence Hall Observance," *Chicago Tribune* and *Evening Times (Sayre, PA)*, 5 July 1967.

31. Solberg, *Hubert Humphrey*, 310.

32. Anderson oral history interview, 8 July 1971, 48–49.

33. "Lady Diplomat Finds Progress in Vietnam," *Minneapolis Tribune*, 4 Dec. 1967.

34. Anderson oral history interview, 8 July 1971, 53.

35. Epigraph: Mondale and Hage, *The Good Fight*, 88. Cohen, *Undefeated*, 294.

36. "We Just Have to Persist," *Press and Sun Bulletin (Binghamton, NY)*, 28 Jan. 1968; "Eugenie Anderson Defends Nation's Role in Vietnam," *Winona Daily News*, 26 Mar. 1968.

37. Califano, *Triumph and Tragedy of Lyndon Johnson*, 271; Solberg, *Hubert Humphrey*, 325.

38. Nash, "Ambassador Eugenie M. Anderson," 259; Lamson, *Few Are Chosen*, 194.

39. Freeman, *A Room at a Time*, 232.

40. "What Every Working Woman Needs," *St. Paul Pioneer Press*, 4 Feb. 1968.

41. Schlesinger and Schlesinger, eds., *Letters*, 9 July 1968, 359.

42. Schlesinger and Schlesinger, eds., *Letters*, 13 and 24 July 1968, 367.

43. Chester, Godfrey, and Page, *An American Melodrama*, 152.

44. Louis Menand, "Lessons from the Election of 1968," *New Yorker*, 8 Jan. 2018.

45. Clinton, *What Happened*, 197–98.

46. Mailer, *Miami and the Siege of Chicago*, 209.

47. "Focus on the Future," speech, 28 Aug. 1968, Eugenie M. Anderson papers, box 14.

48. "The High Road," notes, Sept. 1968, Eugenie M. Anderson papers, box 14.

49. Eugenie to Orville Freeman, memo, 14 Sept. 1968, Eugenie M. Anderson papers, box 14; William Ringle, "2 Resign U.S. Posts to Aid Hubert," *Sunday Press (Binghamton, NY)*, 22 Sept. 1968; Walburn, *Miles Lord*, 190; Brenes, "The Tragedy of Hubert Humphrey."

50. "L.B.J., Hubert Views as Different," *Kansas City Times*, 15 Oct. 1968.

51. Nathanson, "Humphrey Aide Norman Sherman Looks Back"; Mondale interview; Mondale and Hage, *The Good Fight*, 86.

52. Walburn, *Miles Lord*, 193–94.

53. Eugenie to Hubert H. Humphrey, 13 Nov. 1968, Eugenie M. Anderson papers, box 6.

54. Hubert H. Humphrey to Eugenie, 20 Dec. 1968, Eugenie M. Anderson papers, box 6.

55. Kirkpatrick, *Political Woman*, 242.

56. Freeman, *We Will Be Heard*, 3.

57. "Minnesotan Again Leads Attack on Sex Barrier," *Minneapolis Tribune*, 1 Oct. 1971; Freeman, *We Will Be Heard*, 15.

58. Freeman, *A Room at a Time*, 235.

Notes to Chapter Seven: Passing the Standard

1. Epigraph: Mondale interview. Cohen, *Undefeated*, 459.

2. Eugenie to Margaret K. Anderson, 4 July 1973, Hans P. Anderson collection.

3. Eugenie to Margaret, 19 Oct. 1975, Hans P. Anderson collection.

4. Hans to Eugenie, 26 Oct. 1975, Hans P. Anderson collection.

5. Eugenie to Muriel Humphrey, 18 Jan. 1978, Eugenie M. Anderson papers, box 22.

6. "Founders of DFL Are Gone," *Minneapolis Tribune*, 22 Jan. 1978.

7. "Is Armageddon Near for Party of HHH?" *Minneapolis Star*, 21 Sept. 1978.

8. Collier, *Political Woman*, 120.

9. "DFLers Think Back on Birth, Uneasy Early Days of Party," *Minneapolis Star Tribune*, 15 June 1984; "Mondale Loss Ends an Era of Minnesotans on U.S. Scene," *Minneapolis Star Tribune*, 11 Nov. 1984.

10. "Longtime DFLer Eugenie Anderson Endorses Boschwitz," *Minneapolis Star Tribune*, 28 Oct. 1984.

11. "DFL Convention Glory Days Long in Past," *St. Cloud Times*, 20 May 1990.

12. "First Woman Secretary of State," *Fond du Lac Commonwealth Reporter*, 18 Mar. 1997.

13. "Eugenie Anderson—She Broke Glass Ceiling," *St. Paul Pioneer Press*, 3 Apr. 1997.

14. "Nation's First Woman Ambassador Dies," *Red Wing Republican Eagle*, 1 Apr. 1997; "A Woman—and Diplomat—of Substance," *Minneapolis Star Tribune*, 5 Apr. 1997.

15. "We Just Have to Persist," *Press and Sun Bulletin* (Binghamton, NY), 28 Jan. 1968.

Notes to Afterword

1. Eugenie to Hans, written in 1982, recalled in 1997 eulogy, Hans P. Anderson collection.

2. Eugenie to Hans, 18 July 1958, Hans P. Anderson collection.

3. Eugenie Anderson, Address, Democratic National Convention, Chicago, 1968, Eugenie M. Anderson papers, box 14.

BIBLIOGRAPHY

Unpublished Materials

Anderson, Eugenie M. Papers. Minnesota Historical Society, St. Paul.

Anderson, Hans P. Letters collection. 1953-99. Private.

Anderson family. Letters collection. 1912-99. Private.

Houston, Robert B. Interview transcript. Foreign Affairs Oral History Collection, Association for Diplomatic Studies and Training, Arlington, VA. www.adst.org.

Humphrey, Hubert H. Papers. Minnesota Historical Society, St. Paul.

Johnson, Richard G. Interview transcript. Foreign Affairs Oral History Collection, Association for Diplomatic Studies and Training, Arlington, VA. www.adst.org.

Kampelman, Max. Papers. Minnesota Historical Society, St. Paul.

Moore, Ezekiel Arrowsmith. Memoirs, 1947.

Moore, Flora Belle McMillen. Memoir by Mary K. Moore, 1936.

Oral History Interview with India Edwards by Jerry N. Hess. 16 Jan. 1969. Harry S. Truman Presidential Library and Museum, Independence, MO. https://www.trumanlibrary.org/oralhist /edwards1.htm.

Stuhler, Barbara. Papers. Minnesota Historical Society, St. Paul.

Telegrams to and from Bulgarian legation. *Foreign Relations of the*

United States, 1964–1968. Volume XVII: Bulgaria. Office of the Historian, Department of State. https://history.state.gov/his toricaldocuments/frus1964-68v17/d27.

Tice, Donald C. Interview transcript. Foreign Affairs Oral History Collection, Association for Diplomatic Studies and Training, Arlington, VA. www.adst.org.

Published Sources

Albright, Madeleine, with Bill Woodward. *Fascism: A Warning.* New York: HarperCollins, 2018.

———. *Madam Secretary.* New York: Miramax Books, 2003.

Anderson, Alexander P. *The Seventh Reader.* Caldwell, ID: Caxton Printers Ltd., 1941.

Angell, Madeline. *Red Wing, Minnesota: Saga of a River Town.* Minneapolis: Dillon Press, 1977.

Applebaum, Anne. *Iron Curtain: The Crushing of Eastern Europe, 1944–1953.* New York: Doubleday, 2012.

Arendt, Hannah. *The Burden of Our Time.* London: Secker & Warburg, 1951.

———. *The Origins of Totalitarianism.* New York: Harcourt, 1994.

Baldwin, Louis. *Women of Strength: Biographies of 106 Who Have Excelled in Traditionally Male Fields, A.D. 61 to the Present.* Jefferson, NC: McFarland & Co., 1996.

Beito, Gretchen Urnes. *Coya Come Home: A Congresswoman's Journey.* Los Angeles: Pomegranate Press, Ltd., 1990.

Binder, David. *Fare Well Illyria.* Budapest: Central European University Press, 2014.

Brenes, Michael. "The Tragedy of Hubert Humphrey." *New York Times,* 23 Mar. 2018.

Burns, James MacGregor, and Susan Dunn. *The Three Roosevelts: Patrician Leaders Who Transformed America.* New York: Atlantic Monthly Press, 2001.

Califano, Joseph A., Jr. *The Triumph and Tragedy of Lyndon Johnson: The White House Years*. 1991. Reprint, New York: Touchstone, 2015.

Calkin, Homer L. *Women in the Department of State: Their Role in American Foreign Affairs*. Washington, DC: Department of State Publication, 1978.

Caro, Robert A. *The Passage of Power: The Years of Lyndon Johnson*. Vol. 4. New York: Alfred A. Knopf, 2012.

Chester, Lewis, Hodgson Godfrey, and Bruce Page. *An American Melodrama: The Presidential Campaign of 1968*. New York: Viking Press, 1969.

Clinton, Hillary Rodham. *What Happened*. New York: Simon & Schuster, 2017.

Cohen, Dan. *Undefeated: The Life of Hubert H. Humphrey*. Minneapolis: Lerner Publications Co., 1978.

Collier, Peter. *Political Woman: The Big Little Life of Jeane Kirkpatrick*. New York: Encounter Books, 2012.

Collins, Gail. *When Everything Changed: The Amazing Journey of American Women from 1960 to the Present*. New York: Little, Brown and Co., 2009.

Delton, Jennifer Alice. *Making Minnesota Liberal: Civil Rights and the Transformation of the Democratic Party*. Minneapolis: University of Minnesota Press, 2002.

Dosdall, Jean. *Red Wing, Minnesota, 1857–2007: 150 Years*. Red Wing, MN: Red Wing Republican Eagle, 2006.

Edwards, India. *Pulling No Punches: Memoirs of a Woman in Politics*. New York: Putnam, 1977.

Evans, Sara M. *Tidal Wave: How Women Changed America at Century's End*. New York: Simon & Schuster, 2010.

Farber, Zac. "Politics of the Past: Eugenie Anderson 'Held Her Own in Smoke-Filled Rooms.'" *Minnesota Lawyer*, 28 June 2017. http://minnlawyer.com/2017/06/28/politics-of-the-past-eugenie-anderson-held-her-own-in-smoke-filled-rooms/.

Fraser, Arvonne. *She's No Lady: Politics, Family, and International*

Feminism. Edited by Lori Sturdevant. Minneapolis: Nodin Press, 2007.

Freeman, Jo. *A Room at a Time: How Women Entered Party Politics.* Lanham, MD: Rowman & Littlefield Publishers, 2002.

———. *We Will Be Heard: Women's Struggles for Political Power in the United States.* Lanham, MD: Rowman & Littlefield Publishers, 2008.

Friedan, Betty. *The Feminine Mystique.* 1963. Reprint, New York: W. W. Norton & Co., 1997.

Garrettson, Charles L. III. *Hubert Humphrey: The Politics of Joy.* New Brunswick, NJ: Transaction Publishers, 1993.

Gillon, Steven M. *The Democrats' Dilemma: Walter F. Mondale and the Liberal Legacy.* New York: Columbia University Press, 1992.

Griffith, Winthrop. *Humphrey: A Candid Biography.* New York: William Morrow & Co., 1965.

Gunderson, Dan. "Coya's Story." Minnesota Public Radio, 3 May 2004. http://news.minnesota.publicradio.org/features/2004/05/16_gundersond_coya/.

Harriman, Florence (Mrs. J. Borden). *From Pinafores to Politics.* New York: Henry Holt and Co., 1923.

Haynes, John Earl. *Dubious Alliance: The Making of Minnesota's DFL Party.* Minneapolis: University of Minnesota Press, 1984.

Hedin, Lydia E., Jean M. Chesley, John P. Anderson, and Louise A. Sargent. *Alexander P. Anderson, 1862-1943.* Red Wing, MN: Goodhue County Historical Society, 1997.

Humphrey, Hubert H. *The Education of a Public Man: My Life and Politics.* New York: Doubleday & Co., 1976.

Johnson, Frederick L. *Goodhue County, Minnesota: A Narrative History.* Red Wing, MN: Goodhue County Historical Society Press, 2000.

———. "Professor Anderson's 'Food Shot From Guns.'" *Minnesota History* 59, no. 1 (Spring 2004): 4-16.

Johnston, Patricia Condon. *Pretty Red Wing: Historic River Town.* Afton, MN: Johnston Publishing, 1985.

Kalm, Leah M., and Richard D. Semba. "They Starved So That Others Be Better Fed: Remembering Ancel Keys and the Minnesota Experiment." *Journal of Nutrition* 135, no. 6 (June 2005): 1347–52. https://doi.org/10.1093/jn/135.6.1347.

Kampelman, Max M. *Entering New Worlds: The Memoirs of a Private Man in Public Life*. New York: HarperCollins Publishers, 1991.

Kirkpatrick, Jeane J. *Political Woman*. New York: Basic Books, 1974.

Lamson, Peggy. *Few Are Chosen: American Women in Political Life Today*. Boston: Houghton Mifflin Co., 1968.

Larsen, Susan C., and Neil Juhl Larsen. *Charles Biederman*. Manchester, VT: Hudson Hills Press, 2011.

Leavitt, Judith A. *American Women Managers and Administrators: A Selective Bibliographical Dictionary of Twentieth-Century Leaders in Business, Education, and Government*. Westport, CT: Greenwood Press, 1985.

Leonard, Rodney E. *Freeman: The Governor Years, 1955–1960*. Minneapolis: Hubert H. Humphrey Institute of Public Affairs, 2003.

Mailer, Norman. *Miami and the Siege of Chicago: An Informal History of the Republican and Democratic Conventions of 1968*. New York: World Publishing Co., 1968.

McCarthy, Eugene J. *1968: War and Democracy*. Apple Valley, MN: Lone Oak Press, 2000.

McCullough, David. *Truman*. New York: Simon & Schuster, 1992.

Menand, Louis. "Lessons from the Election of 1968." *New Yorker*, 8 Jan. 2018. https://www.newyorker.com/magazine/2018/01/08/lessons-from-the-election-of-1968.

Mesta, Perle, with Robert Cahn. *Perle: My Story*. New York: McGraw-Hill Book Co., 1960.

Millett, Larry. *Minnesota's Own: Preserving Our Grand Homes*. St. Paul: Minnesota Historical Society Press, 2014.

Mondale, Walter F., with David Hage. *The Good Fight: A Life in Liberal Politics*. New York: Scribner, 2010.

Moskin, J. Robert. *American Statecraft: The Story of the U.S. Foreign Service*. New York: Macmillan, 2013.

Nash, Philip. "Ambassador Eugenie M. Anderson." *Minnesota History* 59, no. 6 (Summer 2005): 249–62.

———. "A Woman's Place Is in the Embassy: America's First Female Chiefs of Mission, 1933–1964." In *Women, Diplomacy and International Politics Since 1500*, edited by Brenda Sluga and Carolyn James, 222–39. New York: Routledge, 2016.

Nathanson, Iric. "The Caucus That Changed History: 1948's Battle for Control of the DFL." *MinnPost*, 26 Feb. 2016. https://www.minnpost.com/politics-policy/2016/02/caucus-changed-history-1948s-battle-control-dfl.

———. *Don Fraser: Minnesota's Quiet Crusader*. Minneapolis: Nodin Press, 2018.

———. "Humphrey Aide Norman Sherman Looks Back at Politics in the Tumultuous '60s." *MinnPost*, 16 Nov. 2015. https://www.minnpost.com/books/2015/11/humphrey-aide-norman-sherman-looks-back-politics-tumultuous-60s.

Owen (Rohde), Ruth Bryan. *Look Forward, Warrior*. New York: Dodd, Mead & Co., 1942.

Pierpont, Claudia Roth. *Passionate Minds: Women Rewriting the World*. New York: Alfred A. Knopf, 2001.

Rasmussen, Christian. *A History of Goodhue County, Minnesota*. N.p.: Higginson Book Co., 1935.

———. *A History of the City of Red Wing, Minnesota*. Red Wing, MN: Red Wing Advertising Co., 1933.

Roberts, Kate. *Minnesota 150: The People, Places, and Things that Shape Our State*. St. Paul: Minnesota Historical Society Press, 2007.

Roosevelt, Eleanor. *The Autobiography of Eleanor Roosevelt*. 1961. Reprint, New York: Harper Perennial, 2014.

Sandbrook, Dominic. *Eugene McCarthy: The Rise and Fall of Postwar American Liberalism*. New York: Alfred A. Knopf, 2004.

Schlesinger, Andrew, and Stephen Schlesinger, eds. *The Letters of Arthur Schlesinger, Jr.* New York: Random House, 2013.

Schlesinger, Arthur M., Jr., *Journals: 1952-2000*. New York: Penguin, 2007.

Schumacher, Michael. *The Contest: The 1968 Election and the War for America's Soul*. Minneapolis: University of Minnesota Press, 2018.

Sevareid, Eric. *Not So Wild a Dream: A Personal Story of Youth and War and the American Faith*. New York: Atheneum, 1976.

Sheed, Wilfrid. *Clare Booth Luce*. New York: E. P. Dutton, 1982.

Solberg, Carl. *Hubert Humphrey: A Biography*. 1984. Reprint, St. Paul, MN: Borealis Books, 2003.

Spangenburg, Ray, and Diane K. Moser. *Niels Bohr: Gentle Genius of Denmark*. New York: Facts on File, 1995.

Steil, Benn. *The Marshall Plan: Dawn of the Cold War*. New York: Simon & Schuster, 2018.

Sturdevant, Lori. *Her Honor: Rosalie Wahl and the Minnesota Women's Movement*. St. Paul: Minnesota Historical Society Press, 2014.

Walburn, Roberta. *Miles Lord: The Maverick Judge Who Brought Corporate America to Justice*. Minneapolis: University of Minnesota Press, 2017.

Weatherford, Doris. *Women in American Politics: History and Milestones*. Washington, DC: CQ Press, 2012.

Winslow, Anne, ed. *Women, Politics, and the United Nations*. Westport, CT: Greenwood Publishing Group, 1995.

INDEX

Mrs. Ambassador was designed and set in type by Judy Gilats. The text type is Cardea and the script is Gioviale. The book was printed by Versa Press.